Theodore Lownik Library
Illinois Benedictine College
Lisle, Illinois 60532

MARTIN HEIDEGGER'S

PHILOSOPHY OF RELIGION

WITHDRAWN

by

JOHN R. WILLIAMS

SUPPLEMENTS / 2

MARTIN HEIDEGGER'S

PHILOSOPHY OF RELIGION

by

John R. Williams

200.1
H465
W724

Canadian Cataloguing in Publication Data

Williams, John Reynold, 1942-
  Martin Heidegger's philosophy of religion

(SR supplements ; 2)

Bibliography: p.
Includes index.
ISBN 0-919812-03-1

1. Heidegger, Martin, 1889-1976.
2. Religion—Philosophy.
I. Title. II. Series.

B3279.H49W484   193   C77-001097-0

©1977 Corporation Canadienne des Sciences Religieuses / Canadian Corporation
for Studies in Religion

Foreward

It is with much satisfaction that the Canadian Corporation for
Studies in Religion publishes Professor Williams' work on Heidegger.
For years the pressure in Canada and elsewhere has grown to provide
scholars with an opportunity to publish the results of their research
in such a way as to make them available to their fellows more
quickly and at an appreciably lower price than has been the custom.
This Corporation was established to provide that opportunity.

Supported financially by donations from some Canadian universities,
religion departments, theological schools and colleges and assisted
by special committees of five Canadian learned societies in the field
of religion to stimulate publication, the aim of the Corporation to
publish "materials to serve the needs of scholars working in both
the French and English languages in Canada in all fields of the
academic study of religion" is indeed being fulfilled. The modest,
yet encouragingly successful beginning made by the Corporation in
connection with that aim was the launching of two series: *SR
Supplements* and *Editions SR*.

Professor John Williams' *Martin Heidegger's Philosophy of Religion*
now joins those works already published by this Corporation which
by their very existence bespeak the feasibility of scholars co-
operating for the purpose of furthering the propogation of research.

I welcome the opportunity of greeting this work and of commend-
ing through it also the work of this Corporation.

Martin Rumscheidt
President
Canadian Corporation for
Studies in Religion

TABLE OF CONTENTS

TABLE OF CONTENTS

Acknowledgements

The preparation and publication of this book would not have been possible without the assistance of the following individuals and organizations, to whom I wish to express my sincere gratitude: the editors of *The Heythrop Journal*, *Studies in Religion/Sciences Religieuses*, and *Eglise et Théologie* for permission to reproduce, in revised form, material which originally appeared in their journals; The Canada Council and Memorial University of Newfoundland for the funds which enabled me to complete the research and writing of this book; and my former instructors in the philosophy of religion, including Augustine Kalberer, O.S.B., Frederick Temple Kingston, Robert Pinto, Laurence Lynch, Leslie Dewart, Arthur Gibson, Gérard Siegwalt, and Maurice Nédoncelle, for the enlightenment and encouragement they provided in my study of philosophy of religion in general and Heidegger in particular.

The book has been published with the help of a grant from the Humanities Research Council of Canada, using funds provided by the Canada Council.

Note Concerning Translations

The English translations of passages cited in this work are my own, except where otherwise indicated (by the notation, 'E.T.') and in the case of *Sein und Zeit* (where the English translation retains the pagination of the German original). The specific translations of Heidegger's own works which are used here are listed in the bibliography for Chapter Three at the end of this work.

Introduction

Martin Heidegger died on May 26, 1976. Although he will write no more, newly published works of his will continue to appear for some years yet. Thus, it is likely that his reputation as one of the most influential philosophers of the 20th century will not soon be forgotten.

The purpose of this work is to describe and evaluate the treatment of religion in Heidegger's philosophy. This task will involve not only an exposition of Heidegger's own discussion of religious topics, but also an examination of the relation between philosophy and religion in general. This is because the religious significance of Heidegger's thought depends in large measure on the nature and validity of the philosophical study of religion.

The word 'religion' is notoriously difficult to define. It is used to refer to more or less clearly delineated faith traditions such as Buddhism, Islam and Christianity; it can also refer to the realm of the divine-human relationship, however that may be understood; finally, it can mean the theoretical study of either (or both) of these two phenomena. The philosophy of religion usually deals with the divine-human relationship, although as we shall see, there is considerable disagreement among philosophers as to the scope of their investigation in this area. One other academic discipline, namely theology, has precisely the same subject-matter as philosophy of religion, and in the course of this work it will be necessary to determine the exact relationship between these two disciplines.

The religious significance of Heidegger's philosophy has been a matter of considerable interest to philosophers and theologians from most of the major world religions, especially Buddhism, Taoism, Judaism and, of course, Christianity (including Orthodoxy, Catholicism and Protestantism). This interest is all the more remarkable in that Heidegger himself claims to have no competence in matters of religion. He has always held that there exists a sharp dichotomy between thinking and faith, and consequently between philosophy and theology, and he has recommended to theologians that they consider philosophy (including his own) as 'foolishness'. That this advice has been widely rejected is evident from even a brief glance at contemporary religious thought, especially in Western Christianity.

A comprehensive assessment of the religious significance of Heidegger's philosophy would necessarily involve the application of his ideas to each of the major world religious systems. This would be an enormous task, and the present work has the more modest

1

objective of exploring Heidegger's impact on Western Christianity. This is, as might be expected, the religious tradition where Heidegger's ideas have received the widest scrutiny. Most of the major 20th century Christian theologians have examined his work, and the resulting evaluations of it manifest a wonderful variety, since they include characterizations of Heidegger's thought as the worst form of atheism and paganism as well as appreciations of its eminent suitability as a foundation for theological speculation. A careful analysis of these evaluations is necessary in order to determine the causes of their diversity, as well as to see which, if any, can serve as a trustworthy guide to the interpretation of Heidegger's religious significance.

In a work such as this which involves both description and interpretation, normally the descriptive part comes first. Thus, one would expect to find here first a presentation of Heidegger's own treatment of religion, and then the interpretation and evaluation of the role of religion in his philosophy. However, there are strong reasons for modifying this procedure in this work. Because of Heidegger's views on the separation of philosophy and religion, he has not developed for himself a specific philosophy of religion. Any systematic presentation of his views on religion must be constructed from his writings on other topics--i.e., it involves from the beginning an *interpretation* of his philosophy. Since, therefore, such a great part of our task is alien to Heidegger's own procedure, and indeed involves the possibility of the rejection of certain of his beliefs, it is necessary in this work to clarify the problems involved in the interpretation and evaluation of his thought before actually setting forth what he has said about religion. These problems fall into two main categories: (1) the inability of Heidegger's interpreters to agree on the religious significance of his philosophy; and (2) the lack of consensus among both theologians and philosophers as to the nature and even the possibility of the philosophy of religion. If these problems are analyzed and clarified in advance, then Heidegger's own views on religion can be presented in such a way as to facilitate a rapid and straightforward evaluation.

The plan of this work follows from the above considerations. The first chapter will be devoted to a survey of previous evaluations of Heidegger's relevance for religious thought. This will show the lack of consensus among his theological interpreters as to the value of his philosophy for their own discipline. Some have considered his philosophy to be atheistic--a denial of God's existence or reality--and therefore to be totally rejected by religious people. Others have felt that this philosophy is neutral with regard to belief in God--it neither affirms nor denies Him. Finally, there are those who hold that Heidegger's thought is positively

theistic in its import and of great value for religion. That
Heidegger has aroused such interest among theologians is indica-
tive of the importance of our topic; however, the great divergence
of these evaluations of his philosophy does require some explanation before we can continue on further.

In examining these religious interpretations of Heidegger's
philosophy, it becomes very clear that there is a fundamental disagreement among both philosophers and theologians as to the validity of the philosophical study of religion. Although religious
matters such as the existence and nature of God have in the past
been treated by almost all philosophers, there are some philosophers today (including Heidegger) who hold that this has been
illegitimate, and that philosophy should not concern itself with
the subject-matter of religious faith. Among theologians, the
separation of philosophy from theology enjoys a much longer tradition, and today is practised by many representatives of this discipline. However, there has always existed the opposite tendency
to attempt an integration of faith and reason and to use philosophy
to interpret religious faith. And so, the interrelationship of
philosophy and religion is evidently one of the principal issues
of disagreement among the interpreters of Heidegger's philosophy,
and it is apparent that no evaluation of the religious import of
his philosophy can be regarded as definitive unless this issue is
clarified.

To emphasize the apparent irreconcilability of the different
attitudes towards the philosophical study of religion is not to
terminate discussion of this matter. Indeed, one recent development in this area offers the possibility of a new approach to this
subject, and promises to be especially useful in the evaluation of
the religious import of Heidegger's philosophy. While Heidegger
himself and most of his interpreters have been working in what may
be termed the mainstream of modern European (especially German and
French) philosophy, and thus share many of the same philosophical
and theological presuppositions, there has arisen within the past
100 years a distinctive American tradition of philosophy, and
especially of philosophy of religion, which may well be able to
shed new light on the difficulties involved in the interpretation
of Heidegger. This tradition may be characterized very briefly as
a 'creative empiricism', which differs both from the 'rationalism'
of continental European philosophy and the 'analytical empiricism'
of British philosophy. For the Americans, the philosophical study
of religion is both possible and necessary. Religious knowledge,
as knowledge, is fundamentally the same as all other types of
knowledge, and is subject to the same laws of description, interpretation and evaluation as these others--i.e., it must originate
from and be referrable to human *experience*. However, this form of

3

empiricism is not content to accept the data of experience as something unchangeable, which can only be analyzed and described; rather, experience is in large measure the product of human creativity, and is to that extent subject to controlled change and development. For religion, this means that mankind is not restricted by its past traditions, but is capable of changing religion to meet the needs of the future. It is possible that this American approach to the philosophy of religion may provide a novel and useful perspective from which to evaluate Heidegger's treatment of religion, and so chapter two of this work will be devoted to a survey of some important American philosophers of religion and a comparison of their approach to religion with the other philosophical approaches.

Having thus clarified the various meanings of the expression 'philosophy of religion', we can then proceed in chapter three to examine Heidegger's philosophy in order to determine in what sense if any it includes a philosophy of religion. Heidegger's own attitude towards this question has already been noted. However, a close examination of his writings does indeed reveal a concern with religious matters. Heidegger offers a vigorous critique of traditional Christian theology, which he feels has been corrupted by its assimilation into Greek metaphysical philosophy. In accordance with his understanding of the relation between thinking and faith, most of his explicit treatment of religious topics is negative—he shows how previous theological formulations have been inadequate but does not say how they can be improved. Nevertheless, if viewed from a perspective other than his own (such as that of American philosophy of religion), certain aspects of his philosophy can be seen as quite suggestive of a religious interpretation. Of particular importance in this regard are his description of man, especially the concept of *death* therein, and his description of Being as a *gift* to man, which implies that there is something beyond Being which is its source. Heidegger does deal explicitly with notions such as the 'holy', 'divinity', 'the gods' and 'God', but this discussion is not directly relevant for religion, since these terms are understood philosophically rather than theologically. However, in another sense they are important for religion, since they refer to the way in which man should live on the earth, which is of major concern to religion.

This investigation of Heidegger's philosophy from the perspective of American philosophy of religion reveals that there does exist a Heideggerian philosophy of religion. The final chapter of this work will be devoted to an evaluation of Heidegger's treatment of religion, with particular reference once again to the American approach to religion. The evaluation will deal first with Heidegger's philosophy of religion in its extant form, and then will suggest how a more complete Heideggerian philosophy of religion might be developed. Finally, the relation of theology to the Heideggerian philosophy of religion will be indicated, in order to round out the treatment of the religious significance of Heidegger's philosophy.

In view of the difficulties involved in the interpretation of Heidegger's thought, as well as the somewhat restricted scope of our topic, this work will not be able to serve as an introduction to Heidegger's philosophy in addition to accomplishing its main purpose--a detailed study of his treatment of religion. Some previous familiarity with Heidegger's thought will be assumed, especially with regard to the contents of his first major work, *Sein und Zeit*, as well as to the role of that work in the development of his philosophy.

Heidegger and the Theologians

I. Previous Evaluations.

The philosophy of Martin Heidegger has been a major factor in the
development of Christian theology in the twentieth century.
Heidegger himself has claimed repeatedly that he is not competent
to deal with matters theological, but his works have nonetheless
evoked spirited responses from the leading theologians of this era.
The early and widespread characterization of Heidegger as an
'existentialist', and indeed an atheistic existentialist like
Jean-Paul Sartre, occasioned a vigorous attack against him by
Protestant theologians such as Karl Barth and several Catholic
theologians too. On the other hand, a closer acquaintance with
Heidegger's lectures and writings has convinced many others that
his philosophy can be used with profit for the elucidation of the
Christian faith in the twentieth century. Of this latter group,
some theologians, notably Rudolf Bultmann, have felt that Heidegger's
philosophy as such is theistically neutral, but that certain of its
elements, such as its description of man, are better suited for the
translation of the biblical message than is the language of traditional theology. Others, like John Macquarrie, believe that Heidegger's philosophy is positively theistic in import, and can serve
as the basis of a valid contemporary natural theology. These
different interpreters of the relevance of Heidegger for theistic
thought have themselves entered into direct confrontation, and this
debate has engaged many of the foremost theologians of this era.
Any adequate treatment of the religious significance of Heidegger's
philosophy must first situate itself with regard to a representative
selection of these previous interpretations of his thought.

It is to be noted that almost all of the interpretations of
Heidegger's philosophy with regard to its religious import have
come from theologians rather than philosophers or historians of
religion. And when non-theologians have offered evaluations of
Heidegger's religious significance, they have generally done so
from a theological, rather than a philosophical, perspective.
The philosopher A. de Waelhens, in his widely circulated introduction to Heidegger, entitled *La philosophie de Martin Heidegger*,[1]
states categorically that Heidegger's description of human existence is totally incompatible with "Christian experience" (which
he does not define):

> ...we believe that we have shown that the theses of Heidegger's
> philosophy are, in fact, the mere transposition of a strictly

7

personal experience of existence, experience which is, without a doubt, the exact contrary of Christian experience....Thus one could demonstrate without difficulty that the Heideggerian ideas of thrownness, of guilt and especially of transcendence (ideas which are major elements of the *notion* of existence for Heidegger) constitute *the experience of the refusal of Christian existence*....The philosophy of Heidegger can serve no other end than its own, and that end is the acceptance of finitude and the exaltation of contingence.[2]

De Waelhens does not attempt a philosophical analysis of the Christian experience of existence as he has done with the Heideggerian description of existence, and so his judgment of the total incompatibility of the one with the other is evidently based on some unexpressed preconceptions of Christian theology which colour his thinking. (In fact, as will be shown in chapter 4 below, Heidegger's description of human finitude and the contingency of being are extremely valuable for religious thought, including that of Christianity.)

Another example of a philosopher evaluating the religous import of Heidegger's philosophy from a naive theological standpoint is the otherwise perceptive book by Helmut Danner, *Das Göttliche und der Gott bei Heidegger* (The Divine and the God in Heidegger).[3] After giving a fairly thorough description of Heidegger's use of the terms God, the God, the divine, the divinities, the holy, etc., Danner concludes that Heidegger's concept of God is inadequate because it is incompatible with the description of God given in the Bible:

...with regard to the *God* and the divine in Heidegger's thought, it must be stated unequivocally that, except for the word itself, they have *nothing in common* with the Jewish-Christian *God*.... Insofar as Heidegger reveals himself in his thinking about the (divine) God, and he indeed asks and seeks after a God, after 'the' God, he comes only to the declaration of 'God's' absence; the God of the Old and New Testaments does not in the least enter into his horizon--which is consistent insofar as the God of Revelation cannot be experienced by thinking.[4]

Danner speaks quite freely of the "God of the Old and New Testaments" without indicating any awareness of the theologically (not to mention philosophically) problematical character of the Biblical concept (or concepts) of God. To speak of the "God of the Old and New Testaments" without any further description implies that there is general agreement as to the meaning of this expression. One need only think of the differences between Judaism and Christianity, not to mention the variety of concepts of God within these two religions, to realise that this assumption is mistaken. For Danner to argue convincingly that Heidegger's concept of God is incompatible

8

with that of the Bible, he would have to be much more precise about his understanding of this latter term.

The final philosophical evaluation of the religious import of Heidegger's philosophy to be noted here is at the same time the shortest and the most influential. It was offered by Jean-Paul Sartre, the French 'existentialist' philosopher. He was responsible for many of the atheistic interpretations of Heidegger because of his celebrated remark that "there are...the existential atheists, amongst whom we must place Heidegger as well as the French existentialists and myself."[5] The extensive use which Sartre made of Heidegger's ideas in his own major philosophical work, *Being and Nothingness*, served to verify in the minds of many of his readers this declaration that Heidegger's philosophy is thoroughly atheistic, and Heidegger's name has been linked to Sartre's in many books on existentialism as an unrepentant atheist.[6]

Apart from these three exceptions, Heidegger's philosophical interpreters have generally avoided a direct evaluation of the religious significance of his thought. Their attitude towards this question is well expressed by William Richardson, who states only that Heidegger is not incapable of a religious interpretation. But as regards *which* interpretation is most adequate, "here the matter is difficult and it must be left to the theologians themselves."[7] As will become evident in the following pages, this view seems to be shared by most theologians as well.

Theological interest in Heidegger's philosophy has not been exclusive to Western Christians. The significance of his thought for the Buddhist and Taoist religious traditions has been the subject of lively discussion among some oriental scholars,[8] and well-known representatives of other phases of the Judaeo-Christian tradition have offered religious evaluations of his philosophy.[9] However, it will be advisable in this chapter to limit our treatment to representatives of the principal Western Christian theological traditions, since it is Western Christianity which is most closely related to Heidegger's philosophy.

The theological interpreters of Heidegger can be divided easily enough into those who consider him and/or his philosophy atheistic and those who believe that he can be interpreted theistically. There are, however, two important twentieth-century theologians who resist this manner of classification, despite their extensive use of Heidegger's philosophy. The first of these, Paul Tillich, has acknowledged Heidegger as one of the major influences in his theological development:

> When existential philosophy was introduced into Germany, I came to a new understanding of the relationship between philosophy and theology. Heidegger's lectures at Marburg, the publication of his *Sein und Zeit* (Being and Time), and also his interpreta-

tion of Kant were significant in this connection.[10]
Tillich adopted from Heidegger both his concern for Being--the
ontological perspective which had been absent from theology as
much as from philosophy in the early twentieth century--and his
approach to Being through a description of human existence, which
Tillich developed as his method of 'correlation' (in which the
questions posed by the human condition are answered by divine
revelation).[11] In addition to the overall structure of his theology, Tillich has been influenced by Heidegger's philosophy in many
specific aspects of his theological system, such as his concept of
death.[12] All in all, Heidegger's influence on Tillich has been
very extensive,[13] and yet Tillich has generally avoided a direct
evaluation of the religious significance of Heidegger's philosophy.
Apart from occasional references to "Heidegger's emphatic atheism,"[14] Tillich seems content to regard Heidegger as just a
philosopher, and he is not surprised that Heidegger does not attempt
to give religious answers to the questions raised by his philosophy,
questions which Tillich feels can be answered only by the theologian.

The second major theologian who has refused to judge the religious import of Heidegger's thought is Karl Rahner. Although
Rahner's theological vocabulary is permeated with Heideggerian
terminology and his 'theological anthropology' closely parallels
Heidegger's philosophical treatment of human existence, his explicit interpretation of Heidegger's philosophy is apparently
limited to one essay, published in 1940.[15] Even at this relatively
early stage in the development of Heidegger's thought, when he had
published only one full-length book, *Kant und das Problem der
Metaphysik*, and a few shorter essays, notably *Was ist Metaphysik?*
and *Vom Wesen des Grundes*, since the appearance of *Sein und Zeit*
in 1927, Rahner displayed an accurate perception of the direction
in which Heidegger was moving, especially with regard to the
primacy of the question of Being and the limited importance of his
analysis of human existence. Rahner points out that this fundamental ontology of Heidegger will be very different from traditional metaphysics, which Heidegger refers to as "onto-theology"
because it identifies the foundation of being as God. Heidegger's
own ontology will scrupulously avoid the problem of God; he asserts
that his description of *Dasein* is theistically neutral. Thus,
Rahner feels that the theistic import of Heidegger's thought will
be revealed only as his ontology develops. He sees two basic
possibilities: if the interpretation of *Dasein* as radically finite
extends to the description of Being in terms of nothingness, then
Heidegger will have ended up with an atheistic nihilism such as
Nietzsche's. If, however, the analysis of *Dasein* reveals a human
transcendence open to the absolute, placed before a choice between

eternal death and eternal life before God, and not simply before nothingness, then Heidegger's philosophy will have a most profoundly religious meaning. In this article, Rahner does not predict which possibility will prevail, and he seems not to have returned to this question in any of his later writings, even though the direction of Heidegger's thought has become much clearer in subsequent years.[16]

Most of the theologians who have dealt with Heidegger have been less hesitant than Tillich and Rahner to judge the religious import of his thought. In what follows, we shall deal first with the unfavourable evaluations, then with the favourable. In each case, a tripartite division among the theologians treated here suggests itself: Catholic theologians, Karl Barth and his followers, and Rudolf Bultmann and his associates. The remainder of the chapter will be devoted to an examination of these evaluations in order to determine why they differ to such a great extent, and which of them, if any, offers a trustworthy guide to the theological use of Heidegger's philosophy.

A. Negative Evaluations of Heidegger's Philosophy.

1. Catholic Theologians.

Among those Catholic scholars who have addressed themselves to Heidegger's thought, there is just as wide a spectrum of interpretations as will be evident among Protestant theologians. Heidegger has apparently never been subjected to any official condemnation by the Catholic Church, although as a baptized Catholic (and former seminarian) he would have been liable to such measures when they were in vogue. Nevertheless, the opposition to Heidegger from within this Church has been led by the proponents of its 'official' philosophy and theology, Thomism.

The early interpretation of Heidegger as an existentialist, and indeed an atheistic existentialist like Sartre, met with a vigorous condemnation from a French Thomist, Régis Jolivet. In his book, *Le problème de la mort chez M. Heidegger et J.-P. Sartre*, Jolivet derives from Heidegger's characterization of *Dasein* as Being-towards-death the conclusion that the Heideggerian absolute is Nothing (*le néant*). Heidegger's silence with regard to the post-mortem condition of *Dasein* is interpreted by Jolivet as a denial of all existence after death and, consequently, a denial that man has an immortal soul; thus, this philosophy is at bottom a species of materialism. According to Jolivet, "The only imaginable destiny for *Dasein* is to tend toward this return to nothing [i.e., death] which gives it its true meaning;"[17] for this reason, he describes Heidegger's philosophy as a "neo-Stoicism." And he

11

offers as a refutation of Heidegger (and Sartre) a proof of the immortality of the soul, based on "the experience that we have of ourselves...[as] an incarnate *soul*."18

A more perceptive critique of Heidegger, one which takes into account the later developments of his thought, has been offered by another French Thomist, Maurice Corvez, in his book, *L'Être et la conscience morale*. Corvez's assessment of Heidegger's philosophy is just the opposite of Jolivet's: far from being a materialist, Heidegger is in reality an idealist. Indeed, Corvez seems to admit of just two metaphysical categories: idealism and (Thomistic) realism; since Heidegger's phenomenology is something quite different from the latter, he must be an idealist.19 The most damaging evidence of this is the fact that "Heidegger's thought is imprisoned by a narrow subjectivism insofar as it recognizes as ontological and ontic determinations of the world only that which proceeds from the human subject."20 For Corvez, phenomenology is subjectivism, and for that reason is incapable of authentic contact with reality, God included. Corvez attempts to show that there is no place for God in Heidegger's philosophy: Being is not God, since Being has need of beings, and, moreover, is in process. Nor is the Heideggerian 'Nothing' a name for God, since it is but another term for Being. Heidegger's investigation of Being, man, and the world has turned up no trace of God, and he has in addition rejected the God of the Western metaphysical tradition as a being unworthy of the name. Indeed, he does not reject the possibility of an encounter with the true God, but he feels that this can take place only on the level of faith, not of thought (which deals only with the finite). However, thought can and, indeed, must prepare the way for this encounter by thinking the essence of divinity, for it is only within this sphere that God can appear. Corvez concludes that this attempt by Heidegger to prepare for the coming of God is misfounded, since in reality he has "furiously cut all the bridges which lead to Him."21

A number of German Catholic theologians, including Gustav Siewerth, J. B. Lotz and Hans Meyer, have also interpreted Heidegger's philosophy as incompatible with Christianity.22 These theologians all evaluate Heidegger from the same Thomistic perspective, and Meyer's critique, as expressed in his book, *Martin Heidegger und Thomas von Aquin*, may be regarded as representative of their common approach. Meyer does not hesitate to characterize Heidegger's philosophy as atheistic, since it speaks of nothing beyond Being, which is finite and therefore not God. Like Corvez, he admits that Heidegger attempts to prepare the way for the coming of God by thinking from the truth of Being to the essence of the Holy, and from the essence of the Holy to the essence of divinity, but Meyer feels that this procedure restricts the problem of God to

12

the course of human history. He also thinks that Heidegger's criticism of the God of the Western metaphysical tradition does not apply to Aquinas' concept of God: "It is quite evident that Thomas Aquinas refused to adopt the description of God as *causa sui*,"[23] the name which Heidegger feels is most characteristic of the Western metaphysical God. Nor does Thomas' description of God as the supreme good subject him to Heidegger's condemnation of the concept of God as the ultimate *value* of man. Meyer feels that the respective concepts of Being and God are correlative in both Thomas and Heidegger. For Thomas, God is infinite Being. For Heidegger, Being is finite and therefore not God. However (according to Meyer), finite Being entails a finite God. And so Heidegger's attempt to separate philosophy and theology must be judged unsuccessful, for a philosophy which permits only a finite God cannot coexist with a theology which believes in an infinite God.[24]

The criticism of Heidegger from the Thomistic viewpoint is well summed up by Cornelio Fabro in his massive history of modern atheism, *God in Exile*. Fabro judges the theistic potential of a philosophy according to its allowance for divine transcendence (immanence equals atheism). By this criterion, "the Heideggerian *Sein selbst* (Being itself)...is atheistic in content, structure and position, inasmuch as it is the coming-to-presence of the finite by the instrumentality of a finite being condemned to a finite destiny like man's."[25] Fabro feels that Heidegger has completely subjected Being to man: "There is no abandonment of the reference of the truth of being to the essence of man; rather is this very reference made the central determining factor of the definition of Being itself."[26] He admits that Heidegger does not exclude all openness to God, but for all practical purposes "God is foreign to and banished from philosophy."[27] Fabro also grants the validity of Heidegger's criticism of the history of Western metaphysics--for everyone, that is, except Thomas Aquinas. Heidegger has correctly pointed out the primacy of the question of Being for philosophy (as did Aquinas), but he has erred grievously in separating the question of Being from the question of God. For Heidegger, Being has no content, and is therefore Non-being. This is just the opposite of Aquinas' description of God as the plenitude of Being. No matter where else Heidegger may try to find God, Fabro concludes, his failure to describe Being in terms which would identify it with God means that he is an atheist.

2. Barth and the Barthians.

Karl Barth's opposition to the theological use of Heidegger stems from his radical rejection of any philosophical intrusion into the realm proper to theology--the relation of God and man. Barth feels that in this relationship God is absolutely primary; philosophy, however, starts with man, and is therefore capable of only a perverted expression of this relationship. Theology must guard its autonomy against philosophy: there can be no such thing as "natural theology" or "theological anthropology."[28] The *analogia entis* must be rejected, since it reduces God to a philosophical category, a human creation. The relation of God to man depends entirely on God: he gives himself to man in the way he chooses (pre-eminently in the person of Jesus Christ), and man is absolutely incapable of evoking this relationship by his own means (such as philosophy).

Barth has dealt with Heidegger's philosophy in particular in section III/3 of his *Kirchliche Dogmatik* (1950).[29] There he judges that Heidegger's philosophical equivalent of the Christian God is Nothing (*Nichts*). Barth derives this conclusion from Heidegger's 1929 lecture *Was ist Metaphysik?* in which the concept of Nothing is introduced as a possible approach to the question of Being. He feels that this concept is the key to Heidegger's whole philosophy, and it enables him to treat Heidegger together with Sartre as a philosophical atheist. Despite Heidegger's protest against being called an atheist, Barth holds that his philosophy contains implicitly the same atheism which Sartre makes explicit, in that his trinity of beings, *Dasein* and Nothing leaves no room for God. Heidegger does not go so far as to say explicitly that Nothing is God, but Barth has no doubt that his philosophy must be so interpreted.[30] Even though Heidegger, in his 1946 *Letter on Humanism,* shows that Nothing is no different than Being itself, but just another name for Being, Barth holds that this concept is antipathetic to the Christian understanding of God. In fact, its use is equivalent to "proclaiming the devil as the source of all beings and all *Daseins*."[31]

Barth is therefore adamantly opposed to the use of Heidegger's philosophy by Rudolf Bultmann. Bultmann felt that Heidegger's existential analytic of human existence expressed in contemporary language the same understanding of man that the New Testament expressed in mythological language, and so was suitable for use as a "preunderstanding" (*Vorverständnis*) of the gospel message. In a pamphlet entitled, *Rudolf Bultmann: Ein Versuch, ihn zu verstehen* (An Attempt to Understand Him), Barth reproaches Bultmann for paying undue honour to Heidegger by equating his writings with the New Testament. Furthermore, he claims that Bultmann has not taken into account the later development of Heidegger's thought, which reveals that the existential analytic holds only a subordinate place in his philosophy. He chides Bultmann for "canonizing" a philosophical view of man which has been rejected in America and Russia. And he points out the great danger of every theological use of philosophy--that a theology which allows itself to become dominated by philosophy is no longer a theology at all, but is itself philosophy (he does not accuse Bultmann of having gone this far, however).[32]

The Barthian polemic against philosophical theology in general and Heidegger in particular has been continued by his followers. Hermann Diem has also described Heidegger's incompatibility with Christianity in terms of his concept of Nothing: "In contrast to Christian thought, for which God is he who transcends every worldly being and the one with whom man can enter into relation as his Creator, for Heidegger every transcendence is *Nothing*."[33] Heidegger's later description of Nothing as Being plays the same role in his philosophy as the concept of God did in the old metaphysics. Neither, however, is equivalent to the Christian God.[34]

A more subtle rejection of Heidegger has been offered by a pupil of Diem, Gerhard Noller. In his doctoral thesis, *Sein und Existenz*, Noller attempted to show that the use of Heidegger's philosophy by Rudolf Bultmann and Friedrich Gogarten in their theology of demythologizing involved an extensive misunderstanding of Heidegger, particularly with regard to their anthropological interpretation of the existential analytic of *Sein und Zeit*. As to a positive appropriation of Heidegger, Noller reiterates the criticisms of Diem and Barth with regard to Heidegger's concept of Nothing.[35] He also lists and evaluates the four possible approaches of theology to Heidegger's philosophy: 1) It can understand itself as an ontic science, whose object is God (a being); but if it did this, it would be subject to a fundamental ontology whose object is Being as such. 2) It can identify its concept of God with Heidegger's concept of Being; but this would involve numerous difficulties, including the appearance of God as the devil. 3) It can separate the existential analytic of *Sein und Zeit* from the later thought of Heidegger, in order to use the former for its own sake; but Heidegger's thought is too much of a unity for this to be possible--the early Heidegger necessarily entails the later. 4) Theology can take Heidegger's (and St. Paul's) advice to consider philosophy as foolishness; Noller offers no criticism of this suggestion.[36]

3. Bultmannians.

Our last set of interpretations of Heidegger as an atheist comes from a theological perspective which has for the most part been very receptive to Heidegger's philosophy--the school of Rudolf Bultmann. One such evangelical theologian, Helmut Franz, has categorized all theological uses of Heidegger as either *eclecticism* or *glossism*. The former category includes the work of Bultmann himself, who used only the early writings of Heidegger, and also that of Heinrich Ott (see below). The principal representative of glossism, by

15

which Franz means the appropriation of Heidegger's theory of language, is Ernst Fuchs. Fuchs holds that Heidegger's description of inauthentic language points to a true language, which for theology is the language of faith, but Franz feels that Fuchs is in danger of subordinating to the *content* of biblical language the fact that it is *Jesus* speaking.[37]

According to Franz, Heidegger's characterization of all theology as metaphysics is true of medieval-scholastic theology but not of modern evangelical theology. More precisely, metaphysics is only the *past* of theology.[38] For the Greeks, metaphysics was theology in the sense that God and the world were correlative: the world precisely as world was a God-world. This God, however, was the metaphysical supreme being, the *causa sui*, a description which Heidegger rightly feels is unworthy of the true God. Heidegger himself describes briefly some essential characteristics of the true God (*der göttliche Gott*), but Franz feels that this description is no more accurate with regard to the Christian God than is the metaphysical *causa sui*.[39] He also disagrees with Heidegger's contention that the true Christian message was corrupted by its contact with Greek philosophy, even before the writing of the New Testament contents. Theology would deprive itself of its very foundation (the New Testament) if it took Heidegger's advice to re-search the primitive Christian experience by thinking à la Heidegger into the essence of the relationship between man and the true God. In conclusion, Franz interprets the New Testament message as a call out of the world, and therefore Heidegger's suggestion that theology address itself to the world as experienced by the Christian is completely foreign to the nature of genuine theology.[40]

Perhaps the most severe criticism of all those directed against the theological appropriation of Heidegger is that offered by a former pupil of Heidegger and associate of Bultmann, Hans Jonas. Like Franz, Jonas rejects all previous attempts of theologians to profit from Heidegger's thought, especially that of Heinrich Ott. Jonas claims that Heidegger has derived many of his key concepts from Christianity; therefore it is not for him to judge theology from the standpoint of his own philosophy, but rather philosophy must examine the philosophical validity of Heidegger's borrowing from theology. Jonas opposes an eclectic approach to either philosophy or theology; the theologian "must ask whether one can take half of his story without falsifying the whole--as he will in time have to ask conversely whether Heidegger's philosophy can be assimilated in part without taking in the whole."[41] Jonas himself obviously feels that he cannot.

According to Jonas, Heidegger's understanding of Being excludes every Christian interpretation. The apparent similarity of the

self-unveiling of Being and the revelation of God masks a deeper
incompatibility: Heidegger speaks of the appearance of Being to
man in terms of *fate*, but

the Christian is said to be saved from the power of fate...and
that which saved him was, by the understanding of faith as
distinct from the understanding of the world, not an event of
the world and thus not an event of fate, nor destined ever to
become fate or a part of fate itself, but an event invalidat-
ing all dicta of fate and over-ruling the words which fate reveals to man, including the words of self-revealing Being.[42]

Jonas identifies the Being whose fate Heidegger ponders as "the
quintessence of the world," against which "theology should guard
the radical transcendence of its God, whose voice comes not out of
Being but breaks into the kingdom of Being from without."[43] Thus
he sees as irreconcilable Heidegger's statement, "Being reveals itself," and the Christian belief that "the world is God's handiwork."

Jonas feels that Heidegger's attempt to overcome metaphysics and
especially its subject-object dichotomy is ill-founded: "The
subject-object *relation*...is not a lapse but the privilege, burden
and duty of men. Not Plato is responsible for it but the human
condition...."[44] This refusal to accept the subject-object relation is but one example of

the seeming, false humility of Heidegger's shifting the initiative to Being, so seductive to Christian theologians, but in
fact the most enormous *hybris* in the whole history of thought.
For it is nothing less than the thinker's claiming that through
him speaks the essence of things itself, and thus the claim to
an authority which no thinker should ever claim.[45]

In sum, Jonas thinks that Heidegger's thought is pagan rather than
atheistic because it deifies the world--it amounts to saying that
"revelation is immanent in the world, nay, belongs to its nature;
i.e., that the world is divine."[46]

B. Positive Evaluations of Heidegger's Philosophy.

1. Bultmann and Bultmannians.

It has long been a theological commonplace that the theology of
Rudolf Bultmann is greatly dependent upon the philosophy of Heidegger. However, as is the case with Tillich and Rahner, there are
remarkably few direct allusions to Heidegger in Bultmann's own
writings, and those critics who have dealt specifically with the
relation of these two thinkers, notably John Macquarrie and Gerhard
Noller, have either felt it unnecessary or have been unable to cite
specific passages to illustrate Bultmann's attitude towards Heidegger's philosophy.[47] Such passages do exist in Bultmann's writ-

ings, however, and they indicate both the extent and the limits of Heidegger's influence on this theologian.

The decisive period of encounter between Bultmann and Heidegger were the years 1923-1928, when they both taught at the University of Marburg. According to Bultmann, there was much fruitful cooperation between members of the philosophy and theology faculties at Marburg at this time, and he readily acknowledges the influence of Heidegger on his own thought:

The work of existentialist philosophy, which I came to know through my discussion with Martin Heidegger, has become of decisive significance for me. I found in it the conceptuality in which it is possible to speak adequately of human existence and therefore also of the existence of the believer.[48]

Bultmann is here referring to the analysis of existence which Heidegger published in 1927 under the title of *Sein und Zeit*. Since this book was the outcome rather than the origin of a dialogue between Heidegger the philosopher and several Christian theologians, Bultmann felt no qualms about appropriating its contents for theology:

Heidegger's existential analysis of the ontological structure of being would seem to be no more than a secularized, philosophical version of the New Testament view of human life. For him the chief characteristic of man's Being in history is anxiety. Man exists in a permanent tension between the past and the future. At every moment he is confronted with an alternative. Either he must immerse himself in the concrete world of nature, and thus inevitably lose his individuality, or he must abandon all security and commit himself unreservedly to the future, and thus alone achieve his authentic Being. Is not that exactly the New Testament understanding of human life? Some critics have objected that I am borrowing Heidegger's categories and forcing them upon the New Testament. I am afraid this only shows that they are blinding their eyes to the real problem. I mean, one should rather be startled that philosophy is saying the same thing as the New Testament, and saying it quite independently.[49]

The criticism to which Bultmann alludes in this passage has to do with the conflict over the relation of philosophy and theology which had shattered the post-World War I alliance between Barth and Bultmann, among others. Although Barth himself did not issue his public condemnation of Bultmann's use of Heidegger until much later, the Barthian critique was directed against Bultmann already in 1929 by Gerhardt Kuhlmann, in an article entitled, "The Theological Problem of Existence. A Question to Rudolf Bultmann."[50] Kuhlmann felt that Bultmann's use of Heideggerian philosophy as a propaedeutic to faith was a threat to theology: "Philosophy understood as the

18

science of the meaning of Being renders theology at the most superfluous."[51] The "atheistic metaphysics" of Heidegger contains an understanding of the self which Kuhlmann feels is in no way suitable for the man of faith. Bultmann is wrong to identify revelation with Heidegger's "call of conscience."[52]

Bultmann responded immediately to this criticism of Kuhlmann in an article entitled, "The Historicality (*Geschichtlichkeit*) of *Dasein* and Faith. Answer to Gerhardt Kuhlmann."[53] There he distinguishes philosophy and theology according to how each treats man: philosophy deals with the natural man; theology, with the man of faith. Thus a philosophy is not properly speaking theistic or atheistic. From the point of view of theology, philosophy should exhibit the conditions of the possibility of faith in man, but it cannot prove or disprove the object of this faith. Phenomenological philosophy is particularly well-suited for theological use, since

in this case, theology...does not simply take over some philosophical system of dogma, but rather lets itself be referred by philosophy to the phenomenon itself; it lets itself be taught by the phenomenon, by man, whose structure philosophy seeks to disclose."[54]

Against Kuhlmann, Bultmann insists that the theological explication of existence in faith must fall back on the philosophical analysis of man; otherwise theology would not be a science. And, in fact, every previous theology *has* depended on some philosophy for its understanding of man, whether or not it has recognized this dependence.[55]

With regard to Heidegger's philosophy in particular, Bultmann acknowledges his debt to Heidegger for the all-important concept of the historicality of man. He attempts to mediate the concept of man as "being-towards-death" of Heidegger with that as "being-towards-the-other" (love) of Friedrich Gogarten, and concludes that the apparent opposition of these concepts is due to the fact that

Heidegger speaks as an ontologist and therefore has neither the occasion nor the right to speak of love. Gogarten, on the other hand, speaks as a theologian of the ontic; and it is in this sphere alone that love, in the radical sense in which he understands it, is to be found.[56]

Bultmann therefore imposes certain limits on the theological use of Heidegger's analysis of existence, but he feels that it is valid within those limits and can be used with profit by the theologian to interpret the existence of the man of faith.

Some twenty years later, Bultmann's use of Heidegger was sharply criticized by the philosopher Karl Jaspers:

Because Bultmann confines philosophy to one book by Heidegger [i.e., *Sein und Zeit*], and, as I suspect, misunderstands that book when he emphasizes its 'scientific', objective, scholastic

19

aspects, he in effect cuts himself off from all philosophy....
His conception of philosophy, which I believe foreign to Heidegger himself, is that of nineteenth-century academicians or
Hellenistic doxographers. Heidegger himself would surely be
surprised at any theology based on it.[57]

Bultmann was quick to defend himself against this accusation. He
refers to Gogarten's work, *Entmythologisierung und Kirche*, as proof
that "we do not necessarily subscribe to Heidegger's philosophical
theories when we learn something from his existentialist analysis."[58]
Heidegger attacks a problem which is crucial for modern theology--
the problem of history--and if theology can benefit from Heidegger's
analysis, it should do so. Bultmann objects to Jaspers' claim that
he limits all philosophy to Heidegger: "Needless to say, we may
learn from others besides Heidegger. If we can learn those things
better elsewhere, it is all to the good. But they have to be
learned."[59] And in a recent volume of essays in his honour, Bultmann reiterates his independence with regard to Heidegger:

My theology does not become dependent on a philosophical system
by my seeking to make fruitful use of the concepts of the so-
called philosophy of existence, particularly of Heidegger's
analysis of existence in *Being and Time*. I learned from him
not *what* theology has to say, but *how* it has to say it, in
order to speak to the thinking man of today in a way that he
can understand.[60]

As we have seen, one of the major criticisms of Bultmann's use of
Heidegger is that he has ignored the later developments in Heidegger's thought which are implied by the existential analytic of *Sein
und Zeit*. Allusions to the later writings of Heidegger are not,
however, totally absent in Bultmann's works. In an essay entitled,
"The Idea of God and Modern Man," which deals with the 'Death of
God' movement, he refers to Heidegger's interpretation of Nietzsche's
expression "God is dead" as the culmination of two thousand years
of metaphysical subjectivism. Bultmann seems to agree with Heidegger
that modern atheism is a result of this subjectivism, according to
which the world seen as an object is subordinated by man as subject
to a system which is based on the values which man himself posits.
He feels that religion, too, has been victimized by this subjec-
tivity.[61] And in another recent essay, "Apropos of a Philosophical
Theology," Bultmann wonders if perhaps the thought of the later
Heidegger with regard to Being might not provide a formal determination of the concept of God. He realizes that Heidegger himself does
not identify Being with God, but the rejection of the metaphysical
idea of God as *causa sui* would seem to leave open the possibility
of a non-metaphysical concept of God based on the concept of Being.
Or again, perhaps the idea of God is to be determined within the
relation of Being and Nothing.[62] Bultmann does no more than pose

20

these questions, and it appears that he did not develop any systematic approach either to the question of God or to the later philosophy of Heidegger.

Bultmann's pioneering adaptation of Heideggerian philosophy for theology has been continued and developed by the members of his demythologizing 'school', notably Ernst Fuchs and Gerhard Ebeling. These men have moved beyond Bultmann by addressing themselves to the thought of the later Heidegger, especially with regard to the significance of *language*. In their application of Heidegger's theories of language to theological discourse and the interpretation of the Bible, they have given new life to that ancient though underdeveloped branch of theology--hermeneutics.

Heidegger himself had borrowed the term 'hermeneutic' from theology and used it in *Sein und Zeit* to designate the phenomenological interpretation of *Dasein* which he would undertake there. In that work, language is considered as just one of the constitutive features of human existence (alongside 'thrownness' and 'projection'), but in his later writings, Heidegger comes to treat language as the central element of his description of man (since it is the primary locus of Being's revelation to man). Thus hermeneutic becomes the process of man's self-understanding--the linguistic interpretation of linguistically-constituted human existence.[63]

Ernst Fuchs has taken over this latter meaning of hermeneutic and has made it the centre of his theology. He agrees with Bultmann that theology must begin with an existential interpretation of human existence, such as that provided in *Sein und Zeit*. Unlike Bultmann, however, Fuchs considers *language* to be the primary factor of human existence and the indispensable means for carrying through the whole project of demythologizing the New Testament message. Heidegger's description of authentic and inauthentic existence in *Sein und Zeit*, which Bultmann found so useful for interpreting the New Testament distinction between the unbeliever and the man of faith, is assimilated by Fuchs into the later Heidegger's analogous distinction between the everyday language of the subject-object dilemma and the uncorrupted language of Being. Fuchs feels that such a linguistic interpretation "makes it possible to bring something like the existential interpretation of human *Dasein* into the scope of a *theological* problematic, so that we can henceforth renounce the motto of the existential interpretation."[64] He thus rejects the exclusively existentialist interpretation of Heidegger in favour of a hermeneutical interpretation. According to this interpretation:

Man exists linguistically between call and answer. In this relation language advances him what he may really 'let be.' Reality certifies for him only that which has been linguistically advanced to him. His behaviour towards reality is the mirror of the answer which he has given to the call of language which went

21

out to him.[65]
Language is thus constitutive of self-understanding, and Fuchs is
able to show the correlation of inauthentic language with the life
of unfaith and authentic language with the life of faith. Heidegger's analysis of metaphysical language corresponds to the former,
while Fuchs finds authentic language in Jesus' language of love,
as expressed in the New Testament.[66]

The relation of this hermeneutical theology to the philosophy of
Heidegger is analysed systematically by Fuchs' colleague, Gerhard
Ebeling, in an article entitled, "Verantworten des Glaubens in
Begegnung mit dem Denken M. Heideggers" (Vindication of Faith in
its Encounter with the Thinking of Heidegger). With regard to the
relation of philosophy and theology in general, Ebeling feels
that, despite the different historical origins and supposedly different subject-matter of these two disciplines, a genuine separation
between the two is problematical. First of all, each has greatly
influenced the other's historical development. Furthermore, the
two were not distinct for the ancient Greeks, and even after the
encounter with Christianity, philosophy still retained its 'theological' interests. In addition, it is difficult to define either
philosophy or theology in general; how then can their differences
be precisely delineated? It is necessary rather to confront a
particular philosophy with a particular theology. But both philosophy and theology have predetermined concepts of each other. From
which point of view is the comparison to be made? One obstacle to
dialogue between the two is that philosophy does not deny the
possibility that it may overcome theology. Theology does not want
to enter into dialogue on such terms. But in opposition to the
Barthian viewpoint, Ebeling believes that such a dialogue *is* possible, and he suggests some conditions for a fruitful dialogue: too
much time should not be spent on the actual structure of the relation between these two sciences instead of on individual problems;
the concept of *time*, which is central to both, should be discussed;
there should also be discussed the concept of *word* and the role of
speech in philosophy and theology.[67]

With regard to Heidegger's philosophy in particular, Ebeling
thinks that the overcoming of the Western metaphysical tradition by
questioning what was unquestioned in that tradition opens up a completely new dialogue situation for theology. However, this does
not necessarily mean that the problem of the relation of philosophy
and theology has been dissolved. Heidegger's philosophy can rightly
accuse metaphysical theology of the 'death of God,' and can raise
the question whether true Christian faith is compatible with such
a theology. If there is to be a valid encounter between theology
and philosophy today, it must be grounded in the overcoming of
metaphysical thinking in *both* disciplines.[68]

22

Ebeling wants to relate Heidegger's philosophy to Lutheran evangelical theology, the basis of which is "the distinction between law and gospel as the basic experience of faith."[69] According to this distinction, Heidegger's thinking would be an interpretation of the law. As such, it expresses the condition of man without faith and is useful therefore for showing the opposition between faith and unfaith. Ebeling notes that Luther himself had already begun to overcome metaphysical thinking in an effort to attain the true, biblical faith. But the main benefit of Heidegger's philosophy for theology is that it indicates the limits of the thinking about Being, and thereby frees theology for thinking the subject-matter of faith. Heidegger's emphasis on the importance of language is readily translatable into a theological concern for the word of the gospel. Theology can also be certain now of what it formerly only suspected—the unsuitability of metaphysical language to describe God. Finally, theology should not mistake Heidegger's interpretation of the ontological difference between Being and beings for the traditional metaphysical distinction between the spiritual world and the material world. This would only confuse the important theological distinction between man the sinner and God the justifier.[70] In sum, Ebeling feels, as does Fuchs, that a cautious use of Heidegger's philosophy, especially his interpretation of *language*, can be of great benefit to theology, as long as it is realized that Heidegger is competent to speak only of sinful human existence, and not of existence illuminated by the Christian faith.

2. Heinrich Ott.

Perhaps the most comprehensive attempt to demonstrate the relevance of Heidegger's philosophy for theology is that produced by none other than the student and successor of Karl Barth at the University of Basel, Heinrich Ott. Already in his doctoral thesis, *Geschichte und Heilsgeschichte in der Theologie Rudolf Bultmanns* (History and Salvation History in the Theology of Rudolf Bultmann), Ott had criticized Bultmann for his exclusively 'existentialist' understanding of Heidegger. Ott suggested that the weaknesses in Bultmann's theology, especially his dichotomy of history and nature, could be overcome by moving beyond this existentialist understanding into the areas explored in the thought of the later Heidegger—Being, thinking and language. In effect, Ott was criticizing Bultmann's theology from the point of view of Karl Barth's theology, and was claiming that the later Heidegger (and indeed the whole of Heidegger's thought, which Ott regards as a unity) is more compatible with Barth than with Bultmann. To illustrate this latter point, Ott published in 1959 a major study of the later Heidegger and his significance for theology, entitled, *Denken und Sein. Der Weg Martin Heideggers und der Weg der Theologie* (Thinking and Being. The Way of Martin Heidegger and the Way of Theology).

The bulk of this book is devoted to an exposition of the philosophy of the later Heidegger--his approach to the question of Being, the historicality of Being, and the four central concepts of Heidegger: Being itself, thinking, language and world. In each of these areas Ott sees a possible correlation between Heidegger and theology. The question which is at the very basis of Heidegger's thought--Why is there any being at all and not much rather nothing?-- is easily convertible into *the* theological question--Why is there any God at all and not much rather nothing?[71] Ott equates the formulation of Heidegger's phenomenological method--"to let that which shows itself be seen from itself in the very way in which it shows itself from itself"[72]--with the old Protestant principle, *Scriptura sacra sui ipsius interpres*; thus "Theology is phenomenology!"[73]

Ott denies that Heidegger's thought is atheistic. The God which Heidegger rejects is only the God of the Western metaphysical tradition--the *ens supremum* or *causa sui*. Ott feels that theology must imitate Heidegger in overcoming metaphysics. It can do that by interpreting the contingency of beings--as Heidegger says, "the wonder of all wonders: that beings *are*"[74]--as God's creation. Faith in the Creator is not the answer of a metaphysical subjectivism to Heidegger's basic question, but is rather the continuing experience of the strangeness that things are, "the uncompromising persistence of the basic question as to 'why is there any being at all and not much rather nothing?'"[75] Just as the term 'Being' means for Heidegger the awareness that beings *are* at all, so the term 'creation' means for Ott the awareness that all creatures are God's creation.

Ott also tries to fit the Christian concept of God into Heidegger's philosophy. Like Heidegger, he refuses to equate God with Being; God must rather be *a* being: God *is*. This formulation, however, would seem to require some form of *analogia entis*, which Barth had so strongly rejected. But Ott shows that Heidegger's concept of Being is different enough from that of Barth to allow a non-analogical use of the term 'Being' to describe God:

The Being of God, according to our [Heideggerian] understanding of 'Being', means *an occurrence of revelation*: that God reveals himself to thinking as who he is; that he himself comes upon thinking as a destiny and gives himself to thinking as matter for thought; that he approaches thinking as a demand and requires from the thinking man a correspondence in freedom. And the thinking which is come upon by the Being of God is the thinking of faith.[76]

Ott sees a correlation between Heidegger's concept of primal or authentic thinking (as opposed to calculative or technological thinking) and the thinking of theology. For Heidegger, primal thinking is an experience, an encounter, an occurrence. It does not objectivize its matter-for-thought. Likewise, theology is based on an encounter--the encounter with God that is faith: "Theology is the movement of faith wishing to clarify itself: *fides quaerens intellectum.*"[77] It does not attempt to objectivize God, but recognizes its dependence upon him. The attitude of faith towards God is one of response, and this corresponds to Heidegger's concept of language as a summons of Being upon man. Ott holds that the call of God upon man is formulated in the words of the Bible and transmitted to each individual by preaching, where the appropriate response is prayer. These three functions of Biblical interpretation, preaching and prayer are combined in the person of the theologian. For Ott, all theological speech is ultimately prayer.[78]

Although Ott disagrees sharply with Fuchs and Ebeling in their assimilation of the later Heidegger into the Lutheran theological framework based on the distinction of 'law' and 'gospel', he shares their conviction regarding the importance of Heidegger's concept of language for theology. Thus, in an essay entitled, "What is Systematic Theology?" he emphasizes the interpretative function of theology: "The nature of theology as a whole is hermeneutical."[79] In this essay he distinguishes systematic theology from exegesis by assigning to the latter the task of interpreting individual Biblical texts, and to the former the task of interpreting the texts all together. And in another essay, "Language and Understanding," he reiterates his belief that "theology in its very essence is hermeneutics," with the rider that "theology itself is essentially directed towards the preaching of the church."[80] In both these works he bases his interpretation of theology's task on the understanding of thinking and of language offered by Heidegger.[81] Although Ott has modified somewhat his original project of a Heideggerian theology, and has adopted instead Heidegger's own proposal of an *analogia proportionalitatis* between philosophy and theology: as philosophical thinking is related to Being, when Being speaks to thinking, so faith's thinking is related to God, when God is revealed in his word;[82] it is evident that he regards Heidegger's philosophy as amenable to a theistic and theological interpretation, especially with regard to the theology of Karl Barth.

3. Catholic Theologians.

Of the relatively few English-language theologians who have addressed themselves to the philosophy of Heidegger, the most prolific is undoubtedly John Macquarrie, the co-translator of *Sein und Zeit* and the author of numerous articles and books on Heidegger

25

and his significance for theology (especially with regard to Bultmann).[83] In his own major work, *Principles of Christian Theology*, Macquarrie acknowledges that

for many of the philosophical categories employed in this book, I am indebted to the writings of Martin Heidegger. As it seems to me, his way of philosophizing and the concepts he has developed provide the basis for a viable twentieth-century philosophical ('natural') theology, and can be used further for the articulation and elucidation of the whole body of Christian truth in a contemporary way.[84]

Thus, Macquarrie stands apart from the Protestant (especially Barthian) rejection of natural theology. However, he does recognize the limitations of such a use of philosophy for theology:

This does not mean in the very slightest that our theology is being made subservient to a philosophy; but it does mean that, like theologians of the past, we can avail ourselves of such current philosophical work as will best serve to express the faith in terms that communicate with the secular culture of our time.[85]

Macquarrie follows Bultmann very closely in appropriating Heidegger's analysis of human existence for the starting-point of his theology. With regard to his interpretation of *revelation*, too, he points out that

the outlines of the scheme reflect the philosophy of Martin Heidegger, though there are considerable differences in detail and the scheme as here presented is much more explicit than one finds in Heidegger. Nevertheless, it is important to notice that this discussion of revelation can go on in terms drawn for the most part from secular philosophy.[86]

He also indicates the importance for theology of Heidegger's interpretation of *language*, a topic which he develops more systematically in another book, *God-Talk*.

But Macquarrie's most distinctive contribution to the development of a 'Heideggerian philosophical theology' is his attempt to relate Heidegger's concept of Being to the Christian concept of God. According to Macquarrie, the best way to describe Being is in terms of its characteristic of "letting-be": "Being, strictly speaking, 'is' not; but Being 'lets be'". This expression means something "positive and active, as enabling to be, empowering to be, or bringing into being." As men, we have an analogous experience of this characteristic of Being:

Because we ourselves are and our being is open to us, we have some understanding of what it means to let-be; and moreover, because we do have this peculiar mode of being as existents, we even have some idea in our experience of what it means for us to let-be, in a limited way.[87]

26

The letting-be of Being can be experienced by man either as grace--i.e., as a gift--or as the imposition of a burden. Being is present to beings in that it manifests itself through them according to their participation in it. In sum, "Being 'is' the incomparable that lets-be and that is present and manifests itself in and through the beings."[88]

Macquarrie stipulates that Being as thus described is not necessarily synonymous with God, since some people experience Being as indifferent or alien: "Such people do not call Being 'God', for to use the word 'God' means that one has taken up a certain attitude towards Being, namely, the attitude of faith."[89] However, Being can signify God to the believer:

It will be claimed that if we use the word 'God', it does designate Being; but we should be clear to begin with that 'God' is not a neutral designation, as 'Being' is, but one that carries important existential connotations of valuation, commitment, worship, and so on. We could, however, say that 'God' is synonymous with 'holy Being'...[90]

in the sense of Rudolf Otto's analysis of the 'holy', *mysterium tremendum et fascinans*. Macquarrie admits that Heidegger refuses any identification of Being and God, but he feels that this restriction applies only to the traditional, metaphysical concept of God: "One might say that the 'forgetting of Being' which Heidegger regards as characteristic of our Western culture has shown itself... in the tendency of theology to think of God as *a* being rather than as Being."[91] However, the identification of Being and God does require an interpretation of--a step beyond--Heidegger himself:

In Heidegger's own philosophy, Being tends to replace God and draws to itself the attributes traditionally assigned to God. The question posed for theology is whether the theologian too must not fight against the forgetting of Being, and try to reconceive God not as *a* being, however exalted, but as Being, which must in any case be more ultimate that any being.[92]

Macquarrie obviously thinks this is both possible and necessary, and that Heidegger's description of Being, interpreted as gracious and holy, can well express the Christian concept of God.

A brief but extremely valuable interpretation of Heidegger's relevance for theology is given by the Roman Catholic theologian, Thomas O'Meara, in an article entitled, "Heidegger on God." O'Meara feels that "nothing could be more unseemly" than an attempt to create "a Heideggerian theology or theodicy," but he does see "a certain unity in approach, presupposition, and message" in Heidegger's scattered treatment of the God-problem;[93] on the basis of this it is possible to discern the direction in which a solution of this problem might lie. O'Meara argues that an appropriate Heideggerian understanding of God would be that of a God *beyond*

27

Being. The identification of God and Being is ruled out by "the role of participation in Being's presence, the ambiguous role of Being outside the lighting process of knowing truth, [and] Being's dimension in time determined by temporality."^{94} To identify Being and God would be "ultimate theological Hegelianism," rather than a return to the sources of the Western metaphysical tradition. Heidegger's treatment of Being and its relation to the holy opens up the possibility of a two-pronged approach to the question of God: "From one point of view, Being is preliminary to the holy and far below the divine; for another, as yet undeveloped thinking, Being is open beyond the finite."^{95}

O'Meara agrees with Heidegger's contention that the traditional metaphysical concept of God is no longer adequate:

> We wonder whether the God of religious experience or revealed religion is existentially or ontologically identifiable with an ultimate cause, whether the easy identification of theology's and philosophy's objects has not overlooked the dimension of religious experience, grace, and mystery in God's historical communicative self-disclosure.^{96}

Nietzsche was right to do away with God the supreme being, the supreme value, the dialectical God of Hegel, and the Platonic God of the supernatural realm. However, he was wrong to replace these Gods with the superman or the will to power. These Gods are not easily replaced: "there is no quick substitute for the Platonic univocal God. First we must understand what Being really is."^{97} This is what Heidegger seeks to do--first to attain the truth of Being, then the truth of the holy, and only then the dimension where reflection on God can begin. Heidegger himself does not venture into this realm; he only indicates its existence as the appropriate locus of theological reflection upon God. O'Meara refers to Heidegger's 1962 lecture, "Zeit und Sein," as evidence that "Being in the later works of Heidegger (though finite in relationship to man) is now somehow open. Beyond Being through the Holy is something more ineffable."^{98} Thus, O'Meara indicates a new possibility with regard to a theistic interpretation of Heidegger: God is to be conceived neither as Being nor as a being, but rather as beyond Being.

Our final interpretation of Heidegger's significance for Christian theology can serve in addition as a preamble to our evaluation of all these interpretations, since the author, Jean-Paul Resweber, offers pertinent criticisms of many of the authors already cited. In his recent work entitled, *Essai sur le discours théologique à la lumière de la critique heideggérienne de la métaphysique* (Essay on Theological Discourse in the Light of the Heideggerian Critique of Metaphysics), Resweber indicates where he thinks Karl Rahner and Rudolf Bultmann have misunderstood Heidegger:

Rahner proposes a *theoretical* model of understanding, in contrast to Bultmann who offers us a *practical* model. The two theologians remain within the metaphysical limitations of Kantianism by giving preference either to the theoretical side of reason, following Maréchal, or to the practical side, following Luther and Kierkegaard. To be sure, each has followed one of the two methodological paths of *Sein und Zeit*: the existential path and the transcendental path. But for Heidegger these two orientations are, first of all, linked to each other: the ontic primacy of *Dasein* (the existential aspect) underlies understanding (the transcendental aspect) which, in determining the being-there [*Dasein*], offers the point of departure for every ontological problematic. Secondly, these two directions converge towards the hermeneutical path traced by the ontico-ontological structure of the being-there: every understanding of a being or an object is an interpretation, because it is 'a moment constitutive of the understanding which the being-there has of itself.'99

In other words, the theological adaptations of Heidegger's philosophy by Rahner and Bultmann, despite their differences, are both inadequate for the same reason--they have maintained the traditional philosophical dichotomy between theoretical and practical reason which Heidegger has attempted to overcome. Thus, they remain prisoners of the metaphysical tradition of Christian theology which Heidegger has criticized so severely.

Resweber's own special interest in the philosophy of Heidegger centers on its relevance for theological language, and so he examines with particular care the interpretations of Heidegger's theory of language by Ernst Fuchs and Gerhard Ebeling. Although these two theologians have made good use of Heidegger's ideas in explaining the role of hermeneutics in the development of Christian theology, Resweber feels that they, too, have failed to surpass traditional metaphysical theology in one important respect--its dichotomy between (the language of) faith and (the language of) reason:

Fuchs and Ebeling...share the same model which, from Luther to Barth, Bultmann and his followers, governs their perception of Christian doctrine: the relationship between philosophy and theology is considered as a reflection of that which opposes and unites the law and the gospel. The philosophy of Heidegger would be an interpretation of the law which is in contradiction with theology....We believe, on the contrary, that it is not the dichotomy which is original--the eschatological breach after which discourse ceaselessly endeavours to strike a compromise. There exists an original unity of language founded on symbol, which the metaphysical schism has destroyed....In other words, if philosophy is an interpretation of the law, let us recognize

29

that it is *normative*, not on the level of content, but on the level of models, and that philosophical discourse actualizes the metaphorical and symbolical law of religious language.[100]
For Resweber, then, the separation of philosophy from theology and faith from reason is not a primary datum of human consciousness, but is the result of a certain interpretation of the nature of consciousness, especially on the level of language. Thus, a correct philosophical explanation of the function of language applies equally to theological language and to other types of language. To say that Heidegger's analysis is valid only for non-theological language (the 'law' as opposed to the 'gospel') is to introduce into his philosophy a remnant of metaphysical theology which does not belong there.

Resweber's own appreciation of Heidegger's philosophy follows from this criticism. He feels that Heidegger's interpretation of language is the best philosophical interpretation available, and since theological language, as language, is no different than philosophical language, any adequate doctrine of theological language must take into account the writings of Heidegger. This is especially the case with regard to his criticism of traditional metaphysical language, based on the radical separation of subject and object. In place of this 'objectivizing' form of language, both philosophy and theology must adopt a more 'symbolic' form: "...we think that philosophical discourse and theological discourse, although they develop in separation from one another because of their different aims and different objects, draw upon symbolical language for a common model of expression."[101] Such a symbolical form of language is based on the understanding that all language, be it scientific, philosophical or theological, involves an element of interpretation, and if the theologian refuses to recognize that his encounter with the Bible involves his own personal interpretation of its message, then he is succumbing to the metaphysical interpretation:

...the thought of Heidegger, as we have analyzed it, asks us not only to go from the metaphysical interpretation to the essence of faith; it tells us that faith itself *is an interpretation....* *Interpretation establishes the act of belief as such.*[102]
Thus, Resweber feels that an acquaintance with Heidegger's philosophy is essential for any theologian who wishes to deal with the subject of theological language.

II. Evaluation of These Evaluations.

The most noticeable feature of the foregoing survey is the great variety of these religious interpretations of Heidegger's philosophy. The only common feature to be found there is the theologians' conviction that Heidegger's philosophy cannot be ignored, but must be dealt with in one fashion or another. In all other respects these theologians have failed to agree on any specific aspect of Heidegger's thought, much less on his thought as a whole. In the absence of any definitive interpretation, we must therefore examine the above interpretations to see why each has failed to receive general acceptance, and to determine if this is an indication that a new approach to this question is justified.

Our evaluation of the previous theological interpretations of Heidegger shall proceed in the following manner: first, we shall examine the different positions taken by the theologians on the four specific religious issues called into question by Heidegger's philosophy, namely: 1) the nature of man, 2) God, 3) language, and 4) revelation; then we shall seek to clarify the principal source of the theologians' disaccord on these four issues, namely, their differing views on the validity of the use of philosophy by theology, and indeed, of the philosophical study of religion in general; finally, we shall look to philosophy to see whether we can find there the consensus regarding the conditions for the definitive interpretation of Heidegger's religious significance which is missing among the theologians, or, failing that, whether one particular approach to the philosophical study of religion emerges as the best standpoint from which to evaluate Heidegger's treatment of religion.

A. Theological Evaluations of Heidegger's Philosophy.

Underlying all the particular theological issues raised by Heidegger's philosophy is his general criticism of 'metaphysical' thinking, which he applies in equal measure to traditional Western philosophy and traditional Christian theology. Indeed, he sees the two as so interconnected that they are really the same "onto-theo-logy" (see below, chapter 3). In his view, both philosophy and theology must overcome this way of thinking if they are to have any positive value in the future.

There is more agreement among the theological interpreters of Heidegger on this issue than on any other. Even some of his most outspoken critics agree that his criticism of past theology is valid, at least up to a point. Cornelio Fabro, for the Catholics, feels that most previous philosophers and theologians have failed to deal adequately with the notion of Being, although in his view Thomas Aquinas is exempt from this criticism. And Helmut Franz, among the Lutheran evangelical theologians, thinks that Heidegger's critique is valid for medieval-scholastic theology (including, no doubt, Thomas Aquinas) but not modern evangelical theology. Most of the theologians who feel that Heidegger's philosophy is amenable to a positive religious interpretation agree that traditional theology is inadequate in many important respects, including those pointed out by Heidegger. The only real opposition to this view comes from the Catholic theologians, Maurice Corvez and Hans Meyer, who feel that there is no other God than the one described by previous theologians such as Aquinas, and Hans Jonas, who holds that metaphysical thinking is part of the human condition and therefore not surpassable.

The extent of this agreement among Heidegger's theological inter-preters with regard to previous theology should not be over-estimated. As Jean-Paul Resweber has pointed out, neither Karl Rahner, Rudolf Bultmann, Ernst Fuchs or Gerhard Ebeling has fully overcome the limitations of traditional metaphysical theology, despite their express intention to do so. An examination of the specific theological topics mentioned above will indicate more precisely the degree to which this metaphysical thinking still holds forth.

1. Man.

Among the theologians who have investigated Heidegger's description of *Dasein* in *Sein und Zeit* with respect to its compatibility with the Christian doctrine of human existence, there is an equal split between positive and negative evaluations. The debate be-tween Rudolf Bultmann, the most celebrated proponent of this use of Heidegger's philosophy, and his Barthian adversary, Gerhardt Kuhlmann, illustrates the lack of agreement on this issue. John Macquarrie has followed Bultmann in his theological use of the *Daseinsanalyse*, although he has gone beyond Bultmann in subordinat-ing this aspect of Heidegger's philosophy to the question of Being (and its relation to the question of God). Finally, the Catholic theologian, Régis Jolivet, has condemned Heidegger's description of *Dasein* on the grounds that it requires a neo-Stoical attitude towards death, since it has no place for an essential element of the Christian description of man--his immortal soul.

The preoccupation with this one aspect of Heidegger's thought, as evidenced by Bultmann and Jolivet, is a symptom of what has be-come known as the 'existentialist misunderstanding' of Heidegger. The many interpretations of Heidegger as an existentialist were due principally to the reading of *Sein und Zeit* in isolation from his later works, all the while ignoring his repeated assertions in that book that he is not doing philosophical anthropology or psychology, but is laying the foundations for an inquiry into the meaning of Being.[103] The description of *Dasein* in that work is an *ontological* rather than an *ontic* description--it concerns the basic structures of human existence, its essential possibilities, rather than its concrete actions. Thus, the description of Heidegger as an 'existentialist'--i.e., as one who is primarily concerned with man's subjectivity--involves a fundamental misunderstanding of his philosophy, and any theological interpretation which is based on such a misunderstanding, such as that of Jolivet, is necessarily inadequate.

Rudolf Bultmann has also been accused of such an existentialist misunderstanding and appropriation of Heidegger's thought, but he has defended himself by claiming simply that the description of human existence in *Sein und Zeit* is suitable for theological use apart from any ontological considerations that Heidegger might derive from this description in his later philosophical words. Gerhard Noller and Hans Jonas oppose this 'eclectic' approach to Heidegger; they regard his thought as a unity, which must therefore be accepted or rejected in its entirety. Heidegger's thought is indeed a unity, but this fact need not exclude the procedure of a *discriminating* use of his philosophy for theology. It would be too much to expect of any thinker that he be either entirely right or entirely wrong. There is no reason why the advances evident in his thought cannot be used profitably to overcome the deficiencies therein. Such a procedure must, of course, take into consideration the immediate implications of the thought and concepts which are to be adopted. Bultmann seems not to have been concerned to develop the new concept of God which his description of human existence in Heideggerian terminology demanded, and to that extent his 'existentialist' interpretation of Heidegger is inadequate.

2. God.

The major problem in any Christian interpretation of Heidegger is the location of the concept of God in relation to his thought. Those theologians who accept the traditional description of God in terms of Being are divided according to whether they consider Heidegger's concept of Being to be assimilable to the Christian concept of God, as does John Macquarrie, and those who deny any such resemblance. The latter category includes most of the theological opponents of Heidegger. Heinrich Ott accepts Heidegger's explicit denial of the identity of Being and God, and tries to explain how God can be a being which is not inferior to Being. Thomas O'Meara contends that the only place for God in relation to Heidegger's philosophy is *beyond* Being.

The suggestion by O'Meara that 'Being' is no longer a suitable name for God is not likely to be well-received by the majority of Christian theologians, for this understanding of the divine nature seems to be firmly rooted in the Bible and Christian tradition. However, as will be shown in chapter four, the description of God

33

as beyond Being seems to be the most adequate interpretation of
Heidegger's philosophy with regard to the problem of God, and it is
the logical consequence of his critique of traditional metaphysical
theology, which most of his theological interpreters profess to
accept. It is noteworthy that this rejection of 'Being' as a
description of God comes from an American theologian. This is an
indication that the American tradition of philosophy of religion
may be able to provide the most suitable basis for the religious
interpretation of Heidegger's philosophy (see below, chapter two).

3. Language.

Heidegger's teaching on language is perhaps the most important
aspect of his critique of traditional metaphysics, since it is by
means of language that the metaphysical outlook has permeated the
consciousness of Western mankind. Of those theologians who have
dealt specifically with the significance of Heidegger's philosophy
for theological language, only Hans Jonas offers a negative evaluation. Among the others--Ernst Fuchs, Gerhard Ebeling, Heinrich Ott,
John Macquarrie and Jean-Paul Resweber--there is general agreement
that the traditional naively realistic theory of language, based
on the premise of a primordial separation of knowing subject and
known object, is totally inadequate today for theological discourse
as well as for philosophy. Heidegger's teaching that every description involves an interpretation--i.e., that all language is *hermeneutical*--has stimulated these theologians to examine the (often
latent) presuppositions of theological discourse to see whether
they are in fact justified either theologically or philosophically.
As a result of Heidegger's influence, there is a widespread realization among theologians today that language cannot be totally 'objective', but that the attitudes and preconceptions of the speakers,
whether Biblical writers or present-day theologians, have a great
deal to do with how religious matters are understood and how they
are described.

As was the case with Heidegger's general critique of metaphysical
theology, his teachings on the nature of language have not been
applied to the fullest extent by all of the theologians mentioned
above. Jean-Paul Resweber has shown that both Ernst Fuchs and
Gerhard Ebeling posit as a primary datum of language something
which is really secondary--the distinction between the law and the
gospel, or reason and faith, each with its distinctive form of
discourse. Both Heinrich Ott and John Macquarrie reject this distinction between the law and the gospel, and their application of
Heidegger's theory of language to theology is more extensive than
that of Fuchs and Ebeling. With Ott, though, there is a definite
aversion to any real interdependence of philosophy and theology,

and his description of theological discourse as prayer renders problematic the similarity of his notion of theological language and Heidegger's description of philosophical language.

4. Revelation.

Whereas theological discourse may be described in terms of man speaking about (or to) God, divine revelation has to do with God speaking to man. Revelation is an important concept in traditional Christian theology, and one on which Heidegger's philosophy has shed new light for some of his theological interpreters. Heidegger has used the concept of revelation in his philosophy to describe the essentially passive role of man in his understanding of Being-- this understanding is a gift to man from outside him; it is revealed to him (either by Being itself or by something beyond Being). Both Heinrich Ott and John Macquarrie have found this description of revelation very useful for interpreting the Christian concept of divine revelation, which has traditionally been understood in a rather heavy-handed fashion (at least with regard to the inspira- tion of the Biblical writers). However, Helmut Franz disagrees with the attempts to rethink the nature of Biblical revelation, since the Bible is the foundation of Christianity and must be ac- cepted as it is.

On each of these four theological issues, therefore--the nature of man, God, language and revelation--there is a basic disagreement among the theologians as to the compatibility of Heidegger's phi- losophy with Christian theology. In searching for the source of these disagreements we find as one major factor a difference of opinion regarding the relation of theology to *any* philosophy, Heideggerian or otherwise. It appears that this is the one issue which, more than any other, has prevented the emergence of any generally acceptable religious interpretation of Heidegger's thought.

5. Philosophy and Theology.

Two related issues emerge in any discussion of the relation be- tween philosophy and theology: 1) the validity of the *philosophy of religion*, i.e., the study of religion by philosophers; 2) the validity of *philosophical theology*, i.e., the use of philosophical concepts and terminology by theologians to interpret and explain the Christian faith. Although a complete spectrum of opinions on these matters can be found within Christianity at almost any time in its history, it is especially since the Protestant Reformation that the debate has been, to a certain extent, institutionalized. At the time of the Reformation, Luther and Calvin stressed the weakness of sinful human reason and its consequent inability to achieve true knowledge in religious matters without special divine help. Thus, they rejected the strictly philosophical study of religion, and at the same time tried to curb as much as possible the use of philosophical concepts in their theology. The Catholic Church, on the other hand, maintained that human reason is capable of attaining a valid, though limited, knowledge of religious matters (including the existence of God) without any such special divine aid. And in consequence they were much more open to the use of philosophy than were the Protestants.

This difference of opinion still characterizes the two theological traditions. The most outspoken opponents of both the philosophy of religion and philosophical theology in the 20th century have been Karl Barth and his followers. Of the theological interpreters of Heidegger, only Heinrich Ott has tried to reconcile Barth's theology and Heidegger's philosophy. However, this attempt has failed to win acceptance either from Protestants, who feel that Ott has gone too far in the direction of a philosophy of religion, or from Catholics, who hold that he has not gone far enough.[104]

Although Rudolf Bultmann has been severely criticized by Karl Barth for failing to maintain the necessary gulf between theology and philosophy, he is in reality very close to Barth's position on this matter. Although he makes use of Heidegger's description of human existence, he applies it only to the 'natural man,' not to the 'man of faith.' Like Barth, he rejects the philosophy of religion--philosophy can be neither theistic nor atheistic because it has no competence in religious matters. As is the case with Barth, and with Gerhard Ebeling as well, Bultmann's rejection of the philosophy of religion is based on the understanding of human reason as incapacitated by original sin and unable to attain religious truth without special divine help. The difference, therefore, between the Barthians and the Bultmannians is not with regard to the validity of the philosophy of religion--this they agree in rejecting--but only with regard to the validity of philosophical theology. And even here, the Bultmannians place severe restrictions on the use of philosophical concepts in theology.

In contrast to this Protestant attitude, the Catholic interpreters of Heidegger have no reservations about the validity of philosophical theology. The main point of contention among them is whether *Heideggerian* philosophy is suitable for theological use. Many Catholic theologians have been convinced of the *a priori* superiority of Thomistic philosophy, and have adopted from Heidegger only what they consider to be compatible with Thomas Aquinas (if anything). On the other hand, John Macquarrie and Jean-Paul Resweber are convinced that Heidegger's philosophy is eminently suitable for theological use, and they have contributed greatly to the development of a 'Heideggerian philosophical theology.' However, neither of them has addressed himself to the question of whether there can be a valid Heideggerian philosophy of religion. The neglect of this question is not surprising, since Heidegger himself holds that philosophy has no competence in religious matters. But until this question is raised and discussed, the religious significance of Heidegger's philosophy will not be fully known.

It is obvious, therefore, that Christian theologians have not been able to agree among themselves as to the religious significance of Heidegger's philosophy. The basic source of this lack of consensus is their disagreement as to the validity of the theological use of *any* philosophy, Heideggerian or otherwise. And even those theologians who have attempted to develop a Heideggerian philosophical theology have neglected the other principal aspect of his significance for religion, namely, his importance for the philosophy of religion. Despite, therefore, the great effort which these theologians have put forth in investigating and evaluating the religious elements of Heidegger's thought, it is apparent that they have not provided a satisfactory understanding of his significance for religion. In order to determine in what sense, if any, there exists a Heideggerian philosophy of religion, we shall turn from theology to philosophy, which despite its previous reluctance to deal with this specific question, may at least be able to provide us with a definite understanding of the nature and validity of the philosophy of religion.

B. Philosophers on the Philosophy of Religion.

Even a superficial glance at the history of Western philosophy is sufficient to show that, until the 20th century, almost every philosopher dealt with religious matters. This is true both of those who felt that the task of philosophy is to present a comprehensive interpretation of the whole universe, which necessarily included the role of God therein, and of those whose philosophy had more modest aims, such as the explanation of human knowledge (which has to include knowledge of God). This close interrelation of philosophy and religion in the past has been severely criticized by Heidegger for having been responsible for the degeneration of both philosophy and theology. Whatever one may think of this criticism, it does have as its object an indisputable fact—most philosophers have treated religious matters from a philosophical standpoint.

Up until the 18th century, religion was such an integral part of philosophy that it is difficult to isolate the philosophy of religion as a sub-division of philosophy in general. But during the past 250 years, philosophers have come to regard religion as one specific area of human activity, which can be analyzed and interpreted in relative isolation from other areas. In his book, *The Emergence of Philosophy of Religion*, James Collins treats Hume, Kant and Hegel as the main figures in this movement towards a distinctive philosophy of religion:

> The crucial hundred years for the explicit and systematic development of the philosophy of religion reach from about 1730 to 1830. These dates are significant, since they embrace a period extending from Hume's early reflections on religious issues to Hegel's last lectures on the philosophy of religion. The three central figures are Hume, Kant, and Hegel. They lay the classical foundations for the modern philosophical theories of religion....With them, the philosophy of religion comes of age and takes its place among the basic parts of philosophy.[105]

Collins does not mean to imply that these three philosophers were solely responsible for the development of philosophy of religion, but only that this sub-discipline took its definitive form during their lifetimes and largely under their influence.

The 19th century witnessed the continued popularity of religion as a philosophical topic, although the range of evaluations of religion widened considerably. Philosophers such as Feuerbach, Marx and Nietzsche rejected Christianity as the norm of true religion and in place of the Christian God they substituted man as the most important being in the universe. To the extent that they approved of religion at all, it was a religion of mankind, an atheistic religion, that they recommended. On the other hand, many philosophers continued the traditional identification of the God of philosophy with the God of the Bible, and refused to be convinced by the arguments of the atheistic philosophers. Despite these different evaluations of religion, however, philosophers of the 19th century generally shared the belief that religion is an important philosophical topic.

With the coming of the 20th century, the situation has changed. Many philosophers no longer practise the philosophy of religion, although they have different reasons for not doing so. Among those who continue to treat religion, we find radically different attitudes to the object of their study. In general, we can discern four basic approaches to the philosophy of religion among contemporary philosophers: 1) Some philosophers have no interest in religion, and their conception of philosophy is such that they feel perfectly free to limit their research to one particular branch of philosophy in isolation from all others. This attitude is especially common among British and American philosophers, many of whom feel that philosophy is logic and nothing else. According to this view, there may or may not be such a thing as a valid philosophy of religion, but unless one is genuinely interested in this question, there is no need to pursue it. 2) Other philosophers do not treat religion, but this is not because they have no interest in religion. Rather it is because they believe that philosophy has no competence in religious matters--philosophy and religion are two distinct and unrelated spheres of human activity. This is, of course, the view of Heidegger, but it is shared by other philosophers, notably Ludwig Wittgenstein.[106] Here again, there is no philosophy of religion, not, as in the first case, because of the philosophers' lack of interest, but because of the very nature of philosophy and religion. 3) Still other philosophers *do* practise the philosophy of religion, either as their major preoccupation or as a subordinate part of their overall philosophical outlook. However, their view of philosophy is such that they feel they must deal with religion as they find it--either in the churches or in (usually outdated) theological textbooks. These philosophers analyse and describe religion, and even evaluate it on philosophical grounds--e.g., its internal logical consistency--but they feel that they cannot *change* it. They must either take it or leave it the way it is. This attitude towards religion is found among both its opponents and its proponents. Examples of both are abundant in Great Britain, where there are vigorous philosophical debates over religious issues as traditionally formulated, in which both sides agree that there can be no other possible formulation. A variation of this attitude towards the philosophical study of religion is found among the disciples of Thomas Aquinas, who believe that the basic philosophical and theological truths have already been enunciated by Aquinas, and it only remains for the philosopher to apply these truths in different historical situations. Thus, this third category of philosophers consists of those who consider as valid the philosophy of religion, but have rigid preconceptions as to the nature of the religion which they treat. 4) Finally, there are those philosophers who practise the philosophy of religion without the restrictions of the foregoing attitude towards this activity. They consider that religion is a sphere of human activity which, like all others, is subject to change and development, and that the task of the philosopher is not simply to describe past manifestations of religion but to point the way to new and better ones. Isolated examples of this approach to religion can be found in any list of 20th-century philosophers--the names of Henri Bergson, Karl Jaspers, Gabriel Marcel and Pierre Teilhard de Chardin spring readily to mind--but the most consistent and persistent manifestation of this approach is to be found among American philosophers--from Charles Sanders Peirce to Charles Hartshorne and his followers. Despite the many differences between the Americans and their European counterparts, they do agree that a creative approach to the philosophy of religion is both possible and necessary, and they have contributed greatly to the recent development of this discipline.

It is evident, therefore, that there is no consensus among 20th-century philosophers as to the nature or even the validity of the philosophy of religion. As was the case with the theologians, they do not provide us with definitive criteria for the philosophical treatment of religion according to which we can evaluate Heidegger's philosophy. In the absence of such a common understanding of the nature of philosophy of religion, it is necessary to choose among the four different approaches listed above. The first two must be rejected here on the grounds that such an abrupt ending to our project would be premature—we cannot conclude that a Heideggerian philosophy of religion is impossible until we have exhausted all efforts to construct one. The third approach appears to offer certain advantages, such as a definite concept of religion with which to work. But this advantage is only apparent, since it is necessary to choose beforehand which concept of religion is best, and if the theologians are unable to agree on this point, there is no reason to suspect that philosophers would. And so there remains the fourth alternative, the creative approach to religion. But here it is necessary to choose among the different practition-ers of this approach, and to offer a certain justification for our choice.

A comprehensive description and comparison of all the different creative approaches to the philosophical study of religion in the 20th century is beyond the scope of this work. At this stage in our procedure we can only suggest that one particular approach *may* be useful for evaluating the religious significance of Heideg-ger's philosophy, and then describe this approach and apply it to Heidegger's philosophy to see if it really does work. The approach which will be examined here is that of American philosophy of reli-gion. There are several reasons for making this particular choice: 1) there have been very few previous attempts to evaluate Heideg-ger's thought from this standpoint; 2) this approach to the philosophy of religion is practised not by one or two isolated individuals or schools but has been a characteristic element of American philosophy for almost 100 years; 3) American philosophers are relatively familiar with other philosophical traditions, and often take into account their strengths and weaknesses when for-mulating their own position. And so, without denying that other contemporary philosophers have made great contributions to the philosophy of religion, we will proceed to describe in some detail the American approach to the philosophy of religion to see if it can provide a suitable basis for an evaluation of Heidegger's significance for religious thought.

1. Published in Louvain by Publications Universitaires de Louvain, first edition 1942, several subsequent (unaltered) editions.

2. de Waelhens, *op. cit.*, pp. 359f.

3. Published in Meisenheim am Glan by Anton Hain, 1971.

4. Danner, *op. cit.*, p. 175.

5. Sartre, *Existentialism and Humanism* (tr. by Philip Mairet), London (Methuen: 1948), p. 26.

6. Cf. Marjorie Grene, *Dreadful Freedom*, Chicago (University of Chicago Press: 1948), A. C. Cochrane, *The Existentialists and God*, Philadelphia (Westminster Press: 1956), and David E. Roberts, *Existentialism and Religious Belief*, New York (Oxford University Press: 1957).

7. Richardson, "Heidegger and God---and Professor Jonas," *Thought* 40 (1965), p. 40.

8. E.g. Keiji Nishitani, "Preliminary Remark" to "Two Addresses by Martin Heidegger," *The Eastern Buddhist* (new series) I (1966), pp. 48-59.

9. Cf. Martin Buber, "Das Problem des Menschen" and "Gottesfinsternis. Betrachtungen zur Beziehung zwischen Religion und Philosophie," in *Werke*, vol. I, *Schriften zur Philosophie*, München (Kösel Verlag: 1962), pp. 307-407 and 503-603, especially pp. 369-378 and 557-561, for Judaism, and Christos Yannaras, *De l'absence et de l'inconnaissance de Dieu*, Paris (Les Editions de Cerf: 1971), for Orthodox Christianity.

10. Tillich, *On the Boundary* (1936), New York (Charles Scribner's Sons: 1966), p. 56.

11. Tillich's philosophical theology will be explained in greater detail in the following chapter.

12. Cf. Tillich, *Systematic Theology* III, Chicago (University of Chicago Press: 1963), p. 53. This description of death is so close to that of Heidegger in *Sein und Zeit* that Tillich is to be criticized for not acknowledging Heidegger in this passage.

13. Cf. Thomas O'Meara, "Tillich and Heidegger: A Structural Relationship," *Harvard Theological Review* 61 (1968), pp. 249-261 for a more complete treatment of this influence.

14. Tillich, *On the Boundary*, p. 57. Cf. also his *Perspectives on 19th and 20th Century Protestant Theology*, London (S.C.M. Press: 1967), p. 70.

15. "Introduction au concept de philosophie existentiale chez Heidegger," *Recherches de Science Religieuse* XXX (1940), pp. 152-171 (tr. by R. Celle). Although the article carries the name of *Hugo* Rahner as author, it seems certain that Karl Rahner actually wrote it, and it is attributed to him in the *Bibliographie Karl Rahner 1924-1969*, ed. by Roman Bleistein and Elmar Klinger, Freiburg (Herder: 1969), and in his biography, *Karl Rahner*, by Herbert Vorgrimler, Montreal (Palm: 1965), p. 31.

16. Cf. Rahner's somewhat ambiguous statements regarding Heidegger's influence in his contribution to *Martin Heidegger im Gespräch*, ed. by Richard Wisser, Freiburg (Verlag Karl Alber: 1970), pp. 48f.

17. Jolivet, *Le problème de la mort chez M. Heidegger et J. P. Sartre*, Abbaye Saint Wandrille (1950), pp. 12f.

18. *Ibid.*, p. 45.

19. Corvez, *L'Être et la conscience morale*, Louvain (Editions Nauwelaerts: 1968), pp. 78-81.

20. *Ibid.*, p. 118.

21. *Ibid.*, p. 146.

22. Cf. Siewerth, "Martin Heidegger und die Frage nach Gott," *Grundfragen der Philosophie in Horizont der Seinsdifferenz*, Düsseldorf (L. Schwann: 1963), pp. 245-259; Lotz, "Das Sein selbst und das subsistierende Sein nach Thomas von Aquin," *Martin Heidegger zum 70 Geburtstag*, Pfullingen (G. Neske: 1959), pp. 180-194, and *Sein und Existenz*, Freiburg (Herder: 1965); and Meyer, *Martin Heidegger und Thomas von Aquin*, München (F. Schöningh: 1964).

23. Meyer, *op. cit.*, p. 71.

24. *Ibid.*, pp. 73-84.

25. Fabro, *God in Exile* (tr. by Arthur Gibson), New York (Paulist-Newman: 1968), p. 929.

26. *Ibid.*, p. 928.

27. *Ibid.*, p. 931.

28. Barth, "Philosophie und Theologie," *Philosophie und Christliche Existenz* (Festschrift for Heinrich Barth), ed. by Gerhard Huber, Basel (Hebling & Lichtenhahn: 1960), pp. 98, 106.

29. Reprinted in *Heidegger und die Theologie*, ed. by Gerhard Noller, München (Chr. Kaiser: 1967), pp. 197-225.

30. *Ibid.*, pp. 214f.

31. *Ibid.*, p. 225.

32. Barth, *Rudolf Bultmann: Ein Versuch, ihn zu Verstehen*, Zollikon (Evangelischer Verlag: 1952), pp. 38-45. Bultmann's reply to Barth is contained in Barth and Bultmann, *Briefwechsel 1922-1966*, ed. by Bernd Jaspert, Zurich (Theologischer Verlag Zurich: 1971), pp. 169-192.

33. Diem, *Gott und die Metaphysik*, Zurich (Evangelischer Verlag: 1956), p. 8.

34. *Ibid.*, p. 9.

35. Noller, *Sein und Existenz*, München (Chr. Kaiser: 1962), p. 160.

36. *Ibid.*, pp. 42-44.

37. Franz, "Das Denken Heideggers und die Theologie," *Heidegger und die Theologie*, ed. by Gerhard Noller, pp. 257f.

38. *Ibid.*, p. 264.

39. *Ibid.*, p. 279.

40. *Ibid.*, pp. 285-287.

41. Jonas, "Heidegger and Theology," *Review of Metaphysics* XVIII (1964), p. 215.

42. *Ibid.*, p. 217.

43. *Ibid.*, p. 219.

44. *Ibid.*, p. 230.

45. *Ibid.*, p. 228.

46. *Ibid.*, p. 219.

47. Cf. Macquarrie, *An Existentialist Theology*, London (S.C.M. Press: 1955), and *The Scope of Demythologizing*, New York (Harper Torchbooks: 1966), and Noller, *Sein und Existenz*, München (1962).

48. Bultmann, "Autobiographical Reflections," *Existence and Faith*, ed. by Schubert Ogden, New York (Meridian: 1960), p. 288.

49. Bultmann, *Kerygma and Myth*, ed. by Hans Werner Bartsch, New York (Harper Torchbooks: 1961), pp. 24f.

50. Kuhlmann, "Zum theologischen Problem der Existenz. Fragen an Rudolf Bultmann," *Heidegger und die Theologie*, ed. by G. Noller, München (Chr. Kaiser: 1967), pp. 33-58. This article appeared originally in the *Zeitschrift für Theologie und Kirche*, Neue Folge, 10. Jg., 1929, pp. 28-58.

51. Kuhlmann, "op. cit." *Heidegger und die Theologie*, p. 54.

52. *Ibid.*, pp. 54-58.

53. Bultmann, "Die Geschichtlichkeit des Daseins und der Glaube. Antwort an Gerhardt Kuhlmann," *Heidegger und die Theologie*, pp. 72-94. This article appeared originally in the *Zeitschrift für Theologie und Kirche*, Neue Folge, 11. Jg., 1930, pp. 339-364. (E. T. by Schubert M. Ogden appears in *Existence and Faith*, pp. 92-110.

54. Bultmann, "op. cit.," *Existence and Faith*, p. 95.

55. *Ibid.*, pp. 97f.

56. *Ibid.*, p. 105.

57. Bultmann and Jaspers, *Myth and Christianity*, New York (Noonday Press: 1958), p. 9.

58. *Ibid.*, p. 58.

59. *Ibid.*

44

60. Bultmann, *The Theology of Rudolf Bultmann*, ed. by Charles W. Kegley, New York (Harper & Row: 1966), p. 276.

61. Bultmann, "L'Idée de Dieu et l'homme moderne" (1966), *Foi et Compréhension* (tr. by André Malet), Paris (Editions de Seuil: 1969), pp. 369-373.

62. Bultmann, "A Propos d'une 'Théologie Philosophique'" (1962), *Foi et Compréhension*, pp. 360f.

63. Cf. James M. Robinson, *The New Hermeneutic*, New York (Harper & Row: 1964), pp. 44f.

64. Fuchs, *Marburger Hermeneutik*, Tübingen (J. C. B. Mohr: 1968), p. 53.

65. Fuchs, *Hermeneutik*, Bad Cannstatt (1954), p. 133, quoted in Robert Funk, *Language, Hermeneutic and Word of God*, New York (Harper & Row: 1966), p. 55.

66. Cf. James M. Robinson, *The New Hermeneutic*, p. 50.

67. Ebeling, "article cited," *Zeitschrift für Theologie und Kirche* 58 (1961), Beiheft 2, pp. 119-121.

68. *Ibid.*, pp. 121f.

69. *Ibid.*, p. 122.

70. *Ibid.*, pp. 123f.

71. Ott, *Denken und Sein*, Zollikon (Evangelischer Verlag: 1959), p. 28.

72. Heidegger, *Sein und Zeit*, p. 34.

73. Ott, *op. cit.*, p. 48.

74. Heidegger, "Nachwort" to "Was ist Metaphysik?" *Wegmarken*, p. 103.

75. Ott, *op. cit.*, p. 88.

76. *Ibid.*, p. 148.

77. *Ibid.*, p. 174.

78. *Ibid.*, pp. 191f.

79. Ott, "article cited," in James M. Robinson and John B. Cobb, Jr., eds., *The Later Heidegger and Theology*, New York (Harper & Row: 1963), p. 78.

80. Ott, "article cited," in Martin Marty and Dean Penman, eds., *New Theology #4*, New York (Macmillan: 1967), p. 126.

81. See also his recent essay on this topic, "Die Bedeutung von Martin Heideggers Denken für die Methode der Theologie," in *Durchbliche. Martin Heidegger zum 80. Geburtstag*, Frankfurt (1970), pp. 27-38.

82. Cf. James M. Robinson, *The Later Heidegger and Theology*, p. 43.

83. Although a member of the Church of England, Macquarrie's theological method is much closer to that of Catholicism than to that of Protestantism, especially with regard to his view of the relation of philosophy and theology.

84. Macquarrie, *op. cit.*, New York (Scribners: 1966), p. ix.

85. *Ibid.*

86. *Ibid.*, pp. 81f.

87. *Ibid.*, p. 103.

88. *Ibid.*, p. 105.

89. *Ibid.*

90. *Ibid.*

91. *Ibid.*, p. 106.

92. *Ibid.*

93. O'Meara, "Heidegger on God," in *Continuum* V (1967-68), p. 688.

94. *Ibid.*, p. 690.

95. *Ibid.*, p. 691.

96. *Ibid.*, p. 694.

97. *Ibid.*, p. 695.

98. *Ibid.*, p. 698.

99. Resweber, *op. cit.*, Lille (Service de Réproduction des Thèses, Université de Lille III: 1974), pp. 465f. The reference is to A. de Waelhens, note to the French translation of *Sein und Zeit*, p. 280.

100. Resweber, *op. cit.*, p. 633.

101. *Ibid.*, p. 592.

102. *Ibid.*, p. 651.

103. Heidegger, *Sein und Zeit*, pp. 37, 183, 231, 241, 314, 333, 357, 372, 436.

104. Cf. James M. Robinson, *The Later Heidegger and Theology*, pp. 63-76 for criticisms of Ott's use of Heidegger's philosophy.

105. Collins, *op. cit.*, New Haven and London (Yale University Press: 1967), p. viii.

106. Cf. his "Lectures on Religious Belief" (1938), in *Lectures and Conversations*, ed. by Cyril Barrett, Oxford (B. Blackwell: 1966).

American Philosophy of Religion

I. Survey of American Philosophy of Religion.

The very existence of a distinctive American philosophy of religion may come as a surprise to some people, even to some Americans. There are many reasons for this surprise: the relative brevity of American civilization; the massive interpenetration of diverse cultures in the American 'melting-pot'; the American preference for action instead of the sort of contemplation usually associated with philosophy; etc. Despite these factors, however, a distinctive American philosophy of religion has emerged within the past century, and although recent years have seen the development of many diverse philosophical and religious movements in America, the movement which will be described in this chapter still holds a dominant position among American philosophers today.

The one word which best characterizes the American approach to philosophy is 'pragmatism'. There is no ready-made definition for this term, however. There are significant differences in its use by the three men of whom it is most often applied--Charles Peirce, William James and John Dewey. In general, though, it refers to the tendency of these three men to emphasize the close relationship between thought and action, and between theory and practice. Pragmatism is empirical--it not only begins with experience but refers all theories and speculations back to experience for verification. It stresses process, life and movement, and eschews unchangeable essences and abstract ideas. It entertains a high opinion of and is in close contact with science. It has been called "the only unique contribution American philosophy has made to the tradition known as Western philosophy,"[1] and a close examination of its main representatives will reveal that this contribution has been a positive one.

The pragmatic aspect of American philosophy of religion by no means exhausts its distinctiveness in relation to other philosophical traditions. Whereas philosophers in Germany, France and Great Britain have often tended to ignore philosophical and religious developments in countries other than their own, the Americans have always looked beyond their own borders for philosophical inspiration. Although the accretions from abroad have not always proven beneficial for the development of American philosophy of religion, in general this openness to outside influences has resulted in a potential for creative development unmatched elsewhere.[2] As will become evident in the following exposition of American pragmatism, the major outside philosophical influence has been British empiricism. The nature of this influence has not been a slavish imitation, however, for the Americans have felt free to make significant alterations in the concept of experience which is the fundamental datum to which the British empiricists appeal. In its willingness, then, to make selective and critical use of other philosophical traditions, insofar as these agree with the tenets of pragmatism, American philosophy of religion stands out as a distinctive approach to the academic study of religion, and one which is by no means necessarily inferior to its senior overseas counterparts.

In America, the birth of the national philosophical tradition is easy to pinpoint. Although a certain amount of philosophical speculation had been practised since the middle of the 17th century, it is only with the end of the Civil War (1865) that an independent philosophical tradition emerged and the 'golden age' of American philosophy began.[3] The major philosophical movement of this period was pragmatism, and its chief representatives were Charles Peirce, William James and John Dewey. These men were strongly opposed by a brilliant representative of the Idealist tradition, Josiah Royce, and by his equally well-known colleague at Harvard, George Santayana, but the passage of time has revealed that the pragmatists have had the more lasting influence on subsequent American thought. And so it is with the philosophical thought of these three men that we shall begin this investigation of American philosophy of religion.

Charles Sanders Peirce (1839-1914).

Although he never obtained a permanent academic post and published no full-length books (save one scientific treatise), Charles Peirce was able to exercise a decisive influence on the development of American pragmatic philosophy. Pragmatism originated among a group of young intellectuals which included Peirce, William James, Oliver Wendell Holmes, Jr. and Chauncey Wright, who met as "The Metaphysical Club" in Cambridge, Mass., between 1870 and 1874. A common focus of attention at these meetings was the definition of Alexander Bain (1818-1903) of belief as "that upon which a man is prepared to act." As Peirce remarked later, "From this definition, pragmatism is scarce more than a corollary."[4] On the basis of this understanding, Peirce prepared a written formulation of his concept of pragmatic philosophy, and the publication of this paper in the November, 1877, and January, 1878, issues of *Popular Science Monthly* marked the first public announcement of the birth of pragmatism.

Since the word 'pragmatism' has come to have different meanings

50

for different philosophers, it is important to know what exactly
Peirce meant by the term. For him, pragmatism[5] signified not a
system or school of philosophy but rather a philosophical *method*,
a means of clarifying ideas. Of his many definitions and descriptions of pragmatism, the following is perhaps the most explicit:
"In order to ascertain the meaning of an intellectual conception
one should consider what practical consequences might conceivably
result by necessity from the truth of that conception; and the sum
of these consequences will constitute the entire meaning of the
conception" (5.9). The practical consequences in question refer
primarily to experimental verification, and if such verification is
not possible, then the conception should be dismissed as meaningless. This is, in fact, one of the principal aims of Peirce--to
rid philosophy of meaningless language. The following dialogue
is illustrative of this point:
  Questioner: What, then, is the *raison d'être* of the doctrine?
  What advantage is expected from it? Pragmatist: It will serve
  to show that almost every proposition of ontological metaphysics
  is either meaningless gibberish--one word being defined by other
  words, and they by still others, without any real conception ever
  being reached--or else is downright absurd; so that all such
  rubbish being swept away, what will remain of philosophy will be
  a series of problems capable of investigation by the observational
  methods of the true sciences... (5.423).
It should not be deduced from the foregoing that Peirce's attitude
towards metaphysics is entirely negative. In the same dialogue he
claims to extract from metaphysics "a precious essence, which will
serve to give light and life to cosmology and physics," not to mention ethics and religion. His arguments for the validity of metaphysics are based on his acceptance of epistemological and metaphysical *realism*. Peirce's pragmatism requires that there exist
real, external counterparts of our conceptions; otherwise, there
would be no possibility of experimental verification of our ideas.
The appeal to realism is strengthened by the success of the experimental sciences which constantly invoke realism in their search
for patterns of regularity in the universe. Peirce firmly believed
that scientific laws exist quite independently of human minds
(5.96ff.).
Peirce applied his pragmatic method to every branch of philosophy,
but not in equal measure. Scarcely one hundred pages of his
Collected Papers are devoted specifically to religion (6.395-587);
however, these writings do demonstrate that for Peirce religion
and pragmatism are entirely compatible. In general, he did "not
approve of mixing up Religion and Philosophy" (5.107). Religion
is not simply a type of knowledge nor even just a belief: "Religion is a life, and can be identified with a belief only provided

51

that belief be a living belief--a thing to be lived rather than said or thought" (5.439). Peirce does not mean, however, that religion is exempt from the requirements of pragmatism, such as a capacity for experimental verification. In fact, religion is expected to display this characteristic just as fully as philosophy or science, since "it is only an application of the sole principle of logic which was recommended by Jesus, 'Ye may know them by their fruits,' and it is very intimately allied with the ideas of the gospel" (5.402 n.2).

Religion, then, must be pragmatic. But this is not the limit of religion's relationship with philosophy. Indeed, the chief object of religious experience, God, is also the ultimate focus of both philosophy and science. But before this can be shown, it is necessary to indicate that there really is a God and how man comes to know him. With regard to the latter point, Peirce holds that "we can know nothing except what we *directly* experience" (6.492). And so our knowledge of God must be empirical: "Where would such an idea, say as that of God, come from, if not from direct experience?...as to God, open your eyes--and your heart, which is also a perceptive organ--and you see him" (6.493).

Peirce's God is more than just an object of individual religious experience; he is the culmination of the pragmatic view of philosophy and science. As we have seen, an essential aspect of pragmatism is its appeal to experimental verification. However, this verification need not be performed immediately; it may have to wait until the indefinite future to be performed by other members of the scientific or philosophical community. It is Peirce's contention that the scientific community, in its continual attempt to formulate the laws of the universe, is engaged in a religious endeavour, since it is ultimately trying to attain God, the source of all law. God is the creator of the universe, and since the universe is still evolving, God's creative activity is still taking place, and is subject to investigation by the scientific community. Thus, the idea of God is capable of pragmatic verification "because it provides a driving religious force for the scientific community."[6] And just as science is properly religious, so religion should be in its own way scientific, a religion of science--"so true to itself, that it becomes animated by the scientific spirit, confident that the conquests of science will be triumphs of its own, and accepting all the results of science, as scientific men themselves accept them, as steps toward the truth" (6.433).

Despite his relative obscurity as a philosopher during his own lifetime, Peirce's influence on William James, John Dewey and others served to consolidate pragmatism as the characteristic American philosophical attitude. Although Peirce's religious views as well as his pragmatism were modified to a considerable extent by his successors, his construction of a pragmatic philosophy of religion provided the prototype of later contributions to this discipline which have proved most fruitful.[7] Peirce lived well beyond the popularization of pragmatism, but received little of the credit for it. The one most responsible for that popularity was Peirce's closest friend, William James.

William James (1842-1910).

Although there are some significant differences between the pragmatism of James and that of Peirce, James never failed to give Peirce the credit for originating the movement, and if anything he minimized the extent to which his philosophy differs from that of his friend.[8] His own concept of pragmatism is best expressed in the following extract from *Some Problems of Philosophy*, an introductory textbook in philosophy which he was working on at the time of his death:

The pragmatic rule is that the meaning of a concept may always be found, if not in some sensible particular which it directly designates, then in some particular difference in the course of human experience, which its being true will make. Test every concept by the question 'What sensible difference to anybody will its truth make?' and you are in the best position for understanding what it means and for discussing its importance. If, questioning whether a certain concept be true or false, you can think of absolutely nothing that would practically differ in the two cases, you may assume that the alternative is meaningless and that your concept is no distinct idea. If two concepts lead you to infer the same particular consequence, then you may assume that they embody the same meaning under different names.[9]

As with Peirce, *verification* is all-important. Pragmatism is not a full-fledged philosophical system but simply a *method*. James explains elsewhere: "No particular results then, so far, but only an attitude of orientation is what the pragmatic method means. *The attitude of looking away from first things, principles, 'categories,' supposed necessities; and of looking towards last things, fruits, consequences, facts.*"[10]

An important aspect of James' pragmatism is his concept of *truth*. Just as verification is not simply a conceptual affair but issues in specific actions, so neither does truth refer to a passive imitation of reality by the mind but involves an active relation of the mind to reality:

The truth of an idea is not a stagnant property inherent in it. Truth *happens* to an idea. It *becomes* true, is *made* true by events. Its verity *is* in fact an event, a process: the process namely of its verifying itself, its veri-*fication*. Its validity

53

is the process of its valid-*ation*.[11]
Truth, then, is a *result* of the pragmatic activity of verification.
There is no such thing as abstract truth by itself; to be true, an
idea must correspond to reality as experienced, or rather, reality
must correspond to the idea. This does not mean that truth is
entirely dependent on the individual knowing subject. James' concept of truth is relative rather than absolute, but it is relative
to *facts*, not to subjective whimsical fancies.

Like Peirce, James held that the pragmatic verification of an
idea is accomplished in the future. But whereas Peirce's realism
entails that this verification is a matter of *discovering* an
already existing truth, for James verification involves a continuous
process of *making* the truth.[12] The concept of truth, therefore, is
an essential element in the differing views of pragmatism held by
Peirce and James. And whereas Peirce's pragmatic method was incorporated into a *realistic* philosophical system, James' pragmatism
was part and parcel of the system he called *radical empiricism*.

As is the case with most of the concepts James employs, one need
not look far to find a concise statement of what he means by
radical empiricism:

Radical empiricism consists first of a postulate, next of a
statement of fact, and finally of a generalized conclusion.

The postulate is that the only things that shall be debatable
among philosophers shall be things definable in terms drawn from
experience. (Things of an unexperienceable nature may exist ad
libitum, but they form no part of the material for philosophical
debate.)

The statement of fact is that the relations between things,
conjunctive as well as disjunctive, are just as much matters of
direct particular experience, neither more so nor less so than
the things themselves.

The generalized conclusion is that therefore the parts of
experience hold together from next to next by relations that are
themselves parts of experience. The directly apprehended universe needs, in short, no extraneous trans-empirical conjunctive
support, but possesses in its own right a concatenated or continuous structure.[13]

That which is radical about this form of empiricism, that in which
it differs from traditional British empiricism, is its widening
the scope of experience to include not just individual things but
also the relations between those things.[14] Radical empiricism
renders obsolete both the more limited empiricism of Locke, Hume
and Mill and also the various rationalist alternatives, especially
that of Kant, since there is no need for a priori categories in the
mind or elsewhere in the universe to explain relations between
things.[15]

James did not hesitate to apply his radical empiricism to the field of religion. His series of Gifford Lectures for 1901-02, *The Varieties of Religious Experience*, is devoted to the description and evaluation of various types of religious phenomena, especially those arising from personal religious experience. (His treatment of religion is characterized by the complete exclusion of the ecclesiastical element and by his distaste for creeds and dogmas.) As a criterion for the truth of religion, James proposes the human utility of the religious individual's actions, and from his study of the most religious of people, the saints, he concludes that their actions are indeed evidence in favour of the truth of their beliefs:

> In a general way, then, and 'on the whole,' our abandonment of theological criteria, and our testing of religion by practical common sense and the empirical method, leave it in possession of its towering place in history. Economically, the saintly group of qualities is indispensable to the world's welfare.[16]

However, the study of saintliness does not provide *conclusive* proof of the truth of religion, and James investigates next another group of religious individuals, the mystics, in an attempt to find further evidence either for or against the truth of religion. This study reveals the certain existence of mystical states of consciousness, but whereas these mystical experiences are absolutely authoritative for the mystics themselves, there is no necessity for others to accept their validity.[17] As with saintliness, therefore, mysticism provides no conclusive evidence either for or against the truth of religion.

A third category of religious individuals are the theologians, but here again James finds no compelling reasons to accept religion:

> I believe, in fact, that the logical reason of man operates in the field of divinity exactly as it has always operated in love, or in patriotism, or in politics, or in any other of the wider affairs of life, in which our passions or our mystical intuitions fix our beliefs beforehand. It finds arguments for our conviction, for indeed it *has* to find them. It amplifies and defines our faith, and dignifies it and lends it words and plausibility. It hardly ever engenders it; it cannot now secure it.[18]

There are some useful services which the science of religions can perform, such as the modernizing of doctrines in the light of human and scientific development. However, the only conclusion that James reaches as to the truth of religion is that it does produce real effects upon its adherents, and as the key concept of most religions is God, therefore "God is real since he produces real effects."[19] Beyond this rather tenuous evidence in favour of

55

religion, James can only invoke the 'right to believe' as the ultimate justification of religious belief--if a man is inclined on emotional or other non-intellectual grounds to believe in God, then he has a right to such a belief. He has a further right to believe, since religion might be such that it cannot become true unless he believes it.[20]

The Varieties of Religious Experience exemplifies a thoroughly empirical approach to the study of religion. Less obvious in that work, but still an essential characteristic of James' treatment of religion, is his pragmatism. The truth of religion, like all other truth, is subject to pragmatic verification:

> The truth of 'God' has to run the gauntlet of all our other truths. It is on trial by them and they by it. Our *final* opinion about God can be settled only after all the truths have straightened themselves out together.[21]

By the pragmatic criterion of truth, the traditional metaphysical attributes of God--his aseity, his necessity, his immateriality, etc.--are meaningless, since they make no difference in the religious life of the believer. God's moral attributes, on the other hand--his holiness, justice, love, etc.--are extremely meaningful: "Pragmatically, they stand on an entirely different footing. They positively determine fear and hope and expectation, and are foundations for the saintly life."[22] James' final conclusion about God is that

> the line of least resistance, then, as it seems to me, both in theology and in philosophy, is to accept along with the super-human consciousness, the notion that it is not all-embracing, the notion, in other words, that there is a God, but that he is finite, either in power or in knowledge, or in both at once.[23]

This latter qualification is necessary to account for evil in the world.

As a philosopher James personified to the highest degree the American capacity for profiting from diverse philosophical traditions. He was personally acquainted with leading philosophers in England, France, Germany and Italy, and he was far in advance of other English-speaking philosophers in dealing with the forerunners of 'existentialism', Kierkegaard and Nietzsche.[24] Although he left behind him no 'school' of philosophy, he did provide American philosophy with a coherent and distinctive philosophy of religion, one which the third major representative of pragmatism, John Dewey, was hard-pressed to surpass.

John Dewey (1859-1952).

The man who was to become known as "America's philosopher"[25] began his philosophical career as a neo-Hegelian. The chief appeal

56

of Hegel for Dewey was his capacity for overcoming the many serious divisions within experience--"divisions by way of isolation of self from the world, of soul from body, of nature from God."[26] The elimination of these divisions was the chief goal of Dewey's own philosophical work, and although he became more and more critical of Hegel in later years, he recognized "that acquaintance with Hegel has left a permanent deposit in my thinking."[27]

Although Dewey had been a student of Charles Peirce during Peirce's stay at Johns Hopkins University (1879-1884), he seems not to have been greatly influenced at this time by Peirce's pragmatism.[28] The philosopher most responsible for weaning him from Hegel was William James. The decisive work of James in this respect was the *Principles of Psychology* (1890); Dewey recognized this work as an enormous advance over previous discussions of mentality, but at the same time he felt that James had not gone far enough. Despite the interpretation of consciousness as a 'stream', rather than a fixed state, which James introduced there, Dewey felt that the retention of a distinct realm of consciousness apart from the body did not solve the traditional mind-body problem. His solution was to stress another aspect of James' thought-- his treatment of man as a vital organism--and so to eliminate the dichotomy between the concepts of man employed by biology and psychology, respectively.[29] The result of this discriminating use of James was a philosophy which in all respects is a thoroughgoing *naturalism*.

Unlike most other naturalisms, which are based on an a priori conception of what constitutes human nature, Dewey's naturalism is thoroughly *empirical*. In this respect he had to contend, as did James, with the narrow concept of experience postulated by the British empiricists which brought forth the Kantian-Hegelian reaction. Kant, Hegel and their successors failed to solve the problems of the old empiricism because they failed to diagnose the real cause of these problems--the supposition that the separation of knower and known, of experience and nature, is primary and irreducible. Although, as Dewey says, "[this] notion is now so established in tradition that to many thinkers it appears to be a datum, not an interpretative classification,"[30] it must be reexamined as critically and empirically as the description of any other human activity. Having done this, Dewey concludes:

The notion that the universe is split into two separate and disconnected realms of existence, one psychical and the other physical, and then that these two realms of being, in spite of their total disjunction, specifically and minutely correspond to each other...presents the acme of incredibility.[31]

With this breakdown of the classical concepts of experience and knowledge, the way is open for a naturalist explanation of these phenomena--one which begins with the unity of experience and nature rather than with their irreversible separation.

If knowledge is not--because it can not be--the conformity of the mind to the thing, then what is it? In his answer to this question, Dewey's pragmatism--or, as it is better known, his *instrumentalism*-- comes to the fore. Knowledge is not primarily contemplative, as was believed by previous philosophers, but *operative, active, instrumental*. The best example of how knowledge operates is modern science: "Knowing, for the experimental sciences, means a certain kind of intelligently conducted doing; it ceases to be contemplative and becomes in a true sense practical."[32] This reconceptualization of knowledge necessitates a new meaning for 'truth', and here again Dewey's pragmatism is evident:

> If ideas, meanings, conceptions, notions, theories, systems are instrumental to an active reorganization of the given environment, to a removal of some specific trouble and perplexity, then the test of their validity and value lies in accomplishing this work. If they succeed in this office, they are reliable, sound, valid, good, true. If they fail to clear up confusion, to eliminate defects, if they increase confusion, uncertainty, and evil when they are acted upon, then they are false. Confirmation, corroboration, verification lie in works, consequences. Handsome is that handsome does. By their fruits shall ye *know* them. That which guides us truly is true--demonstrated capacity for such guidance is precisely what is meant by truth.[33]

Dewey applied his pragmatic experimentalism to all aspects of human activity, including aesthetics, ethics and religion. As an empiricist, he made no a priori assumptions about the validity of religious experience, but was content to subject it to the same pragmatic criterion of truth as any other kind of experience. Against those who criticized this procedure, he suggested that they were perhaps not being entirely honest:

> It seems to me that the great solicitude of many persons, professing belief in the universality of the need for religion, about the present and future of religion proves that in fact they are moved more by partisan interest in a particular religion than by interest in religious experience.[34]

As a naturalist, Dewey's prime religious target is the 'supernatural'. In the past, "religions have been saturated with the supernatural--and the supernatural signifies precisely that which lies beyond experience."[35] To reject the supernatural, however, is not to reject all religion. He states in his book, *A Common Faith*:

> I shall develop another conception of the nature of the religious phase of experience, one that separates it from the supernatural and the things that have grown up about it. I shall try to show that these derivations are encumbrances and that what is genuinely

religious will undergo an emancipation when it is relieved from them; that then, for the first time, the religious aspect of experience will be free to develop freely on its own account.[36] The key to Dewey's treatment of religion is his distinction between religion, a religion, and the religious. To begin with, he rejects the notion of religion in the singular, since he can find nothing which the various religious bodies hold in common.[37] Next he acknowledges the reality of religious experience, although he is adamant that this does not refer to a unique $kind$ of experience: "Any activity pursued in behalf of an ideal and against obstacles and in spite of threats of personal loss because of conviction of its general and enduring value is religious in quality."[38] And finally, he asserts the primacy of the religious over particular religions:

It is the claim of religions that they effect this generic and enduring change in attitude. I should like to turn the statement around and say that whenever this change takes place there is a definitely religious attitude. It is not a religion that brings it about, but when it occurs, from whatever cause and by whatever means, there is a religious outlook and function.[39]

As the title of his book indicates, Dewey speaks freely of $faith$ in connection with religion. His description of religious faith sets him apart from the traditional separation of faith and reason:

Faith in the continual disclosing of truth through directed cooperative human endeavor is more religious in quality than is any faith in a completed revelation....There is such a thing as faith in intelligence becoming religious in quality--a fact that perhaps explains the efforts of some religionists to disparage the possibilities of intelligence as a force. They properly feel such faith to be a dangerous rival.[40]

This faith in intelligence is necessary to sustain Dewey's $meliorism$--"the belief that the specific conditions which exist at one moment, be they comparatively bad or comparatively good, in any event may be bettered."[41] Having no recourse to supernatural aid, man must depend on his own efforts to improve his condition. But without a belief that this condition can be improved, he may not even make the effort. Dewey is reluctant to introduce the word 'God' into his treatment of the religious, since its usual meaning of a supernatural being is unacceptable to him. However, if this word is to be used, he would have it signify "the ideal ends that at a given time and place one acknowledges as having authority over his volition and emotion, the values to which one is supremely devoted, as far as these ends, through imagination, take on unity."[42] As so used, the word 'God' signifies for Dewey, as it does for the traditional religions, the ultimate religious concept.

Although he was not especially interested in religion, Dewey

59

clearly indicated its place in his philosophy of experimental
naturalism. To say that he represents an advance in the development of a pragmatic philosophy of religion requires that no very
specific meaning be given to the word 'pragmatism'. For just as
James differed from Peirce so much that the latter invented the
word 'pragmaticism' to distinguish their respective philosophies,
so also did Dewey's philosophy become more widely known as 'instrumentalism' because of its dissimilarities with James' teaching.
And yet there are many common elements shared by these three men,
so much so that the differences among them are minor compared with
their differences with traditional philosophy, whether empiricist
or rationalist. With Dewey, the term 'pragmatism' practically
disappears, but American philosophy has continued to reformulate
and express the basic tenets shared by Peirce, James and Dewey.
The remaining philosophers to be treated in this chapter have
seldom if ever been called pragmatists, but they have continued
the work of Peirce, James and Dewey in the development of a
characteristic American philosophy of religion.

Alfred North Whitehead (1861-1947).

Although Alfred North Whitehead did not come to America until
he was sixty-three years of age, in 1924, he is justly regarded as
one of the major figures in the history of American philosophy.
As professor of philosophy at Harvard University from 1924 until
1938, his lectures and books provided American pragmatic philosophy with the metaphysical structure it had lacked since the time
of Peirce. And while incorporating into this structure most of
the basic ideas of the pragmatists, Whitehead laid special
emphasis on the notion of *process* which has become so prominent
among subsequent American philosophers and theologians.
   Like Peirce and James, Whitehead's original vocation was that of
a scientist, and it was only after his move to America that he
began to devote himself wholeheartedly to philosophy. Although his
acquaintance there with the three major pragmatists was somewhat
limited,[43] he fitted well into what we have described as the
pragmatic tradition of American philosophy because of his thoroughgoing empiricism, his rejection of the dichotomy between thought
and material nature, and his emphasis on process as a fundamental
characteristic of all being. Like Dewey, he seldom refers to his
philosophy as a form of pragmatism. However, he does on occasion
indicate his general acceptance of the pragmatic criterion of
truth,[44] and he feels that logic is in need of pragmatic verification, since its precise laws and concepts are abstractions from
experience:
   This deductive logic has not the coercive supremacy which is

60

conventionally conceded to it. When applied to concrete instances, it is a tentative procedure, finally to be judged by
the self-evidence of its issues. This doctrine places philosophy on a pragmatic basis. But the meaning of 'pragmatism' must
be given its widest extension. In much modern thought, it has
been limited by arbitrary specialist assumptions. There should
be no pragmatic exclusion of self-evidence by dogmatic denial.
Pragmatism is simply an appeal to that self-evidence which sus-
tains itself in civilized experience.[45]

Thus, Whitehead's philosophy is pragmatic, although he is careful
to indicate the limitations of this title as an overall description of his philosophy.

In common with the other pragmatists, Whitehead is an empiricist.[46]
But he is no less critical than they of traditional British
empiricism, as exemplified by Locke, Berkeley and Hume. These
philosophers claimed to allow experience to be the sole determinant
of valid knowledge, but in point of fact they were unconsciously
employing arbitrary criteria for accepting some forms of experience, especially sense-perception, while rejecting others. Whitehead criticizes this exclusive reliance on sense-perception, since
it allows for no knowledge of the past or future. Furthermore, he
feels that it is a mistake to assign primacy to sense data in the
process of knowledge. Sense-data are, in fact, products of *abstraction*: "The instinctive interpretations which govern human life
and animal life presuppose a contemporary world throbbing with
energetic values. It requires considerable ability to make the
disastrous abstraction of our bare sense-perceptions from the
massive insistency of our total experiences."[47] The point at which
this abstraction becomes disastrous is when the philosopher forgets
that it is an abstraction, and ascribes concrete reality to the
object of the abstractive process. This is an example of what
Whitehead calls the "Fallacy of Misplaced Concreteness," which he
feels has been the basic cause of the inadequacy of modern
philosophy.[48]

The specific abstractions to which concreteness has been assigned
vary from philosopher to philosopher, but Whitehead deals at length
with some of the most common in traditional philosophy. The first
of these is *substance*: "The simple notion of an enduring substance
sustaining persistent qualities, either essentially or accidentally,
expresses a useful abstract for many purposes of life. But whenever
we try to use it as a fundamental statement of the nature of things,
it proves itself mistaken."[49] Another abstraction which has seldom
been recognized as such is the subject-object dichotomy. The knowing subject is not a primary datum of experience, and neither are
the perceived objects: "The primary situation disclosed in cognitive experience is 'ego-object amid objects.' By this I mean that

61

the primary fact is an impartial world transcending the here-now which marks the ego-object...."[50] It is only by a process of abstraction that we can isolate the self as knower from the field of experience which includes the self and other objects as known. By showing that these concepts are abstractions, Whitehead has demonstrated the weakness of traditional empiricism and thereby has prepared the way for a more adequate description of reality, which he incorporates into his own philosophical system.

The "Philosophy of Organism" is the title which Whitehead preferred for his own form of empiricism.[51] He conceived all elements of nature, including consciousness, as essentially interrelated, as parts of one organic whole. This view of reality is a direct consequence of his empiricism, according to which individual entities are not the primary objects of our experience but are abstractions from the welter of confused and overlapping experience of all sorts to which we are constantly subjected. The recognition of the true nature of experience leads immediately to the rejection of the concept of mind as an entity independent of the body and of all other examples of misplaced concreteness. Instead of a world composed of eternal, immutable substances, the philosophy of organism allows for process and evolution at all levels of reality, including the divine. Thus, Whitehead does not hesitate to apply the empirical approach to the field of religion.

In company with the other pragmatist philosophers, Whitehead approaches the study of religion without theological presuppositions as to the truth of religion in general or of any particular religion. As a result, he is perfectly willing to criticize various manifestations of religious thought and behaviour which he considers to be philosophically unjustified. At the same time, he esteems religion very highly, indeed as indispensable to philosophy, since it provides philosophy with a belief in the purposeful order of nature. As in the philosophy of Peirce, Whitehead's God is the culmination of his metaphysics, and as such, it differs significantly from the traditional Christian concept of God.

Whitehead's criticism of traditional religion is based on his philosophical empiricism. All religious phenomena, including God, are subject to the same epistemological and metaphysical conditions as any other entity: "God is not to be treated as an exception to all metaphysical principles, invoked to save their collapse. He is their chief exemplification."[52] The descriptions of God as an eternal, unchangeable, supreme being, the uncaused cause of the universe, and the highest value or perfection are all examples of misplaced concreteness--false abstractions from the world of process which necessarily includes God. They constitute the legacy of the Greek philosophical expression of Christian dogmas, which Whitehead feels has been most unfortunate for both philosophy

62

and theology.[53]

Whitehead's rejection of traditional theism does not mean that he is an atheist or agnostic. On the contrary, his reconstituted concept of God is an essential element in his philosophical system. The primary function which God performs is the provision of *purpose* or *value* for the universe. The world would be meaningless if the particular metaphysical order which it exemplifies could not be explained by reference to some principle. And where there is no meaning, there is no purpose or value. That there is order in the universe can be observed empirically, by noting the existence of physical regularities. To account for these regularities, and for the purpose which they manifest, Whitehead introduces the concept of God: "'God' is that actuality in the world in virtue of which there is physical 'law'".[54] For Whitehead, therefore, God is not just an optional adjunct to a universe which is complete in itself, but is rather the principle without which the universe would be totally meaningless.

Having established the metaphysical need for God, Whitehead goes on to develop a description of God which is fully compatible with the principles of his philosophical system. The first such principle is the empirical basis of all human knowledge: "The general principle of empiricism depends upon the doctrine that there is a principle of concretion which is not discoverable by abstract reason. What further can be known about God must be sought in the region of particular experiences, and therefore rests on an empirical basis."[55] Another basic element of Whitehead's philosophy is the notion of process, and this too must be applied to God: "The notion of a supreme being must apply to an actuality in process of composition, an actuality not confined to the data of any special epoch in the historical field."[56] This concept of a 'process God' is intended to overcome a major inadequacy of the traditional description of God as unchangeable--its failure to allow for any real interaction between God and the world.

The apparent incompatibility between the descriptions of God as the source of value in the universe and as subject to change and development led Whitehead to distinguish two natures in God, *primordial* and *consequent*. The former refers to God's function as the provider of value, but this description is incomplete: "God's 'primordial nature' is abstracted from his commerce with 'particulars', and is therefore devoid of those 'impure' intellectual cogitations which involve propositions....It is God in abstraction, alone with himself. As such it is a mere factor in God, deficient in actuality."[57] Most of Whitehead's discussion of God in his major work, *Process and Reality*, is devoted to the primordial nature, and the consequent nature is treated in just seven pages at the end of the book. Despite this imbalance, however, it is evident that the consequent nature is an essential part

63

of God, and this enables Whitehead to conclude that God and the world are linked together in a processive relationship according to which any change in one necessitates a change in the other.

Over and above the concept of God, the relationship of philosophy and religion in general, according to Whitehead, is one of inter-dependence and mutual benefit:

> Religion should connect the rational generality of philosophy with the emotions and purposes springing out of existence in a particular society, in a particular epoch, and conditioned by particular antecedents. Religion is the translation of general ideas into particular thoughts, particular emotions, and particular purposes; it is directed to the end of stretching individual interest beyond its self-defeating particularity. Philosophy finds religion and modifies it; and conversely religion is among the data of experience which philosophy must weave into its own scheme.[58]

Religion is not exempt from the critical function of philosophy, even the religious concept of God. However, it is only the obsolete and retrogressive expressions of religious dogma that need fear the judgment of philosophy, for it is the purification, not the elimination, of religion that Whitehead intends.

It is evident, therefore, that Whitehead has incorporated the major themes of American philosophy of religion into his philosophical system, and has supplemented the pragmatists' treatment of religion by providing it with a sophisticated metaphysical backing. In his emphasis on the empirical basis of all our knowledge and on the central metaphysical role played by the concept of God, he has shown that a philosophical treatment of religion is both possible and necessary--necessary for both philosophy and religion. But his major contribution to the development of a characteristic American philosophy of religion is, without a doubt, his extension of the notion of *process* to all of reality, including God, and it is through the 'schools' of process philosophy and process theology that his influence has been most widely disseminated.

Charles Hartshorne (1897-   ).

The period between 1925 and 1940, during which Whitehead was elaborating his philosophical system, was not particularly receptive to new developments in the philosophy of religion. The "golden age" of American philosophy was at its end, and more restrictive concepts of philosophy, such as that of logical positivism, were beginning to dominate. At the same time, the most vigorous theological movements were neo-orthodoxy and pietism, neither of which granted any importance to philosophical views of religion. As a result, it was not until after the Second World War that

Whitehead's ideas began to exercise a significant influence on American philosophers and theologians. This statement admits of one very important exception, however, and it is due largely to this man that Whiteheadian process philosophy and theology are so influential today. The philosopher in question is Charles Hartshorne.

Hartshorne's importance for American philosophy of religion extends far beyond his espousal of Whitehead's principal ideas. As co-editor of the Collected Works of Charles Peirce and as a close student of the writings of James and Dewey, he is well versed in the basic tenets of American philosophy. In addition, he has read widely in the history of Western philosophy; he is familiar with modern logic, and shows more awareness of contemporary European philosophy than perhaps any American since William James. His acquaintance with some forms of Eastern philosophical thought, especially the Buddhists, has convinced him of the cultural relativity of the Western tradition. Finally, he has attempted to assimilate all these various influences into his own original approach to the philosophy of religion.

Hartshorne is reluctant to consider himself a pragmatist, but he does not disown the fundamental concept of pragmatism: "From Peirce and James I accept a basic pragmatism (it is also a kind of existentialism); ideas must be expressible in living and behavior or they are merely verbal."[59] Likewise, his emphasis on reality as *process* is a reiteration of a concept fundamental to all the pragmatists. However, he does differ from the pragmatists on one important point, namely, their empiricism. He feels that metaphysics requires certain a priori, necessary principles, and therefore any description of reality which omits the non-empirical, necessary element is incomplete:

I hold that an empirical world-view is at best either science outrunning its empirical warrant, or a self-critical fusion of *a priori* first principles and the conclusions of science. Philosophy has two primary responsibilities: to clarify the non-empirical principles and to use them, together with relevant empirical facts, to illuminate value problems of personal and social life.[60]

The chief instance of necessary principles which he feels is excluded by a thoroughgoing empiricism is God, a concept which is central to his philosophy. But apart from this rejection of empiricism, he accepts the basic tenets of American philosophical pragmatism, and his philosophical approach to religion shares much in common with the other American philosophers already described.

Although Hartshorne makes it very clear that he is a philosopher, not a theologian, nevertheless his writings reveal a predominant concern with the problems of religion, and especially with the concept of God. He feels that philosophers who refuse to deal

65

with the concept of God are incapable of giving an adequate account of reality: "If metaphysics knows anything, it must either know God, or know that the idea of God is meaningless. Neutrality as to God means no metaphysics. The choice is a theistic metaphysics, or an atheistic metaphysics, or a positivistic rejection of both God and metaphysics."[61] Hartshorne, of course, opts for theism, although he soon rejects that particular term because of its association with the classical description of God as absolute in all respects, a description which he, like Whitehead, considers quite inadequate.

In his book, *Man's Vision of God*, Hartshorne divides the various philosophical attitudes towards God into three categories: 1) there is a being who is absolutely perfect in all respects; 2) there is a being who is absolutely perfect in only some respects; 3) there is no being who is absolutely perfect in any respect.[62] He rejects the first type of theism for the same reason as Whitehead--it allows for no real interaction between God and the world. The third possibility must also be rejected, since philosophy requires the existence of a reality that is necessary in at least some respect. God must therefore be absolute in some respects and relative in others. However, even though he is surpassable in some respects, he is surpassable only by himself. God's relativity means that "in no possible state of affairs can there be anything in any fashion superior to God as he is in that same state of affairs."[63] Hartshorne calls this second type of theism 'Surrelativism'.[64]

One of the chief ways in which God can surpass himself is with regard to his knowledge of the future. Hartshorne holds that divine omniscience "does not imply a knowledge 'above time'. There could be a future even to an all-knowing being. When a future event comes to happen, such a mind will know more than it did before, but at both times it will know all that there is, though at the later time there will be a new event to know."[65] In a certain sense, man can be said to be a creator of God, since man produces things for God to know. However, this does not detract from God's superiority to man and to the world. Hartshorne compares the relation of God and the world to that of the human mind and body: "The body of a given mind is *that much of the world which the mind immediately knows and controls and suffers*....God is that mind which enjoys the fullest intimacy with all things, and therefore in an undiluted sense has all the world for body."[66] In order to distinguish this doctrine of God from pantheism, which it resembles superficially, as well as from traditional theism, Hartshorne uses the term 'panentheism', which he defines as "the view that deity is in some real aspect distinguishable from and independent of any and all relative items, and yet, taken as an

66

actual whole, includes all relative items."[67]

For Hartshorne, therefore, if there is a God, he must be relative in some aspects. Now in order to show that there *is* a God, he has recourse to one of the most venerable arguments for divine existence, the ontological argument, which he summarizes as follows: "Deity can be consistently conceived, but only as existent."[68] In other words, if God is conceivable, then he must exist. The only alternative to God's existence is that the term 'God' or 'divinity' has no coherent meaning. The meaning which Hartshorne assigns to this term is expressed in the words--"an inherent harmony capable of logical expression, between the religious and the secular functions of the human mind, and of the world as portrayed in these functions."[69] The only alternative to belief in God is a refusal of meaning to existence; on this point Hartshorne follows Peirce and Whitehead, both of whom described God as the principle of value and meaning in the universe. So Hartshorne feels that the ontological argument provides conclusive proof of the existence of God, but he is careful to point out that the argument is valid only for the surrelative concept of God (and not for the absolutist concept which Anselm of Canterbury attempted to prove[70]).

Hartshorne's treatment of religious topics other than God is relatively cautious. With regard to the validity of divine revelation, he states only that metaphysics is basically open to theology's claim that some persons can know certain things by uncommon experiences, although he holds that such revelatory experiences are not binding on those who have not had them. In general he feels that religious faith is philosophically justifiable:

I discern some degree of rational justification for a religion of complete, all-inclusive devotion to One in whose Life all good and all actuality are embraced, to whom prayer may properly be addressed, and whose loving acceptance even of our sufferings is supremely symbolized in the human life depicted in the Gospels.[71]

In his philosophy of religion, Hartshorne has attempted to develop all the implications of Whitehead's insight that all of reality, including God, is in process. Hartshorne's students have been the leaders in the elaboration of Whiteheadian process philosophy and theology in North America, and under his influence, the main elements of the pragmatist tradition of American philosophy of religion have been passed on to the present. Before considering the current state of process philosophy of religion, however, we must describe the contribution to the American tradition of a man with whom Hartshorne often disagreed, but for whom he had the utmost respect as a philosopher and theologian, Paul Tillich.

67

Paul Tillich (1886-1965).

Like Whitehead, Tillich was not a native-born American. He was already 47 years old when he arrived in the United States in 1933 as a refugee from Nazi Germany, having been expelled by Hitler from his professorship at the University of Frankfurt. Up until that time he was very much a part of the German intellectual milieu, and shared the prevalent feelings of his academic colleagues that nothing significant in philosophy and theology was occurring elsewhere.[72] But he gradually discarded this view, and in later years acknowledged the considerable influence of American culture on his own thinking:

> The spirit of the English language has demanded the clarification of many ambiguities of my thought which were covered by the mystical vagueness of the classic philosophical German; the interdependence of theory and practice in Anglo-Saxon culture, religious as well as secular, has freed me from the fascination of that kind of abstract idealism which enjoys the system for the system's sake; the cooperation with colleagues and students of Union Theological Seminary, Columbia University, and other universities and colleges has provided the experience of a type of Protestant religion and culture very different from that of continental Europe....[73]

In another place he praises the lack of authoritarianism in American society as well as "the American courage to go ahead, to try, to risk failures, to begin again after defeat, to lead an experimental life both in knowledge and in action, to be open towards the future, to participate in the creative process of nature and history."[74]

Although Tillich seldom mentions by name his main predecessors in the American philosophy of religion--Peirce, James, Dewey and Whitehead--it is clear from his above statements that the basic features of what we have described as the American pragmatic tradition had an especial appeal for him. He mentions specifically the interdependence of theory and practice, the inclination towards the experimental life both in knowledge and in action, and the stress on participation in the creative process of nature and history. However, Tillich's ontological and epistemological realism prevents him from a whole-hearted adoption of pragmatism, associated as it is with a thoroughgoing empiricism: "When pragmatism speaks of experience, it surrenders the criteria of truth and the good no less than does vitalistic philosophy. There are for it no norms above the dynamic process of experience, namely, of experienced life."[75] Thus, Tillich's approach to pragmatism is similar to that of Hartshorne: they both accept the principal features of that tradition, with the notable exception of its thoroughgoing empiricism.

As we have already seen, the pragmatic tradition of American philosophy of religion has been represented most adequately in recent years by the philosophers and theologians of *process*. In his later writings, Tillich has taken this movement into account when formulating his own position. As with pragmatism, his attitude towards process thought includes a positive as well as a negative note. In his *Theology of Culture*, he offers a word of approval:

Courage is another important element in American philosophical thought. Perhaps one could say that the emphasis on becoming, process, growth, progress, etc., in American philosophy is the expression of a courage which takes upon itself risks, failures, regressions, disappointments in a way which one can hardly find in the groups which are mostly responsible for Continental philosophy.[76]

However, he explicitly rejects an unlimited application of process to being, since he believes that there must be a *structure* of process, an a priori element according to which process can be understood ontologically.[77] With regard to the notion of a process God, Tillich rejects Charles Hartshorne's contention

that creaturely contingency conditions God in some respect and makes him literally finite in relation to it. My resistance against this doctrine...is rooted in the overwhelming impression of the divine majesty as witnessed by classical religion. This makes any structural dependence of God on something contingent impossible for me to accept.[78]

Unlike the other Americans treated so far, Tillich is better described as a philosophical theologian than as a philosopher of religion. Upon assuming the chair of Philosophical Theology at Union Theological Seminary, he stated: "Philosophical Theology is the unusual name of the chair I represent. It is a name that suits me better than any other, since the boundary line between philosophy and theology is the center of my thought and work."[79] He considered himself a theologian not because he belonged to a particular church or because he was concerned with defending a particular religious tradition, but because "the existential question of our ultimate concern and the existential answer of the Christian message are and always have been predominant in my spiritual life."[80] Tillich believes that neither philosophy nor theology is complete in itself: philosophy's description of the human condition raises questions which it cannot answer. Theology has the answers from divine revelation, but if it ignores the philosophical expression of contemporary culture, its answers will go unheard. Tillich's major work, *Systematic Theology*, is organized in terms of this method of *correlation*--between the questions raised by philosophy and the answers given by theology. A summary

69

of this approach is given in the above-mentioned inaugural address:
  Philosophical theology deals with the concept of reason and the
  categories belonging to it and leads to the existential problem
  implied in reason, to which the answer is: revelation. Philosophical theology deals with the concept of being and the categories belonging to it and leads to the existential concept
  implied in being, to which the answer is: God...
and so on, with the concepts of existence/the Christ, life/the
Spirit, and history/the Kingdom of God.[81]

In his "Introduction" to the *Systematic Theology*, Tillich notes
three points of divergence between the philosopher and the theologian. With regard to their cognitive attitudes towards the objects
of their investigation, the philosopher tries to maintain a detached objectivity towards being and its structure while the theologian is deeply and passionately involved with his object, God. A
second divergence concerns their sources: the philosopher looks at
the whole of reality to discover within it the structure of reality
as a whole, while the theologian examines a particular aspect of
reality, Jesus Christ and the Church. Finally, philosophy and
theology differ with regard to their content: the philosopher deals
with being as it is; the theologian, with being as it should be,
with man's quest for a "new being."[82] Despite these differences,
Tillich maintains that just as every theologian must be a philosopher in order to understand the questions which theology must
answer, so also every philosopher is a theologian when dealing with
existential matters.

It follows from this understanding of the relationship between
philosophy and theology that there can be no valid conflict between
faith and reason or between reason and revelation. As long as it
is recognized that human reason is subject to all the limitations
of finite existence and therefore cannot provide man with all the
answers to his most important existential questions, man will be
open to the possibility of receiving these answers through revelation. Tillich defines revelation as "the manifestation of something within the context of ordinary experience which transcends
the ordinary context of experience."[83] What is revealed does not
contradict reason--it is the answer to the question which reason
can only pose. Revelation is the manifestation of what concerns
us ultimately, and this is what makes it the object of theology
rather than of philosophy, of existential faith rather than of
detached reason.

The source of revelation, God, is described by Tillich in accordance with his method of correlation. He does not begin with the
biblical or classical theological concept of God, but rather describes God as the answer to man's most fundamental existential
question--the question of being. As finite, man is aware of the

contingency of his own being and of all other finite beings. He is therefore threatened by non-being, which remains a constant possibility for him. But in addition to his finitude, man is aware of an unconditional element in the structure of reality, and this leads man to the question of God:

> The question of God can be asked because there is an unconditional element in the very act of asking any question. The question of God $must$ be asked because the threat of nonbeing, which man experiences as anxiety, drives him to the question of being conquering nonbeing and of courage conquering anxiety.[84]

Tillich goes on to describe God as "being itself" and "the ground of being."[85] He is not a being, even the supreme being, but is rather the structure of all being. For this reason, it is impossible to describe God literally, except to say that he is being itself. All other statements about God are symbolic. In the $Systematic\ Theology$, Tillich evaluates the traditional symbols used by Christians to describe God--God as personal, God as trinity, etc.--and finds most of them still adequate, although in need of some reinterpretation. Despite much opposition from other Christian theologians, however, he does not insist on the universal acceptance of these symbols, even the name 'God':

> If that word has not much meaning for you, translate it, and speak of the depths of the source of your being, of your ultimate concern, of what you take seriously without any reservation. Perhaps, in order to do so, you must forget everything traditional that you have learned about God, perhaps even that word itself.[86]

As was pointed out earlier, there are limits to Tillich's reinterpretation of the Christian faith. In particular, he refused to follow Charles Hartshorne in describing God in terms of process rather than in terms of being. Despite this difference, however, Tillich and Hartshorne have much in common, both in their teachings and in the reception their ideas have been accorded. Just as Hartshorne's philosophy of religion met with relatively little response from his contemporaries and has been developed mainly by his own students, so also did Tillich's philosophical theology have to wait two decades or so after his arrival in America to be taken seriously by philosophers and theologians alike. The situation has changed, however, and the most exciting work in American philosophy of religion today is being performed by men who are familiar with both the American pragmatic-process tradition and the work of Tillich and his European predecessors and contemporaries. The remainder of this survey will be devoted to the consideration of four representatives of current American religious thought. It should be noted that each of the four (with the possible exception of the last) is, like Tillich, a theologian rather than a philoso-

71

pher. They have all been positively influenced by both the American and the Continental European philosophical traditions (especially German phenomenology and existence philosophy). But for two of them, John B. Cobb, Jr., and Schubert M. Ogden, the predominant influence comes from Whitehead and Hartshorne, while for the other two, John Macquarrie and Leslie Dewart, Tillich and his European associates (especially Heidegger) have proven most important.

John B. Cobb, Jr. (1925-   ).

The year 1962 marked an important stage in the development of American process philosophy of religion with the publication of Hartshorne's *The Logic of Perfection* and of the first major works of Hartshorne's two most outstanding pupils, Schubert Ogden's *Christ Without Myth* and John Cobb's *Living Options in Protestant Theology*. Although this book of Cobb's did not present a fully-developed philosophy of religion, he did indicate there his objections to the uses of philosophy by theologians such as Barth, Brunner, Bultmann and Tillich. And in subsequent writings he has worked out his own philosophical position in considerable detail, based largely on the ideas of Whitehead.

Like Tillich, Cobb is a theologian rather than a philosopher. The term which he prefers to describe his academic speciality is "natural theology," or, to be more precise, "Christian natural theology." This latter expression means for Cobb

a treatment of questions of importance for Christian theology in which the criteria of philosophical excellence determine what can be said. The argument presented asks to be judged in terms of its philosophical merits, but the selection of topics and the focus of inquiry are determined by theological passion.[87]

In order to construct such a Christian natural theology, the theologian must be able to express the Christian faith in rational terms. This requires the use of a philosophy, and the theologian must choose either to create his own philosophy--a difficult if not impossible task--or else to adopt and adapt some already existing philosophy for his purposes. The two criteria which Cobb suggests for this second alternative are the intrinsic excellence of the philosophies under consideration--their simplicity, their consistency, etc.--and their congeniality to the Christian faith. On both these grounds, Cobb feels that the philosophy of Whitehead is the most suitable one available, although it can be no more than the *basis* of a Christian natural theology.[88]

The logical starting-point for Cobb's Christian natural theology is the doctrine of God, and Whitehead's philosophy, especially as developed by Hartshorne,[89] is particularly appropriate here:

72

The great advantage of the neo-classical theism is that it shows the possibility of a thoroughly coherent view of God which is at the same time just that view which religious insight seems to entail. Hence the God of the neo-classical philosophy *is* the God of religion.[90]
In line with Whitehead's description of God as the provider of purpose for the universe, Cobb speaks of God as "He who calls us to ever-greater love, life and freedom" and "that factor in the universe which makes for novelty, life, intensity of feeling, consciousness, freedom, and in man genuine concern for others, and which provides that measure of order which supports these."[91] In place of Hartshorne's understanding of God's relation to the world in terms of the relation of the human mind and body, Cobb feels that this relation is best understood in comparison with human memory. When we remember an event which occurred in the past, we experience it as past rather than present, and this element of the remembering is nonsensory. If such nonsensory experiences are possible for humans, then it is not inconceivable that they are possible for God. Thus, God could participate in all human experiencing without the limitations of human singlemindedness and weakness of memory.[92]

Since Cobb is attempting to formulate a specifically *Christian* natural theology, he is not content to describe God simply in terms of his function as the provider of purpose in the universe and to explain God's relation to the world, but he also wishes to show how Jesus Christ can be explained in Whiteheadian terms. Whitehead's concept of *presence* requires that God be present in every entity. However, there are different modes of this presence, depending upon God's intention for each entity on any particular occasion and on that entity's response to God. Cobb feels that God's presence in Jesus, who was as fully human as any other man, was unique because of God's determination that he be uniquely present in Jesus and because of Jesus' total acceptance of this aim.[93] Furthermore, the uniqueness of Jesus extends to the structure of human existence which he introduced into the world and which is final and unsurpassable.[94] In his treatment of human existence, as in his treatment of God, Cobb has tried to base his Christian natural theology as fully as possible on the writings of Whitehead. A more eclectic approach to philosophical resources is evident in the second major representative of contemporary American process theology, Schubert Ogden.

Schubert M. Ogden (1928-   ).

Ogden's first published works were concerned with the theological problems raised by biblical scholarship, especially the demytholog-

73

ization debate centering on the writings of Rudolf Bultmann.[95] He
was quick to notice that this debate involved the wider issue of
theological method and especially the relation of philosophy and
theology, and he has taken particular care to familiarize himself
with Bultmann's own philosophical presuppositions, which are
essentially those of the early Heidegger. It is his basic conviction, however, that these philosophical resources are adequate for
only part of the theological task, and need to be supplemented by
the process philosophy of Whitehead and Hartshorne.

Ogden is a theologian, but he insists that theology cannot be
independent of philosophy. There is a difference between these two
activities, but it does not correspond to the difference between
faith and reason. Faith and reason are components of both philosophy and theology: "To exist as a self is possible solely on the
basis of faith, so that the statement, 'Unless you believe, you
shall not understand,' is true in a sense not only of the Christian
or of the religious believer but of every man simply as such."[96]
Therefore, Ogden can define philosophy as "the fully reflective
understanding of the basic existential faith which is constitutive
of human existence."[97] Theology, on the other hand (that is,
Christian theology), has as its task the fully reflective understanding of Christian faith. It differs from philosophy not by
excluding either faith or reason but by having a somewhat different
object--the Christian faith rather than the faith common to all
men. The meeting place of philosophy and theology is philosophical
theology; its task is "so to understand our common faith as to
answer the basic question of the reality of God."[98]

Ogden agrees with Tillich and Cobb that theology cannot function
independently of philosophy:

Not only is it evident that Christian faith alone is an insuffi-
cient ground for theology's assertions, but it is also clear
that such assertions cannot even be established as meaningful
except by establishing a theistic metaphysics which is true
independently of specifically Christian faith.[99]

The major problem with which the theologian must deal is how to
find the "right" philosophy on which to base his philosophical
theology. Ogden feels that only philosophical criteria should be
used in the evaluation of different philosophies, and it is his
opinion that a synthesis of the philosophical positions of Martin
Heidegger and Charles Hartshorne will provide the "right" philosophy for Christian theology.

Like Bultmann, Ogden holds that Heidegger's principal contribution to theology is his description of human existence as set
forth in *Sein und Zeit*.[100] However, Ogden thinks that Bultmann
was overly dependent upon this aspect of Heidegger's thought, and
thus was unable to provide as adequate an account of divine exis-

tence as he did of human existence. Although even in *Sein und Zeit* Heidegger offered a valuable suggestion for the reinterpretation of divine eternity as infinite temporality, which Ogden develops in accordance with Hartshorne's description of God as process,[101] Heidegger has provided no detailed description of God, and so Ogden looks to the philosophy of Hartshorne to supply the missing parts of the "right" philosophy.

According to Ogden, Hartshorne provides an analysis of divine existence that closely parallels and complements what Bultmann says about Heidegger's analysis of human existence:

Just as Bultmann argues that there can be 'a science that speaks of [human] existence without objectifying it to worldly being,' so Hartshorne argues to exactly the same effect about divine existence. And the reasoning is precisely identical: God can be the object of philosophical explication without in any way being objectified to worldly being because what philosophy seeks to explicate is not God as concretely actual, but rather God's abstract essence--just as, by analogy, the object of existential analysis is not man as concrete existence (Existenz) but rather the abstract form or principle of such existence (Existential-ität).[102]

For both Hartshorne and Ogden, God is relative rather than abso-lute--"a reality which is genuinely related to our life in the world and to which, therefore, both we ourselves and our various actions all make a difference as to its actual being."[103] Ogden adopts the analogy put forth by Hartshorne of the universe as God's body, although this is not intended to detract from the preeminence of God in his relationships with the beings of the universe.[104] He feels that this concept of God is the most ade-quate interpretation of the biblical expression, "God is love," and of the belief that God has manifested himself preeminently in the person of Jesus Christ.[105]

Because Ogden allies himself so closely with Hartshorne's con-cept of God, he is generally opposed to the description of God put forth by Paul Tillich, which he feels is too much like that of traditional Christian theism.[106] He does recognize, however, the importance of Tillich's efforts to overcome the mutual neglect of philosophy and theology, and it is fair to say that Ogden is a legitimate successor to Tillich in the development of American philosophical theology. Even more closely related to Tillich, and conversely, somewhat farther removed from the Whitehead-Hartshorne process tradition, is the third representative of con-temporary American philosophical theology to be treated here, John Macquarrie.

75

AMERICAN PHILOSOPHY OF RELIGION

John Macquarrie (1919-   ).

It should be clear by now that one need not be born in the
United States to participate in the development of American philosophy of religion. John Macquarrie was born and educated in Scotland,
and was a lecturer in theology at the University of Glasgow until
he was appointed Professor of Systematic Theology at Union Theological Seminary, New York, in 1962. Unlike his fellow immigrants,
Whitehead and Tillich, Macquarrie has since returned to his native
island, and now teaches at the University of Oxford. But during
the eight years he spent in North America, he distinguished himself
as one of the foremost exponents of philosophical theology, and
has done more than anyone else in America to show the relevance of
Heidegger's philosophy for theology.

Although Macquarrie relies almost exclusively on Heidegger's
philosophy, he is not unaware that process philosophy also provides
valuable resources for Christian theology. In a recent article
entitled, "God and the World: One Reality or Two?"[107] he speaks
favourably of "panentheism" and its "organic" model of the relation
between God and the world. And he gives his qualified approval to
Whitehead's doctrine of the dipolarity or double nature of God as
"a serious attempt to combine--as I think must be combined--the poles
of transcendence and immanence, of eternity and temporality (or
historicity), of impassibility and passibility, and so on."[108]
However, his basic preference for Heidegger's philosophy is evident
in his criticism of Schubert Ogden's book on Bultmann, *Christ Without Myth*:

Whereas I would continue with Heidegger beyond the stage at which
Bultmann has parted company with him, and believe that Heidegger
can provide an existentially based ontology which avoids the
pitfalls of the old-style metaphysics, Ogden looks rather to the
metaphysics of Hartshorne and company.[109]

Macquarrie distinguishes his own proper endeavour, philosophical
theology, from the philosophy of religion. The former is "that
branch of theology which concerns itself with elucidating and examining the philosophical implications of a religious faith," while the
latter is "that branch of philosophy which concerns itself with
interpreting and evaluating religion."[110] The philosophical study
of religion demands a degree of detachment from religion which
would be illegitimate for the theologian, and the philosopher of
religion must be open to the truth claims of all religions whereas
the theologian speaks out of a specific community of faith.[111] The
specific task of philosophical theology is "to show, through
description and interpretation, the conditions of the possibility
of any religious faith whatsoever."[112] This task must be accomplished if theology is to have any intellectual validity at all,

76

but it does no more than provide an existential-ontological language in which the symbolic language of a particular religious tradition can be expressed.[113] Thus, theology is to a certain degree dependent upon philosophy for its expression, but not for its content.

The starting-point for Macquarrie's philosophical theology is human existence. He believes that an analysis of human existence raises certain important questions about the meaning of being in itself and for us, and that these questions can be answered most adequately by drawing upon the resources of Christian faith. But until these questions are posed, faith is irrelevant. In this respect Macquarrie's method is not unlike Tillich's method of 'correlation', and these two theologians share the belief that existentialist philosophy provides the best analysis of contemporary human existence.

In his book, *An Existentialist Theology*, Macquarrie showed how Heidegger's analysis of *Dasein* seems to point to a reality beyond man as the source of human being, but according to his self-imposed limitations as a philosopher, Heidegger was unable to identify that reality as God.[114] Macquarrie agrees with this analysis of human existence, but is convinced that it can and must be completed by the Christian faith. Like Tillich, Macquarrie thinks that the most adequate way to describe God is in terms of 'being': "In asking that we should understand God as Being rather than as *another* being Tillich, it seems to me, overcame or at least pointed the way to overcoming some of the most stubborn difficulties in the way of traditional theism."[115] The most complete interpretation of being in contemporary philosophy is once again that of Heidegger and, as was shown above, Macquarrie feels that this concept of being, with certain modifications, can well express the Christian concept of God.

One further aspect of Macquarrie's treatment of God brings him into contact with the whole American philosophy of religion tradition from Peirce to Ogden, namely, his contention that God is the source of *meaning* for the universe:

> To believe in God is to believe that human existence is set within a wider context of meaning. Or again, one might say that God is to the world as meaning is to a process or series of events.... When I talk of God as meaning, I have in mind a unity that gives order to the world-process and confers significance on its constituent parts; and also the idea that the process has direction and moves towards some goal.[116]

In another place he equates this belief in God with "faith in being," which he considers to be practically equivalent to "what Schubert Ogden means by 'confidence in the final worth of our existence.'"[117] This description of God in terms of meaning is developed more fully by our last representative of contemporary American philosophy of

77

religion, Leslie Dewart.

Leslie Dewart (1922-   ).

A case could be made for the existence of a *Canadian* tradition of philosophy of religion, distinct from that referred to in this chapter as the *American* approach. However, for our purposes it is allowable to include among the major representatives of American philosophy of religion a Spanish-born naturalized Canadian, Leslie Dewart. As professor first of philosophy and more recently of theology at St. Michael's College, Toronto, Dewart has aroused considerable interest among those concerned with the relationship of philosophy and theology by his writings on the concept of God and related issues.[118] Although these writings do not deal explicitly with the major figures in the development of American philosophy of religion (except Tillich), they do manifest a definite kinship between Dewart's ideas and those of his American predecessors.

Dewart is a (Roman) Catholic, and he concerns himself primarily (although not exclusively) with the Catholic tradition of philosophy and theology. As has generally been the case with Catholic thinkers, Dewart feels that philosophy and religion are intimately connected. However, he is dissatisfied with the various titles used by others to designate the philosophical study of religion-- philosophy of religion, philosophical theology, natural theology, and the Catholic title, fundamental theology--and suggests instead a new title, 'theological philosophy'. One of the principal advantages of this term is "its aptness for putting in relief the theological task which philosophy should normally and naturally undertake when it is practiced by the Christian intellect."[119] Thus, despite his dissatisfaction with the titles adopted for their work by the other American philosophers of religion, Dewart agrees with them that the philosophical study of religion is both legitimate and necessary.

The basis of Dewart's treatment of religion is his contention that traditional Christian theology is inadequate today because it has failed to develop in step with the general evolution of human consciousness. The traditional formulation of Christian doctrines made use of the conceptual/linguistic framework of Greek metaphysical philosophy, and although this interpretation of reality has generally been discarded today in favour of other types of philosophy, Christian thinkers have been reluctant to admit that the traditional expression of the Christian faith is no longer adequate. For Dewart, however, the 'dehellenization' of Christianity is absolutely necessary if the Christian faith is to merit serious consideration from now on.

The most basic feature of the traditional expression of Christianity is its *absoluteness*:

Hellenization naturally and logically tended to lend Christianity the conviction that it should not develop further or transcend its hellenic form. For hellenization introduced into Christianity the ideals of immutability, stability and impassibility as perfections that all Christians and Christianity as a whole should strive for, since these were the typical and central perfections of God himself.[120]

To overcome this view of Christian dogma, a radical critique of its Greek metaphysical foundation is needed, and Dewart holds that in place of this foundation we must construct a post- or "meta-metaphysical" type of philosophy. This surpassing of traditional metaphysics is concerned with three concepts in particular--truth, reality and being--and Dewart devotes the better part of his writings to a critique of the traditional understanding of these concepts and a proposal for their reformulation.

According to Dewart, the traditional metaphysical concept of truth as the conformity of the mind to reality is inadequate because it is based on a theory of knowledge which mistakenly posits as a primary datum of consciousness the separation of knowing subject and known object: "Knowledge cannot be the transcending of the dichotomy between object and subject, because that dichotomy takes place within knowledge....The mind does not make the world present to itself; on the contrary, it makes itself present to the world."[121] The concept of truth, like all other concepts, "has an *empirical* basis and...a philosophical theory of truth must proceed empirically, that is...it may not cease to remain constantly in touch with the empirical facts."[122] As with the concept of truth, the traditional metaphysical concepts of being and reality are inadequate and must be reformulated. For traditional metaphysics, 'being' and 'reality' are synonymous; they both refer to the object of knowledge. According to Dewart, however, "Reality is whatever the self can have real relations towards. Being, on the other hand, is the object of thought: it is that which is empirically given as such."[123] Thus, a meta-metaphysical philosophy is able to conceive of a reality beyond being, and so overcome one of the major stumbling-blocks in the way of an adequate description of God for contemporary man.

In traditional metaphysics, God was the supreme *being*. Dewart agrees with atheists such as Marx, Freud and Sartre that this concept of God is unworthy of belief.[124] However, since there can be a reality beyond being, the modern atheist rejection of God is not conclusive. And, indeed, Dewart feels that belief in God is not only not disproved by contemporary philosophy but is actually warranted by religious experience. He defines religious experience simply as "that aspect of ordinary, everyday experience which is the origin of religious belief."[125] One basic fact of ordinary experience is that our existence is contingent—it is possible that we might never have existed. This fact makes the *meaning* of our existence problematical. In at least one very important respect, namely, our coming-to-be, we do not determine our destiny. We may on this account declare our lives to be absurd, meaningless, or we may turn to religion:

> What religious experience really reveals is that the meaning of existence is not to be found within existence itself, but beyond. And when human experience reveals this, human experience has become *religious* belief.[126]

There is a reality beyond being whose function is to make being, especially human life, meaningful. This is the reality which we call God. As Dewart says, "God is that without which man cannot find meaning in his presence to himself."[127] Understood in this way, God must not only transcend man but, in addition, he has no reality outside human experience. Religion is thus "the evolving expression of our evolving consciousness of God...the ever developing, ever growing meaning of the reality of man, in his self-creating existence in the presence of God."[128]

Although there is no opposition between religious experience (i.e., faith) and ordinary experience, nevertheless the two are not identical:

> Precisely because experience is immanent in the being of man, experience has a transcendent dimension, namely, faith. But faith transcends experience only because faith is the transcendence *of experience*. Faith does not transcend experience by ceasing to be experience. Faith is, as it were, the real, ultimate meaning of that which *already* exists, namely, human experience.[129]

With this rejection of a dichotomy between faith and experience (and, implicitly, between faith and reason), Dewart stands in agreement with the other representatives of the American tradition of philosophy of religion. The same is true with regard to his attitude towards traditional (metaphysical) philosophy and theology, especially their classical concept of God, and his stress on the human side of the divine-human relationship. There are many aspects of the pragmatism of Peirce, James and Dewey that Dewart would not accept, any more than would Cobb, Ogden and Macquarrie. However, these four representatives of contemporary American philosophy of religion are clearly within the tradition begun by the pragmatists and augmented by Whitehead, Hartshorne and Tillich. The future existence and vitality of this tradition will depend to no small extent on these four men and the scholars they influence.

II. Evaluation of American Philosophy of Religion.

The purpose of the foregoing survey of American philosophers and philosophical theologians was not just to describe their individual contributions to their disciplines but to show as well how they have all participated in the development of the American philosophy of religion. It now remains for us to say precisely what we mean by this American approach to the philosophy of religion--i.e., to identify its distinctive features--and also to show how it differs from other approaches to the philosophy of religion. In this way we can determine its suitability for evaluating the religious significance of Heidegger's philosophy.

The most obvious feature of American philosophy of religion is that it actually exists--i.e., there is general agreement among all the Americans treated here that religion is a legitimate object of philosophical investigation. Although not all of the philosophers displayed the same interest in religion, nevertheless each of them devoted a certain amount of his published work to a consideration of this topic and its relation to philosophy in general. Thus, they can all be said to have a philosophy of religion. Among the theologians, there is a general willingness to allow philosophers to deal with religion, although as theologians, they feel that they have something to offer which philosophy in itself is unable to provide. Nevertheless, they all state that theology could not function without the aid of philosophy, and they are particularly interested in determining which is the right philosophy for use in Christian theology.

In its investigation of religious topics, American philosophy of religion is not content simply to describe and analyze; it considers itself qualified to evaluate as well. As we have seen, the Americans have not hesitated to criticize manifestations of religion which they consider to be in opposition to their philosophical principles. The basis of this attitude is their conviction that religious experience, as experience, is subject to the same criteria for description and evaluation as any other type of human experience. The Americans are not willing to concede any privileged epistemological status to religion, and they are opposed to the radical distinction between faith and reason which renders faith impervious to logical (and pragmatic) criticism.

The chief target of criticism for American philosophy of religion is the use of Greek metaphysical philosophy in traditional Christian religion. Since this philosophy is inadequate as philosophy, it is ipso facto unsuitable for use by religion. In formulating their own distinctive philosophy, the Americans are constantly reacting against traditional Greek metaphysical philosophy and its remnants in modern empiricism and rationalism. The concept of

81

knowledge as the overcoming of an original separation between knowing subject and known object, the correlative concept of truth as the conformity of the mind to reality, and the appreciation of immutability as a suitable attribute of God are all legacies of Greek philosophy which are contrary to what is revealed by an empirical investigation of reality. These and many other features of Greek philosophy have been adopted by Christianity for the expression of its beliefs, and to that extent, Christianity is a legitimate object of criticism for American philosophy of religion. Although the non-theologians have been particularly vehement in their criticism, nevertheless they agree with the theologians that religion is capable of being purified from its contamination by Greek philosophy and of being reexpressed in more adequate philosophical concepts.

The form of religion which American philosophy of religion is attempting to create has three principal characteristics: it is *empirical*, it is *pragmatic*, and it emphasizes *process*. The concept of experience is of utmost importance in American philosophy in general. It refers primarily to man's interrelation with his environment through his five bodily senses, but it includes as well the knowledge which results from this bodily activity. For the Americans, man is a unity; there is no dichotomy between body and mind. As opposed to the more limited concept of experience in traditional British empiricism, the American concept of experience includes among its objects not just individual things but also the relations between those things. All human knowledge can be explained in terms of experience, and we have no need of any non-empirical, a priori principles to account for certain elements of our knowledge. Even the concept of knowledge itself, and the correlative concept of truth, can be explained in terms of experience, and since both these concepts are of fundamental importance for an understanding of language, it is not surprising that for American empiricism there is no dichotomy between experience and language. Rather, every experience is fundamentally linguistic, and conversely, there could be no language apart from experience. Thus, American philosophy is very critical of other forms of philosophy which fail to realise the empirical character of all human knowledge, including knowledge of God. It is true that some of the Americans treated above, especially Hartshorne and Tillich, have wanted to retain some degree of a priori knowledge, but even they have realized that this must be supplemented by empirical knowledge if it is to have any real content.

Because of its empirical character, American philosophy of religion places great emphasis on religious experience as the source of religious knowledge. But in order for this experience to be considered valid, it must issue in definite actions, and to this

82

extent American philosophy of religion is pragmatic. Although the original pragmatism of Peirce, James and Dewey has been considerably modified by their successors, nevertheless they all attribute great importance to the Gospel maxim, "By their fruits shall you know them." Religious experiences by themselves are not enough to make a person truly religious; in addition, he must *act* religiously; he must perform useful services for mankind.

The third major characteristic of American philosophy of religion is its emphasis on process and becoming. Although the principal spokesmen for this view of reality are A. N. Whitehead and his followers, the rejection of stability and immutability as characteristics of reality goes right back to Peirce and extends throughout the American tradition. It is true that Tillich and Macquarrie continued to regard 'being' as superior to 'becoming', but they specifically mentioned that their concepts of being are not opposed to becoming but rather include it. The American preference for process over stability accounts in large measure for the importance they assign to religious experience, which is always in a state of flux, and also for their confidence that they can produce better forms of religion in the future, since religion is as much subject to change and development as anything else.

The principal features of American philosophy of religion are all incorporated in its treatment of God. To be sure, there is considerable disagreement as to the exact nature of God, but the Americans agree that the traditional Christian concept of God has been determined in large part by the categories of Greek philosophy and must therefore be reinterpreted to a considerable extent. There is general agreement among both philosophers and theologians that the 'God of philosophy' cannot be other than the 'God of the Bible' or the 'God of theology'. Likewise, there is complete accord that an essential element of both the philosophical and the theological description of God is his function as the source of meaning and value in the universe. There is less agreement on the relation of God to the world, however. The rejection of immutability as a characteristic of divinity meant for William James that God is finite, for Whitehead that God has two natures, for Hartshorne that God is becoming ever more perfect, and so on. Tillich and Macquarrie both describe God's relation to the world in terms of the relation of Being and beings, while Dewart contests this interpretation and speaks of God in terms of 'presence' to the world. The application of the basic tenets of American philosophy to the concept of God evidently has not received its definitive form. But there is general agreement that God is a legitimate object of philosophical investigation, and that any adequate reconceptualization of God must originate from the critique which American philosophy of religion has provided of the traditional Christian concept of God.

Having completed this brief summary of the principal features of American philosophy of religion, we are now in a position to compare the American approach with the other approaches mentioned in the previous chapter. It is not our intention here to give a complete evaluation of American philosophy of religion, but only to show whether its understanding of the relation of philosophy and religion can provide a useful standpoint from which to evaluate the religious significance of Heidegger's philosophy. A more detailed evaluation of American philosophy of religion will be given below, in chapter four.

In opposition to those philosophers who do not practise the philosophy of religion, either because they have no interest in doing so or because they feel that philosophy has no competence in religious matters, the Americans treated here think that the philosophy of religion is both possible and necessary. It is possible because religion is a human activity and is therefore subject to philosophical investigation, and it is necessary for two reasons: 1) religion is a fact, and must be taken into account in any complete description of human existence; 2) any attempt to determine the limits of philosophical speculation invariably comes into contact with the notion of God, which is also the ultimate religious concept. As Hartshorne says, the only alternative to a philosophy that deals with the question of God is a positivistic rejection of both metaphysical philosophy (and, indeed, of meta-metaphysical philosophy) and God.

American philosophers of religion also differ from those philosophers who are willing to treat religion, but only that form of religion which they encounter in churches or in traditional theology. For the Americans, philosophy is not only descriptive; it is creative as well. They see no reason to recognize as definitive for all time any particular formulation of religious experience, since religion is just as subject to change and development as any other human activity. No doubt, certain historical events have been decisive in the development of particular religious traditions, but it is obvious that history did not end at the time of those events, and even the meaning of those events has been subject to many different interpretations since they took place. American philosophers recognize that in the past, as now, one's understanding of the religious significance of certain events is greatly determined by his philosophical presuppositions. Whereas in the past, these presuppositions were accepted uncritically and hence were not recognized as presuppositions, today we are better able to discriminate among different presuppositions and thereby exert a measure of control over the future development of religion.

It was mentioned in the previous chapter that American philosophy of religion is not the only example of the creative approach to the philosophical study of religion. In view of its longevity and its present-day strength, however, it seems particularly well-qualified to serve as a representative of this approach. The final question which remains to be answered in this chapter is: to what extent is American philosophy of religion suitable for evaluating the religious significance of Heidegger's philosophy?

A complete answer to this question will have to wait until after the examination of Heidegger's philosophy in the next chapter. However, a general answer can be given here as a result of the foregoing comparison of the American approach with the other general approaches to the philosophy of religion. It is evident that if there is going to be any philosophical analysis of Heidegger's religious significance, it will have to reject both the positivistic neglect of philosophy of religion and Heidegger's own position that philosophy is incapable of dealing with religion. Furthermore, any attempt to reconcile Heidegger's philosophy with traditional formulations of religion will produce no conclusive result, as is abundantly clear from our study of previous theological evaluations of Heidegger. Thus, the creative approach to philosophy of religion, despite its rejection by Heidegger, is, in fact, the only possible way to determine his significance for the philosophy of religion. We must approach his philosophy free from theological presuppositions as to the truth of any particular manifestation of religion; we must look in his philosophy for God or the equivalent; we must see to what extent his description of human existence treats of religious experience; and so on. Our study of American philosophy of religion has convinced us that there is such a thing as the philosophy of religion, and so we are justified in investigating Heidegger's philosophy in order to determine to what extent, if any, we can find therein a philosophy of religion.

1. Edward C. Moore, *American Pragmatism*, New York (Columbia University Press: 1961), p. vii.

2. An American observer of international religious studies has remarked: "The Germans read the Germans, the British read the British and the Germans (sometimes), and the Americans read the Germans, the British, and the Americans—and the reasons for this have little to do with the quality of scholarship. The consequence is that American scholarship is in a uniquely 'ecumenical' position, and tends to draw upon a richer complex of traditions than is in practice available to European scholarship." Claude Welch, "Theology," in *Religion* (Humanistic Scholarship in America: The Princeton Studies), ed. by Paul Ramsey, Englewood Cliffs, N.J. (Prentice-Hall: 1965), p. 284.

3. The expression is that of Charles Frankel, ed., *The Golden Age of American Philosophy*, New York (George Braziller: 1960). According to Frankel, the golden age extends from 1870 to 1930. This period has also been called the "classical period" of American philosophy. Cf. Max H. Fisch, ed., *Classic American Philosophers*, New York (Appleton-Crofts: 1951).

4. *Collected Papers of Charles Sanders Peirce*, ed. by Charles Hartshorne and Paul Weiss, Cambridge, Mass. (Harvard University Press: 1931-35), vol. 5, para. 12. These volumes, which were supplemented by the addition of volumes 7 and 8, edited by Arthur Walter Burks, in 1958, will henceforth be cited by volume and paragraph number.

5. Peirce later coined the word 'pragmaticism' to distinguish his use of the term from others (cf. 5.414).

6. Joseph P. DeMarco, "God, Religion, and Community in the Philosophy of C. S. Peirce," *The Modern Schoolman* XLIX (1972), p. 344.

7. John E. Smith, "Philosophy of Religion," in *Religion*, ed. by Paul Ramsey, p. 384: "The influence of pragmatism on the philosophy of religion is difficult to overestimate. It extends far beyond the original work of William James and the introduction of the concept of religious experience. The emphasis upon action and the need to translate belief into conduct that characterized the pragmatist position were well in accord with the already established tendency on the American scene to think of religion in wholly practical terms. Pragmatism provided an intellectual justification for the conviction

that religion means essentially a way of living; for many it served to reinforce the idea that creeds and theological formulas are secondary in importance."

8. Cf. Ralph Barton Perry, *The Thought and Character of William James* (briefer version), New York (George Braziller: 1954), p. 282: "James, who liked to dwell on doctrinal similarities and philosophical cooperation, emphasized the likeness while Peirce, who cared more for the precision of his views than for their general physiognomy, emphasized the unlikeness." This is especially true of their attitudes towards the pragmatism of each other.

9. James, *The Writings of William James*, ed. by John J. McDermott, New York (Random House: 1967), p. 238.

10. James, *Pragmatism: A New Name for Some Old Ways of Thinking* (1907), *The Writings of William James*, p. 380.

11. James, *Pragmatism...*, *The Writings of William James*, p. 430.

12. *Ibid.*, pp. 438f.

13. James, *The Meaning of Truth* (1909), *The Writings of William James*, p. 314.

14. Cf. David Hume's contention that "all our distinct perceptions are distinct existences, and that the mind never perceives any real connexion among distinct existences." Hume, *A Treatise of Human Nature*, ed. by Ernest C. Mossner, Harmondsworth, Middlesex (Penguin: 1969), p. 677. James criticizes Hume for rejecting conjunctive relations while retaining disjunctive relations.

15. James, *Essays in Radical Empiricism* (1912), *The Writings of William James*, p. 196: "Radical empiricism, as I understand it, does full justice to conjunctive relations, without, however, treating them as rationalism always tends to treat them, as being true in some supernal way, as if the unity of things and their variety belonged to different orders of truth and vitality altogether."

16. James, *The Varieties of Religious Experience* (1902), London (Fontana: 1971), p. 364.

17. *Ibid.*, p. 407.

18. *Ibid.*, p. 419.

19. *Ibid.*, p. 491.

20. Cf. James, *The Will to Believe* (1897), New York (Dover: 1956).

21. James, *Pragmatism...*, *The Writings of William James*, p. 399.

22. James, *The Varieties of Religious Experience*, p. 429.

23. James, *A Pluralistic Universe* (1909), *The Writings of William James*, p. 803.

24. On Kierkegaard, cf. *Essays in Radical Empiricism, The Writings of William James*, p. 231; on Nietzsche, cf. *The Varieties of Religious Experience*, p. 361.

25. Cf. Sidney Hook, *John Dewey: An Intellectual Portrait*, Westport, Conn. (Greenwood Press: 1971), p. 4.

26. Dewey, "From Absolutism to Experimentalism" (1930), *The Golden Age of American Philosophy*, ed. by Charles Frankel, p. 389.

27. *Ibid.*, p. 391.

28. Sidney Hook, *op. cit.*, p. 12: "Years later, after he had developed his own distinctive ideas, Dewey was to return to the writings of Peirce to find independent support for his philosophy of experimentalism."

29. Dewey, "From Absolutism to Experimentalism," *loc. cit.*, pp. 393f.

30. Dewey, *Experience and Nature*, New York (W. W. Norton & Co.: 1929²), p. 239.

31. *Ibid.*, pp. 267f.

32. Dewey, *Reconstruction in Philosophy*, Boston (Beacon Press: 1967²), p. 121.

33. *Ibid.*, p. 156.

34. Dewey, "From Absolutism to Experimentalism," *loc. cit.*, p. 390.

35. Dewey, "What I Believe" (1930), *Pragmatism and American Culture*,

ed. by Gail Kennedy, Boston (D. C. Heath & Co.: 1950), p. 24.

36. Dewey, *A Common Faith* (1934), New Haven (Yale University Press: 1960), p. 2.

37. *Ibid.*, p. 7.

38. *Ibid.*, p. 27.

39. *Ibid.*, p. 17.

40. *Ibid.*, p. 26.

41. Dewey, *Reconstruction in Philosophy*, p. 178.

42. Dewey, *A Common Faith*, p. 42.

43. Whitehead seldom if ever mentions Charles Peirce in his writings, and he seems not to have entered into any serious philosophical dialogue with John Dewey; only with the works of William James does he show extensive familiarity and appreciation.

44. Cf. Whitehead, *Process and Reality* (1929), New York (The Free Press: 1969), p. 210.

45. Whitehead, *Modes of Thought* (1938), Cambridge (Cambridge University Press: 1956), pp. 144f.

46. Cf. Whitehead, *Adventures of Ideas* (1933), New York (MacMillan: 1933), p. 228: "...all knowledge is derived from, and verified by, direct intuitive observation. I accept this axiom of empiricism as stated in this general form."

47. *Ibid.*, pp. 281f.

48. Whitehead, *Science and the Modern World* (1925), New York (The Free Press: 1967), p. 51. Cf. Whitehead, *Process and Reality*, p. 397: "The chief danger to philosophy is narrowness in the selection of evidence."

49. Whitehead, *Process and Reality*, p. 96.

50. Whitehead, *Science and the Modern World*, p. 151.

51. Whitehead, *Process and Reality*, p. v.

52. *Ibid.*, p. 405.

53. Whitehead, *Modes of Thought*, p. 112: "The final outcome has been that philosophy and theology have been saddled with the problem of deriving the historic world of change from a changeless world of ultimate reality. Our whole conception of knowledge has been vitiated. The final wisdom has been pictured as the changeless contemplation of changeless reality. Knowledge in abstraction from action has been exalted. Action is thereby conceived as being concerned with a world of shadows."

54. Whitehead, *Process and Reality*, p. 334.

55. Whitehead, *Science and the Modern World*, p. 178.

56. Whitehead, *Modes of Thought*, p. 128.

57. Whitehead, *Process and Reality*, p. 39.

58. *Ibid.*, p. 19.

59. Hartshorne, *Creative Synthesis and Philosophical Method*, London (S.C.M. Press: 1970), p. xvi.

60. *Ibid.*, p. xiv.

61. Hartshorne, *Reality as Social Process*: Studies in Metaphysics and Religion (1953), New York (Hafner Publishing Co.: 1971), p. 176. In a later book, *The Logic of Perfection* and Other Essays in Neoclassical Metaphysics, LaSalle, Ill. (Open Court: 1962), he reduces these three alternatives to two by eliminating atheistic metaphysics.

62. Hartshorne, *Man's Vision of God* and the Logic of Theism (1941), Hamden, Conn. (Anchor Books: 1964), pp. 11f.

63. *Ibid.*, p. 48.

64. Hartshorne, *The Divine Relativity*: A Social Conception of God (1948), New Haven and London (Yale University Press: 1967), p. 21.

65. Hartshorne, *Man's Vision of God*, p. 104.

66. *Ibid.*, p. 200.

67. Hartshorne, *The Divine Relativity*, p. 89. He adds: "I scarcely need to say that surrelativism and panentheism are logically the same doctrine with only a difference of emphasis."

68. Hartshorne, *Creative Synthesis and Philosophical Method*, p. 290.

69. Hartshorne, *Man's Vision of God*, pp. 78f.

70. Cf. Hartshorne, *The Logic of Perfection*, pp. 28-117, "Introduction" to *Saint Anselm: Basic Writings*, tr. by S. N. Deane, 2nd edition, LaSalle, Ill. (Open Court: 1962), pp. 1-19, and *Anselm's Discovery*, LaSalle, Ill. (Open Court: 1965).

71. Hartshorne, "A Philosopher's Assessment of Christianity," in *Religion and Culture: Essays in Honor of Paul Tillich*, ed. by Walter Leibrecht, New York (Harper & Bros.: 1959), p. 180.

72. Tillich criticizes this view in his essay, "The Conquest of Intellectual Provincialism: Europe and America," *Theology of Culture* (ed. by Robert C. Kimball), New York (Oxford University Press: 1959), pp. 159-176.

73. Tillich, *The Protestant Era* (tr. by James Luther Adams), Chicago (University of Chicago Press: 1948), p. x.

74. Tillich, "Autobiographical Reflections of Paul Tillich," in *The Theology of Paul Tillich*, ed. by Charles W. Kegley and Robert W. Bretall, New York (Macmillan: 1952), p. 20.

75. Tillich, *The Protestant Era*, pp. 152f. Cf. also Tillich, *Systematic Theology*, Chicago (University of Chicago Press: vol. 1: 1951, vol. 2: 1957, vol. 3: 1963), vol. 3, pp. 28f.

76. Tillich, *op. cit.*, p. 172.

77. Tillich, *Systematic Theology*, vol. 1, p. 167.

78. Tillich, "Reply," in *The Theology of Paul Tillich*, p. 340.

79. Tillich, *The Protestant Era*, p. 83.

80. Tillich, "Autobiographical Reflections...," *loc. cit.*, p. 10.

81. Tillich, *The Protestant Era*, pp. 92f. The five major divisions

of the *Systematic Theology* correspond exactly to these five topics.

82. Tillich, *Systematic Theology*, vol. 1, pp. 22-24.

83. *Ibid.*, vol. 1, p. 109.

84. *Ibid.*, vol. 1, p. 208.

85. *Ibid.*, vol. 1, pp. 235, 238.

86. Tillich, *The Shaking of the Foundations* (1941), Harmondsworth, Middlesex (Penguin: 1966), pp. 63f.

87. Cobb, *A Christian Natural Theology*, Philadelphia (Westminster Press: 1965), p. 17.

88. *Ibid.*, p. 269: Whitehead "never organized his work extensively around the doctrine of man or the doctrine of God. Hence, the theologian approaches Whitehead's work, asking questions the answers to which are not readily available. He must piece together fragments from here and there. Furthermore, at certain points, more crucial to the theologian than to Whitehead, the questions are simply unanswered or are answered in ways that do not seem philosophically satisfactory when attention is focused upon them."

89. *Ibid.*, p. 20: "What is philosophically valid and valuable in my proposals for developing Whitehead's doctrine of God is due chiefly to Hartshorne."

90. Cobb, "Perfection Exists: A Critique of Charles Hartshorne," *Religion in Life* 32 (1963), p. 301.

91. Cobb, *God and the World*, Philadelphia (Westminster Press: 1969), pp. 65, 96.

92. *Ibid.*, pp. 73-76.

93. Cobb, "A Whiteheadian Christology," in *Process Philosophy and Christian Thought*, ed. by Delwin Brown, Ralph E. Jones, Jr., and Gene Reeves, Indianapolis, Ind. (Bobbs-Merrill: 1971), pp. 388-394.

94. *Ibid.*, p. 398. Cf. also Cobb, *The Structure of Christian Existence*, Philadelphia (Westminster Press: 1967).

95. Cf. especially his book, *Christ Without Myth*, London (Collins: 1962).

96. Ogden, "The Task of Philosophical Theology," in *The Future of Philosophical Theology*, ed. by Robert A. Evans, Philadelphia (Westminster Press: 1971), p. 56. Ogden italicizes the entire passage.

97. *Ibid.*, p. 59.

98. *Ibid.*, p. 65.

99. *Ibid.*, p. 80.

100. Ogden, "Bultmann's Demythologizing and Hartshorne's Dipolar Theism," in *Process and Divinity*, ed. by William L. Reese and Eugene Freeman, LaSalle, Ill. (Open Court: 1964), p. 512.

101. Ogden, *The Reality of God*, New York (Harper & Row: 1966), pp. 144-163.

102. Ogden, "Bultmann's Demythologizing and Hartshorne's Dipolar Theism," *loc. cit.*, pp. 506f. The quotation from Bultmann is taken from *Kerygma und Mythos* 2, p. 187.

103. Ogden, *The Reality of God*, p. 47.

104. *Ibid.*, pp. 59f. and 178.

105. *Ibid.*, pp. 68-70.

106. *Ibid.*, p. 124.

107. In *Theology* 75 (1972), pp. 394-403.

108. *Ibid.*, p. 396.

109. Macquarrie, *Studies in Christian Existentialism*, Montreal (McGill University Press: 1965), p. 165.

110. Macquarrie, *Twentieth Century Religious Thought*, London (S.C.M. Press: 1971^2), p. 15.

111. Macquarrie, *Principles of Christian Theology*, New York (Charles Scribners Sons: 1966), p. 2.

112. *Ibid.*, p. 137.

113. *Ibid.*, p. 168.

114. Macquarrie, *An Existentialist Theology*, London (S.C.M. Press: 1955), p. 149.

115. Macquarrie, *God and Secularity* (New Directions in Theology Today III), London (Lutterworth Press: 1968), p. 32. Macquarrie allies himself with Tillich against process philosophy's adoption of *becoming* as the chief metaphysical category: "becoming is included in being, not the other way round." *Principles of Christian Theology*, p. 190.

116. Macquarrie, "God and the World: One Reality or Two?" *loc. cit.*, p. 400.

117. Macquarrie, *God and Secularity*, p. 150.

118. Cf. especially his *The Future of Belief*, New York (Herder & Herder: 1966) and *The Foundations of Belief*, New York (Herder & Herder: 1969).

119. Dewart, *The Foundations of Belief*, p. 12.

120. Dewart, *The Future of Belief*, p. 134.

121. Dewart, *The Foundations of Belief*, pp. 317f.

122. *Ibid.*, p. 302.

123. *Ibid.*, p. 399.

124. *Ibid.*, p. 362.

125. *Ibid.*, p. 426.

126. *Ibid.*, p. 442.

127. *Ibid.*, p. 470

128. *Ibid.*, pp. 470f.

129. *Ibid.*, p. 457.

Heidegger's Philosophy of Religion

A complete treatment of all aspects of religion is not to be found in the writings of Heidegger, any more than in those of Peirce, James, Dewey or Whitehead. Nevertheless, the major elements of the philosophy of religion, according to the American understanding of this term, are all dealt with to some extent in Heidegger's works, and so it should be possible to construct a Heideggerian philosophy according to the American model. The four principal aspects of Heidegger's thought which will be analyzed in this chapter are: 1) the relation of philosophy and religion; 2) his attitude towards traditional philosophy and theology; 3) his description of man; and 4) his discussion of theism.

I. The Relation of Philosophy and Religion.

Philosophy "can no more be theistic than it can be atheistic. This...is not because of any indifferent attitude but out of respect for the limits which have been set upon thought as thought...."[1] These words express Heidegger's lifelong attitude towards matters of religion. He has always maintained that there exists an irreducible dichotomy between faith and thinking. Religion pertains exclusively to faith, and the philosopher, as a thinker, is not competent to deal with matters such as God and the divine-human relationship. Thus, for Heidegger there can be no such thing as the philosophy of religion, and he also places severe restrictions on the use of philosophy in theology.

The chief expression of Heidegger's views on this topic is his 1927 lecture entitled, *Phenomenology and Theology*. Since this work was published as recently as 1969,[2] it is evident that Heidegger's understanding of this matter has not changed since the period in which he composed *Sein und Zeit*. Otto Pöggeler has shown that as early as 1921, Heidegger had adopted Luther's attitude towards the relation of philosophy and theology (as formulated in his theses for the Heidelberg Disputation of 1518),[3] and it is not surprising that Lutheran theologians such as Rudolf Bultmann were the first to welcome Heidegger's ideas.[4]

In *Phenomenology and Theology* Heidegger describes theology as one of the 'positive' sciences, since it deals with a particular realm of being or *Positum*. Thus, it differs absolutely from philosophy, which deals with Being as such.[5] The object of theology is the Christian *faith*, described by Heidegger as "a

95

mode of existence of human Dasein which, according to its own witness--which belongs essentially to this mode of existence-- does *not* come *from* Dasein and is *not* produced *by* Dasein of its own accord, but results from that which is revealed in and with this mode of existence--that which is believed."[6] The Christian faith is an event of *participation* of the believer in what is believed--Christ, the crucified God. It is a *way of life*, and so is entirely beyond the scope of philosophy. This is not to say that there cannot be a *science* of faith, namely theology. Theology is at one and the same time historical, systematic and practical--i.e., it is indeed a rigorous science, but one which is totally independent from the other positive sciences because of the nature of its object, the revelation of God.[7]

Although the Christian *faith* is independent of philosophy, Heidegger feels that the science of faith, theology, has need of philosophy in what concerns its scientific character. Philosophy can judge the logical consistency of theology (but not its over- all truth), and can also supply theology with correctly defined terms in which the faith may be expressed, such as the concept of guilt as an ontological determination of Dasein according to which the specifically Christian (ontic) concept of sin may be under- stood. But this adoption of philosophical categories in no way subordinates theology to philosophy.[8] And whereas these services of philosophy are important for theology, they are not essential to philosophy: thus philosophy is independent with regard both to the Christian faith and to theology: "there is no such thing as a Christian philosophy, any more than there is a 'square circle'".[9]

Heidegger has insisted repeatedly that the mutual independence of faith and thinking entails the theistic neutrality of his analysis of Dasein in *Sein und Zeit*. In *Vom Wesen des Grundes* (On the Essence of Ground--1929) and again in the *Letter on Humanism* (1947), he stated that "through the ontological inter- pretation of Dasein as Being-in-the-world there is neither a positive nor a negative resolution of a possible Being toward God."[10] This restriction applies to the dialectical theology of of the 1920s just as surely as to the scholastic theology of the Middle Ages.[11] Heidegger claims that his thinking is not atheistic or indifferent because it refuses to address itself to the problem of God; this is an area in which thinking as such has no competence.

If Heidegger were perfectly consistent in this matter, he would probably say nothing at all about faith or theology. But in fact he has challenged theology to rid itself of its pseudo-philosophical heritage and to understand itself as the science of *faith*. Chris- tian theology has for too long been based on Greek metaphysics, and Heidegger feels that theologians should take seriously the words of the Apostle Paul that this sort of philosophy is foolishness for the believer.[12] Philosophy is no substitute for theology, and so

a 'Christian philosophy' is a round square and a misunderstanding. There is, to be sure, a thinking and a questioning elaboration of the world of Christian experience, i.e., of faith. That is theology. Only epochs which no longer fully believe in the true greatness of the task of theology arrive at the disastrous notion that philosophy can help to provide a refurbished theology if not a substitute for theology, which will satisfy the needs and tastes of the time.[13]

Heidegger seems to display a concern more theological than philosophical that theology become true to itself as the science of faith. His message remains always the same, however--theology is independent from philosophy because faith is distinct from thinking.

II. Critique of Metaphysical Philosophy.

A. The Onto-Theo-Logical Nature of Metaphysics.

Heidegger's criticism of the use of Greek metaphysical philosophy by Christianity in the development of its theology is but a prelude to his criticism of Greek metaphysics as *philosophy*. The basis of these two critiques is the same--in metaphysics there is no distinction between philosophy (understood as *ontology*--the science of beings) and theology. Metaphysics is thus 'onto-theology', and as such, must be surpassed by philosophy as well as by theology.

The onto-theo-logical character of metaphysics is not simply an accidental feature of this type of philosophy but belongs to its very nature: "Every philosophy is theology in the original and essential sense that the comprehension (*LOGOS*) of beings in general asks about the source [Grund] of Being and this source is named *THEOS*, God."[14] Although Heidegger at first referred to his own philosophy as metaphysics and as ontology, he later abandoned these apellations because of their association with the onto-theo-logical tradition. Indeed, even the term 'philosophy' is inadequate for the same reason, and he entitles his own endeavour simply 'thinking'. For Heidegger, philosophy, metaphysics, ontology and theology are all basically the same, and their most proper title is 'onto-theo-logy'.[15]

The theological character of metaphysics dates from the beginning of Greek metaphysics--Plato and Aristotle:

The highest and first cause is called by Plato and accordingly

97

by Aristotle *TO THEON*, the divine. With the interpretation of
Being as *IDEA*, thinking on the Being of beings is metaphysical,
and metaphysics is theological. Theology means here the interpretation of the 'cause' of beings as God and the location of
Being in this cause....[16]

With the coming of Christianity, this theological character of
metaphysics was reinforced by the identification of the creator
God of the Bible with the first cause of Aristotle. When
medieval Christian theology gave God the name of supreme being
(summum ens), the union of ontology and theology became so obvious that a reaction set in, and modern philosophy has engaged
in a vigorous struggle for its independence from theology. The
predominance of reason over faith and the corresponding valuation
of the *mathematical* (logic) as the bearer of certainty (rather
than divine revelation or the Church) in modern philosophy would
seem to indicate that this struggle has been successful, but
Heidegger feels that modern philosophy, no less than medieval, is
essentially onto-theo-logical:

Since the ascendancy of Christianity in the West, not only
throughout the medieval period but also through all of modern
philosophy, nature and universe were considered as created.
Modern metaphysics from Descartes to Kant, and also the
metaphysics of German Idealism after Kant, are unthinkable
without the Christian ideas that underlie them....[Para.] It
is natural to arrange the whole state of modern metaphysics
in the following way. For this form of metaphysics two concepts are essential: 1) the Christian conception of entities
[beings] as *ens creatum* and 2) the basic mathematical character. The first instance concerns the content of metaphysics,
the second its form. However, this characterization according
to content and form is entirely too facile to be true. For
this structure as determined by Christianity forms not only the
content of what is treated in thought, but also determines the
form, the how. Insofar as God as creator is the cause and the
ground of all that is, the how, the way of asking, is oriented
in advance toward this principle. Vice versa, the mathematical
is not only a form clasped on over the Christian content, but
it itself belongs to the content.[17]

The Western metaphysical tradition culminated in the philosophy
of Friedrich Nietzsche. More than any of his predecessors
Nietzsche recognized the theological character of Western philosophy, but no more than they was he able to liberate philosophy from
theology. Despite his affirmation of the 'death of God', Nietzsche
remains a theologian, according to Heidegger:

Nietzsche's metaphysics, too, is *as ontology*, although it seems
to be far removed from scholastic metaphysics, *at the same time*

> theology....This metaphysical theology is indeed a special kind of negative theology. Its negativity is evident in the expression: God is dead. This is not an expression of atheism, but the expression of the onto-theo-logy of that metaphysics in which authentic nihilism is consumated.[18]

Because of its preoccupation with beings, which necessarily involves a concern for God (or his equivalent) as the highest being and/or the ground of being, metaphysics is unable to ask the most important question for thinking--the question of Being. In opposition to every representative of Western philosophy from Plato to Nietzsche (and most of his contemporaries as well), Heidegger sees that the question of Being must be asked in isolation from the question of God, and in order to make this separation, he devotes himself to a relentless critique of Western metaphysics and especially of the role that Christianity has played therein.

B. Christianity and Metaphysics.

The identification of God with the uncaused cause of Greek metaphysics is but one instance of the wholesale adoption of this philosophy by Christian theology for its interpretation of the faith. Heidegger agrees with Nietzsche that the traditional theological distinction between the natural and the supernatural realms of being has its origin in the metaphysics of Plato:

> With his distinction between the 'true world' [on the one hand] and the world of change as an only apparent world [on the other], Nietzsche is referring to the metaphysics of Plato and all subsequent metaphysics, which he understands as 'Platonism'. He characterizes this as a 'two world doctrine': above the here and now, changeable, sensible world stands the supersensible, unchangeable world of the beyond....Insofar as Christianity [Christentum] teaches that this world, as a vale of tears, is only a temporal passage to a future eternal salvation, Nietzsche can characterize Christianity in general as Platonism (the two world teaching) for the people.[19]

Heidegger is careful to distinguish, as did Nietzsche, between Christianity as a way of life based on the Christian *faith* [Christlichkeit] and institutional Christianity [Christentum]. His criticisms apply solely to the latter, since the Christian faith, as faith, is entirely distinct from metaphysics. Thus, "the condemnation of Christianity [Christentum] is in no way an unqualified criticism of Christians, just as a critique of theology is not necessarily a critique of faith, of which theology is supposed to be an interpretation."[20] Despite this qualification, however, Heidegger feels that his criticisms of Christianity are doubly justified: not only is Christianity largely responsible for the dominance of Greek metaphysics during the past 2000 years, but it adopted this metaphysical outlook despite the radical incompatibility of this outlook with its own New Testament faith.

The Christian appropriation of Greek metaphysics is to be found even in the New Testament, at least according to later interpretations of its contents. Heidegger feels that the description of speaking in tongues in Acts 2, 3-4, reflects Aristotle's concept of language: "The biblical concept of language referred to here follows from that Greek characterization of the essence of language to which Aristotle gave the authoritative definition."[21] The use of the term 'LOGOS' by St. John the Evangelist to describe the role of Jesus as mediator between God and men has also been interpreted from the standpoint of Greek metaphysics by traditional Christian theology. However, Heidegger feels that this metaphysical interpretation of the New Testament is completely unjustified:

LOGOS in the New Testament does not, as in Heraclitus, mean the being of the essent [das Sein des Seienden], the gathering together of the conflicting; it means *one* particular essent, namely the son of God. And specifically it refers to him in the role of mediator between God and men. This New Testament notion of the LOGOS is that of the Jewish philosophy of religion developed by Philo whose doctrine of creation attributes to the LOGOS the function of MESITES, the mediator....A whole world separates all this from Heraclitus.[22]

The theological meaning which Christianity has given to terms such as LOGOS has completely obliterated their original (philosophical) meaning, and Heidegger feels that we must go back to the period before onto-theo-logy was developed--i.e., to the pre-Socratic thinkers--in order to encounter non-theological philosophy in its original purity.

Another example of Christianity's harmful influence on the development of philosophy is its definition of man as the image and likeness of God. Although this particular definition of man is no longer universally accepted, still the idea that man can be defined in relation to other *beings*, whether God, animals, or whatever, rather than in relation to *Being*, holds sway in anthropology, psychology and biology. In this way, Christianity has contributed to the neglect of the question of Being--*the* question of philosophy.[23]

Although the theological domination of philosophy was most evident in medieval scholastic philosophy, it has continued throughout all of modern philosophy, from Descartes to Nietzsche. The modern quest for certitude in knowledge is the direct correlate of the religious quest for certitude with regard to eternal salvation, which was one of the primary theological motives of

100

the Protestant Reformation. Far from being opposed to one another, the certitude of knowledge is a direct consequence of the certitude of faith:

This demand for the preservation of man's natural continuity solely through his own efforts does not constitute a revolt against the teaching of faith; it is rather the necessary consequence of the belief that the highest truth has the character of the certitude of salvation. The change of the essence of truth to certitude of ideas is determined through the essence of Being as actus purus. Therefore, in the history of modern times the world of the Christian faith in manifold variations remains the standard for the establishment and the maintenance of the real (for civilization), and also for the interpretation of the real in its reality (for modern metaphysics). Modern civilization, therefore, is Christian, even when it is unfaithful.[24]

Even Nietzsche, the great enemy of institutional Christianity, did not escape this theological influence: "Justification in the sense of the Reformation and Nietzsche's concept of righteousness as truth are the same."[25] Thus, the attempts of modern philosophers to dissociate their thinking from the domination of theology have all been unsuccessful. Despite the waning influence of Christianity in modern times, the theological stamp that it has put on Western philosophy has been most difficult to efface. Heidegger's vigorous criticism of institutional Christianity has as its sole aim the purification of philosophy from its onto-theo-logical heritage so that it can be free to deal with its proper subject-matter, Being. That he is no enemy of religion is evident from the distinction he makes between the Christian way of life and institutional Christianity, and the respect he has for the former. Nevertheless, the need to rid philosophy from the domination of institutional Christianity requires that he persist in his critique of the latter, even to the extent of showing that it has been responsible for the 'death of God'.

C. The Death of God.

The entire Western metaphysical tradition is summed up in the philosophy of Nietzsche. He expressed the failure of onto-theology in the phrase, "God is dead." According to Heidegger, this phrase is not a declaration of atheism but a judgment against the history of philosophy:

God is the name for the realm of ideas and ideals. This realm of the supernatural has been considered since Plato, or more precisely since the later Greek and Christian interpretation of Platonic philosophy, as the true and really real world. In

101

comparison with it the natural world is only the here-and-now, changeable and therefore merely apparent and unreal world.... [Para.] The phrase, 'God is dead,' means: the supernatural world is without effective power. It bestows no life. Metaphysics, i.e., for Nietzsche, Western philosophy understood as Platonism, is at its end.[26]

In this passage, Heidegger is using the word 'God' in a figurative sense. Nevertheless, he feels that this usage is justified because of the extent to which Christian theism has permeated Western philosophy (and, indeed, all of Western culture). The prominence accorded to the concept of God in traditional metaphysics requires that this God must be attacked if metaphysics is to be overcome, and Heidegger does not hesitate to demonstrate the manifold inadequacy of the traditional onto-theo-logical concept of God.

Among the many functions assigned to God in metaphysics is that of 'first cause':

The ultimate reason for Nature, the uttermost, highest and consequently the first existing cause [Grund] of the nature of things is that which we usually name God. [Para.] The role of a cause [Grund] in the nature of a thing determines that the thing is rather than that it is not. God is called the cause [Grund] as the first existing cause [Ursache] of all beings.[27]

Since, as first cause, God cannot have a cause beyond himself, he is referred to as his own cause (causa sui). This description of God, despite its acceptance by both philosophy and theology is, in Heidegger's opinion, inadequate for both:

This is the cause [Ursache] as causa sui. This is the proper name for God in [metaphysical] philosophy. To this God man can neither pray nor offer sacrifice. Before the causa sui man can neither fall to his knees nor sing and dance. [Para.] Therefore, the god-less thinking which must abandon the God of philosophy, God as causa sui, is perhaps closer to the divine God. Here this means only that it is freer for Him than onto-theo-logy would like to admit.[28]

As will be shown below, Heidegger holds that the rejection of God as the metaphysical first cause is not a declaration of atheism, and indeed there may well be a 'divine God' available only to religious faith. But it is clear that the description of God as causa sui represents an unfortunate confusion of Christian faith and metaphysical philosophy, and by pointing out the inadequacy of this concept of God for theology, Heidegger wants to show that it has no place in philosophy, either.

The metaphysical role of the traditional Christian concept of God is also evident in the description of God as the highest value or the supreme good. Although these terms seem to exalt God in his relationship with men, they in fact do just the opposite, for

it is exactly through the characterization of something as 'value' that it loses its dignity. This is to say that through the estimation of something as a value, one accepts what is evaluated only as a mere object for the appreciation of man.... All valuing, even when it values positively, subjectivizes the thing. It does not let beings be, but makes them valuable as the object of its action.[29]

The exaltation of the human subject is especially characteristic of modern philosophy, but Heidegger feels that it is deeply rooted in the very nature of metaphysics, in that it represents a concern for beings (in particular, the human subject) rather than for Being. Thus, values are determined by man in metaphysical philosophy, rather than by Being (or by God). This is especially true of the metaphysical concept of God:

...the interpretation of God as the highest value is not thought out of Being itself. The ultimate insult to God...consists in this, that God, the being of beings [das Seiende des Seienden], is degraded to the highest value. The crudest insult to God is not to consider God as unknowable, not to prove that God's existence is indemonstrable, but to promote the God who is held as real to the supreme value.[30]

Both theology and philosophy are at fault for this description of God as value: theology, because it has interpreted the God of the Bible in philosophical categories which are entirely inadequate, and philosophy, because it has allowed a concept alien to its very nature (i.e., the God of faith) to distract it from its primary task--the asking of the question of Being.

The prophetic insight of Nietzsche that the onto-theo-logical philosophy of the Christian West has been a failure is practically a truism today. The metaphysical concept of God has fallen into disrepute, and since Christianity had allied itself so closely to metaphysical philosophy, particularly with regard to the concept of God, the rejection of the one was bound to result in the rejection of the other. What has happened is that "on the one hand the worldview is dechristianized, insofar as the world-ground was considered as the infinite, the unconditioned, the absolute; and on the other hand institutional Christianity reinterprets its Christian faith as an ideology (the Christian *Weltanschauung*) and thus makes itself contemporary."[31] Needless to say, Heidegger considers this a far from satisfactory solution for Christianity, but this is a problem for the theologians, not for him. His concern is the purification of philosophy from its contact with Christianity, and he feels that if Christian theology will maintain its proper distance from philosophy, then there is less danger that philosophy will be tempted to solve its problems by resorting to the doctrines of the Christian faith.

As a philosopher, Heidegger can demonstrate the inadequacy of the metaphysical concept of God for both philosophy and theology precisely because of its metaphysical character. But beyond that he has nothing positive to say about how God can be described apart from metaphysics. For philosophy, the death of the metaphysical god has resulted in the *absence* of God (Fehl Gottes). This expression means

that there is no God which clearly and unambiguously gathers men and things to itself and in this gathering governs world history and human dwelling. But even worse things are announced in the absence of God. Not only have the gods and God departed, but the splendour of divinity is obliterated from world history. This time of world night is the needy time, since it becomes ever more needy. It has already become so needy that it is no longer capable of recognizing the absence of God as an absence.[32]

The absence of divinity is significant for philosophy as well as for theology, since it is just one facet of the technological worldview which characterizes Western civilization today. Technology refers to the domination of beings by man, and as such it completely obscures the object of genuine thinking, Being. But in another sense the departure of God can be advantageous for philosophy, since it provides an opportunity for philosophy to rid itself of its theological concerns and thereby free itself for dealing with its own proper subject-matter--the question of Being.

It is evident, therefore, that Heidegger's critique of the theological character of traditional metaphysics follows directly from his understanding of the distinction between theology and philosophy (i.e., between faith and thinking). The interpenetration of philosophy and theology in the past has been disastrous for them both, and Heidegger feels that the separation of these two activities must be accomplished if either of them is to develop as it should. That this critique of onto-theo-logy is not merely negative, but is rather the first step in the development of more adequate expressions of both philosophy and theology, is evident from the positive aspects of Heidegger's philosophy of religion with which we shall deal now--his description of man and his discussion of God.

III. Heidegger's Description of Man.

Whereas it is easy to see the relevance of Heidegger's critique of traditional metaphysics for the philosophy of religion, the

104

same cannot be said of his description of man. True to his understanding of the dichotomy between philosophy and theology, Heidegger offers no treatment of human religious experience as such. Nevertheless, as is evident from the theological interpretations of his thought treated above, Heidegger's description of man is not inimical to a religious interpretation, and so it is necessary to examine this description with particular care in order to determine its significance for the philosophy of religion.

The concept of man is not the primary concern of Heidegger's thought; that position has always been occupied by the question of Being (Sein). Man is discussed only insofar as he is related to Being.[33] This relation is essential to both man and Being, however, and Heidegger has found it necessary to devote much of his written work to developing a non-metaphysical description of man which will provide an adequate approach to the question of Being. The principal aspect of this new description of man is the concept of *death*.

The importance of death in Heidegger's description of man is evident in the two principal titles he uses for man: "Being-towards-death" (in *Sein und Zeit*) and the "mortal" (in his later works). Death is, as well, an essential element in most religious interpretations of human existence, and so a discussion of Heidegger's concept of death will serve not only to illuminate his own proper concern--the question of Being[34]--but also to demonstrate the relevance of his description of man for the philosophy of religion. In what follows, we shall first treat Heidegger's concept of death as it develops from his earlier writings to his later, and then situate this concept with regard to the other aspects of his thought which are of primary importance for the philosophy of religion, especially the interrelation of thinking, language and Being.

A. Heidegger's Concept of Death.

1. Death in *Sein und Zeit*.

The express purpose of *Sein und Zeit* was to determine the meaning of Being, the traditional basic concept of philosophy which has for so long been taken for granted by philosophers. Since Being cannot be observed in itself but only in the beings which make up the world, Heidegger chose as the starting-point of his inquiry the one particular being whose description is most likely to lead to an understanding of Being as such. This favoured being is Dasein, the one which can ask the question of Being. And so *Sein und Zeit* consists of a phenomenological investigation of

105

Dasein, since Heidegger believes that the descriptive-interpreta-
tive method of phenomenology is best suited for revealing the
essential aspects of such an object.

The most basic feature of Dasein is that its Being is a *Being-
in-the-world*, and the first section of *Sein und Zeit* deals with
the everyday, undifferentiated character of this manner of Being
which is immediately available for phenomenological analysis.
This preliminary existential analysis reveals that the average,
everyday character of Dasein is but the *inauthentic* mode of human
existence, wherein the total potentialities of Dasein are not
fulfilled. Thus a further analysis is required: "If the interpretation of Dasein's Being is to become primordial, as a foundation for working out the basic question of ontology, then it must
first have brought to light existentially the Being of Dasein in
its possibilities of *authenticity* and *totality*."[35] This is the
aim of the second section of *Sein und Zeit*, entitled "Dasein and
Temporality".

The reason why everydayness is unable to achieve the totality
of Dasein is that "everydayness is precisely that Being which is
'between' [and therefore does not include] birth and death."[36]
The totality of Dasein must include its death, but this would
seem to mean that the totality can never be attained. For as
soon as Dasein reaches its death, it is no longer Dasein, no
longer Being-in-the-world. It is apparent that the understanding
of death as the mere ceasing-to-be of Dasein is not sufficient
for the attainment of the totality of Dasein.

Perhaps this totality can be revealed by the experience of the
death of others, since Being-with-others is a constituent feature
of Being-in-the-world. This is not the case, however. The other
person does not cease to be for us at death; he is present as a
corpse, and perhaps also as an object of remembrance and affection.
We do not experience the Being-come-to-an-end, the dying, of the
other. Every Dasein must experience his own death for himself.

Death signifies the relation of Dasein to its end, but it is not
an ending in the sense of fulfilment. For at death Dasein loses
its possibilities, and for the most part ends in unfulfilment.
Nor is death an ending in the sense of a stopping, a getting
finished, or a disappearing. The ending that is death is not
Dasein's Being-*at*-an-end but its Being-*toward*-its-end. In Heidegger's terminology, the end of living things other than Dasein
is called 'perishing' (Verenden). Dasein never simply perishes,
as do other animals, but it can end without authentically dying;
this ending is called its 'demise' (Ableben). The term 'dying'
(Sterben) stands for "that *way of Being* in which Dasein *is towards*
its death."[37] Thus death, now understood as dying, is a phenomenon of life.[38]

Since this death is such an essential aspect of Dasein's Being, it manifests itself in both the authentic and the inauthentic modes of existence. Everyday, average Dasein is dominated by the other Daseins it encounters in the world; it considers itself as one among many, one of the 'they' (das Man). The 'they' speaks of death in the phrase, "one dies." Here death is understood as "an indefinite something which, above all, must duly arrive from somewhere or other, but which is proximally *not-yet-present-at-hand* for oneself, and is therefore no threat."[39] The 'they' dictates the 'correct' attitude in the face of death--the courage for anxiety is not permitted, only indifferent tranquillity as to the 'fact' that one dies. The 'they' cannot deny the certainty of death. But this is simply an empirical certainty of demise, and evades the authentic Being-certain of Dasein's own death. The 'when' of death is put off to the remote future, and so the fact that death is possible at any moment is covered up.

Authentic Being-towards-death, on the other hand, is a Being towards a possibility. Dasein conducts itself towards this possibility not by actualizing it (i.e., by bringing about its own demise), nor by brooding over how it may finally be actualized, but by *expecting* it (im Erwarten). To expect death is to comport oneself towards it in such a way that, in and for one's Being, death reveals itself as a genuine possibility, the possibility, indeed, of the impossibility of any existence at all. Heidegger calls the Being towards this possibility *anticipation* (Vorlaufen); it is "the possibility of understanding one's ownmost and uttermost potentiality-for-Being--that is to say, the possibility of *authentic existence*."[40] Anticipation individualizes Dasein and allows it, in this individualization of itself, to become certain of the totality of its own potentiality-for-Being. Heidegger summarizes the role of authentic Being-towards-death thus: "Anticipation reveals to Dasein its lostness in the they-self, and brings it face to face with the possibility of being itself... in an impassioned *freedom towards death*."[41]

Authentic Being-towards-death is, therefore, an existential possibility for Dasein, but is it ever actualized? How can everyday Dasein, lost in the 'they', be shown to itself in its possible authenticity? It can do so through the *call of its conscience* (Gewissenruf), which summons everyday Dasein to its ownmost potentiality-for-Being-its-Self. Heidegger refers to this appeal of conscience as "wanting to have a conscience" or "resoluteness" (Entschlossenheit). Resoluteness exists as a resolution (Entschluss), which is "precisely the disclosive projection and determination of what is factically possible at the time."[42] Thus, the call of conscience summons us not to some empty ideal of existence but to a definite situation.

107

How is resoluteness related to anticipation (authentic Being-towards-death)? What is the connection between wanting to have a conscience and Dasein's authentic potentiality-for-Being-a-whole? Anticipation deals with Dasein's Being as a totality (from birth to death), while resoluteness pertains to Dasein's Being in a definite situation. Authentic Dasein approaches each situation conscious of its fundamental mortality and all that this entails. *Sein und Zeit* is not a work of ethics nor even of meta-ethics, and so Heidegger is not concerned with the actions of individuals in particular situations. He means only to show how his theoretical analysis of human existence is related to the actual conduct of life. One who thinks of his existence as a Being-towards-death will act differently from one who lives only for the present moment.

In the final chapters of *Sein und Zeit*, Heidegger relates anticipatory resoluteness to temporality. Temporality is the basis of Dasein's historicality, and anticipatory resoluteness, as Being-free-for-death, allows Dasein to grasp the finitude of its existence, and thereby enables Dasein to understand its superior power—i.e., its power to choose the powerlessness of abandonment to its thrownness. In this way, death unites Dasein's past (its facticity—thrownness) to its future. Death, therefore, is the basis of Dasein's historicality, and as such is of crucial significance in Heidegger's investigation of man and the question of Being towards which that investigation is directed.

The published text of *Sein und Zeit* ends without any explicit answer to the question of the meaning of Being. It is necessary to examine Heidegger's analysis of death more closely in order to ascertain whether or not death reveals to us anything beyond ourselves, such as Being. Three characteristics of Being-towards-death—facticity, certainty, and finitude—suggest themselves as pertinent for this inquiry.

a) Facticity.

The facticity of death means that Dasein does not procure for itself the possibility of its absolute impossibility, but on the contrary exists as already *thrown* into this possibility. This thrownness into death is revealed in the mood of anxiety. That which anxiety reveals as the basis of Dasein's thrownness into death is not, however, Being itself, but rather *nothing* (Nichts): "The 'nothing' with which anxiety brings us face to face, unveils the nullity by which Dasein, in its very *basis*, is defined; and this basis itself 'is' as thrownness into death."[43] *Sein und Zeit* does not analyze the phenomenon of 'nothing' with regard to its significance for the question of Being; this is done in the 1929

lecture *What is Metaphysics?* and subsequent works. But although
the significance of the thrownness of Being-towards-death for
the disclosure of the meaning of Being is not made explicit in
Sein und Zeit, the very fact of thrownness means that Dasein is
not the master of its origin, that our Being is given to us from
without. From where, then, does our Being come? This question
cannot be answered at this stage of Heidegger's thought.

b) Certainty.

Authentic death is certain and yet indefinite. Like every
Dasein I must die, but the circumstances of my death are essentially indefinite. There is no one moment until which I can
postpone my preparation for death, since death can strike at any
time. The indefinite certainty of death poses a constant threat
to me as Dasein, as Being-in-the-world. Thus, just as Dasein is
not the master of its origin, neither is it the master of its
ultimate (worldly) destiny. Is there indeed any such master? Is
there some reality beyond Dasein which allots to each man his
'appointed' times of birth and death? Heidegger does not speak of
fate in this context; fate is rather a power of Dasein.[44] But if
it is not fate which accounts for the circumstances of Dasein's
death, then it must be some definite reality, perhaps Being itself. *Sein und Zeit* does not answer this question of the master
of death, but it seems to require some reality beyond Dasein to
fulfil this role.

c) Finitude.

The characteristics of facticity and indefinite certainty are
united in the description of death as finite. Although finitude
refers to Dasein primarily insofar as it is temporal, Dasein is
temporal precisely because it is Being-towards-death. As thrownness and as indefinite certainty, death reveals the basic finitude
of Dasein. Dasein requires an 'other' for its origin and for its
destiny; it neither enters nor leaves the world on its own.
Authentic Dasein must exist in full awareness of these limitations;
its appropriate stance is that of anticipatory resoluteness. Heidegger speaks of *infinity* only as the (inauthentic) correlate of
Dasein's authentic temporality, and not as a description of the
source of Dasein's Being. So once again, as with facticity and
certainty, we have no direct access to the 'whence' of finite
Dasein, but only a further characterization of Dasein in terms
which seem to require such a 'whence'. The description in *Sein
und Zeit* of Dasein as Being-towards-death definitely points beyond Dasein to some greater reality. Since the intention of the

109

book was to investigate the meaning of Being, we might conclude
that Being is the reality indicated by Dasein's finitude. However,
nowhere in the unfinished version of *Sein und Zeit* is this equa-
tion made. It remains, therefore, to look beyond *Sein und Zeit* to
Heidegger's later writings in order to determine whether his
description of Dasein as Being-towards-death can reveal and identify some ultimate, trans-human reality.

2. Death in the Later Heidegger.

The first instance of Heidegger's application of his concept of
death to the question of Being is his 1929 study, *Kant and the
Problem of Metaphysics*. In this initial approach to Being through
the history of philosophy, the essential *finitude* of Dasein which
death reveals is described as the basic limiting factor in our
knowledge of Being. Heidegger contrasts an infinite knowledge
which would be able to create things (i.e., give them their Being)
with our finite knowledge, which can only encounter things against
an already presupposed horizon of Being. To be able to know
things in our proper (finite) manner, we must have a knowledge of
Being.[45] Thus, finitude can be understood only in relation to
our power of understanding Being, and vice versa: "we do not even
have to ask ourselves about the relation of the comprehension of
Being to the finitude in man. This comprehension of Being itself
is the innermost essence of finitude."[46]

In his later writings, even those dealing with Kant, Heidegger
abandons the term 'finitude'.[47] Nevertheless, he continues to
combat the exaltation of man which is characteristic of modern
philosophy, and his principal weapon in this combat is his concept of death. In his 1935 summer lectures, published in 1953 as
An Introduction to Metaphysics, Heidegger describes death as man's
ultimate limitation:

[Death] is an end beyond all consummation, a limit beyond all
limits. Here there is no breaking-out or breaking-up, no cap-
ture or subjugation. But this strange and alien thing that
banishes us once and for all from everything in which we are at
home is no particular event that must be named among others
because it, too, ultimately happens. It is not only when he
comes to die, but always and essentially that man is without
issue in the face of death. Insofar as man *is*, he stands in the
issuelessness of death.[48]

As long as man is aware that he is going to die, he can have no
illusions that he is the master of the universe. He is thus open
to the possibility of an encounter with something beyond himself.
For Heidegger, as a philosopher, this reality beyond man is Being,
and his description of death is intended to prepare man for the

thinking of Being. Unfortunately, we are so much under the domination of traditional metaphysics that we are unable even to speak of Being (since the very structure of our language is metaphysical). For this reason, Heidegger has recourse to poetry in order to describe the (metaphysically) indescribable relation of man and Being.

Heidegger's favourite poet is Friedrich Hölderlin (1770-1834), since his poems deal with the essence of poetry.[49] In his study of Hölderlin, Heidegger was fascinated by his designation of man as 'the mortal' (der Sterbliche), and beginning with his own essays on Hölderlin, he substituted that term for 'Dasein'. By his use of this term he wishes to indicate above all the finite way in which man understands Being--i.e., through beings, or, in Hölderlin's phrase, as "sons of the earth."[50]

In contrast to the negative view of death so prominent in this technological age, Heidegger finds in another German poet, Rainer Maria Rilke, a positive appraisal of death: "Death is the *side of life* which is turned away from us, not illuminated by us."[51] As a phenomenon of human life, death reveals the great privilege of man to be capable of knowing Being. But at the same time it reminds man that his knowledge of Being is limited--he is not the master of beings, not even of his own Being. The poetic description of death brings out the essential relationship of man and Being, but it leaves no doubt as to Being's superiority therein.

Heidegger's investigation into the nature of poetry refocussed his abiding interest in *language* onto the problem of Being. Man has long been distinguished from other living things by his power of speech. For Heidegger, though, this characteristic of man cannot be understood in isolation from man's relation to death:

The mortals are those who can experience death as death. Beasts cannot do this. Beasts are also unable to speak. The essential connection between death and language flashes forth, but is still unthought. Nevertheless, it can give us a hint as to the way in which language gathers us to itself and thus relates us to itself, so that death belongs together with that which gathers us.[52]

This description of the interconnection between death and language would be incomprehensible from the viewpoint of metaphysical philosophy, since for metaphysics death is precisely that which all living things (including man) have in common--the end of life-- and as such is entirely unrelated to the power of speech. According to Heidegger, however, both the concept of death and the concept of language in metaphysics are inadequate, because they both contribute to the neglect of the question of Being. In his own thought, these two concepts are essentially related precisely because they are both important elements of the asking of this question.

The significance of language in the relationship of man and Being is one of the major themes of Heidegger's thought:

Language is the house of Being. In its home man dwells. Whoever thinks or creates in words is a guardian of this dwelling. As guardian, he brings to fulfillment the unhiddenness of Being insofar as he, by his speaking, takes up this unhiddenness in language and preserves it in language.[53]

It is only because he is linguistic that man can ask the question of Being. This linguisticality, however, presupposes man's mortality, since as fundamentally temporal (i.e., as thrown Being-towards-death), man is thrown into a linguistic environment. And it is only within this environment and by means of language that man can pose the question of the meaning of Being. One can also say that man is the mortal because he is linguistic. To be mortal is to come to know death as it really is. But to know something as it really is requires for man an understanding of Being. And man's capacity of understanding Being is grounded in his power of speech, as was shown in *Sein und Zeit*.[54] Linguisticality and mortality, therefore, are both rooted in man's understanding of Being; neither is thinkable without the other.

In the poetry of Hölderlin, men are described as the mortals in contrast with the 'immortals' (die Unsterblichen)--the gods. In his essays, *Das Ding* (The Thing--1950) and *Bauen Wohnen Denken* (Building Dwelling Thinking--1951), Heidegger expands this twosome into the *quadrant* (das Geviert),[55] namely, earth, heavens, divinities and mortals. These four elements constitute the *world*. 'World' here signifies the structure in which Being is revealed: the earth represents the tendency towards hiddenness and false disclosure; the heavens represent the openness of unhiddenness; man, the mortal, is the one who brings about the unhiddenness, but only with the help of the divinities. Every thing in the world participates in its quadrant-nature. Heidegger gives the example of a jug: the earth provides the water or wine which it holds; the heavens provided the necessary sun and rain; the mortal man's thirst requires satisfaction from the contents of the jug; and the divinities are sometimes honoured by the offering of the wine. The essence of the jug is the interplay of these four elements, each one of which implies the other three.[56]

The specific relation of man to the quadrant is called by Heidegger *dwelling* (Wohnen): "Men *are* in the quadrant insofar as they *dwell*."[57] Dwelling is not just a passive mode of existence but requires a strenuous effort on the part of man: "The authentic necessity of dwelling requires that mortals must first seek again and again the essence of dwelling, that they *must first learn to dwell*."[58] Dwelling involves a fourfold relation of men to

112

things, which Heidegger calls 'caring' (Schonen). Mortals dwell 'caringly' in the world by respecting the earth, by welcoming the gifts of the heavens (e.g., sun and rain), by awaiting the divinities, and by going towards their death.[59] Heidegger describes the goal of authentic dwelling in the expressions "serenity with regard to things" (die Gelassenheit zu den Dingen) and "openness to the mystery" (die Offenheit für das Geheimnis).[60] This is the exact opposite of the attitude towards things of modern technology, which sees nature as something to be overcome. Such an attitude results in a rootlessness, a basic homelessness or alienation of man from the world. Men can regain their roots only by an authentic dwelling as mortals on the earth, under the heavens and for the divinities.

When Heidegger spoke of man as the mortal in his writings on poetry and language, he wished to signify above all the finite relationship of man to Being. In connection with the quadrant, however, he relates the mortal specifically to death: "Men are called mortals because they are able to die. To die means: to be capable of death as death."[61] Here again, Heidegger is distinguishing dying from mere perishing. And, as before, this distinction is grounded in man's unique capacity of understanding Being. To be capable of death means to understand it in relation to Being. And this signifies that, at bottom, Being-towards-death and the understanding of Being are one and the same.

Man's response to death as described in this way should be to recognize his essential finitude, and to act accordingly with regard to other beings, to himself, and to Being. To understand oneself as mortal is not primarily something negative--a realization that someday as Dasein he will be no more--but rather something positive--that man is the privileged being who is able to know Being. This is what Heidegger means by "a good death."[62]

B. Man and Being.

In order to determine the religious significance of Heidegger's concept of man, we must describe more precisely the relation of man and Being. Whether or not Being can be understood as God, it is nevertheless the central concept in Heidegger's philosophy, and is of crucial importance for the understanding of what man is. Conversely, it is by means of an analysis of human existence that Heidegger first tried to ask the question of the meaning of Being, and throughout his entire philosophical career he has always treated these two concepts--man and Being--together. Since the concept of death is an essential element in Heidegger's description of man, it is also very important for understanding the meaning of Being.

113

The close interrelationship of Being, man and death is to be found already in *Sein und Zeit*. There man is defined precisely in terms of his relation to Being--as *Dasein* (there-Being):

The entity which each of us is himself and which includes inquiring as one of the possibilities of its Being, we shall denote by the term 'Dasein'....Dasein is an entity which does not just occur among other entities. Rather it is ontically distinguished by the fact that, in its very Being, that Being is an *issue* for it....*Understanding of Being is itself a definite characteristic of Dasein's Being.*[63]

And since the most precise definition of Dasein is as "Being-towards-death," it follows that Being cannot be understood in isolation from the concept of death. In *Sein und Zeit*, Dasein is described in terms which seem to require an 'other' as the source of its Being. But no such 'other' was named therein, not even the most likely candidate for the position--Being itself.

In his writings immediately after *Sein und Zeit*, namely, *Kant and the Problem of Metaphysics*, *Vom Wesen des Grundes* and *What is Metaphysics?*, Heidegger describes the *finitude* of Dasein, which is the necessary consequence of his concept of death, in terms of man's capacity for understanding Being. There, Being is presented as the correlate of Dasein's finitude, but only on the level of knowledge, and not as the source of Dasein. Indeed, Being is described at this stage as itself finite,[64] since it can only come to presence in a finite manner--i.e., according to the capacity of Dasein to know it.

The finitude of Being is only one aspect of it, however--the aspect which appears to man. Because we can encounter only this finite side of Being, Heidegger says that Being is concealed even in its revelation. Can we know anything more about Being than the finite side which we encounter in things? Certainly not by the means afforded by traditional metaphysics, which considers only the Being *of beings* and not the *Being* of beings. But with the help of poets such as Hölderlin and the pre-metaphysical thinkers, Heraclitus, Parmenides and Anaximander, Heidegger has attempted to free himself from the domination of metaphysics and to attain a more original understanding of Being. Although he seldom uses the term 'Dasein' in his later works, his concept of man is still an essential part of the understanding of Being, especially with regard to man's powers of language and thought.

The best expression of the relation between language, thinking and Being is to be found in Heidegger's 1946 *Letter on Humanism*. In this work, Heidegger is at pains to dispel the common misinterpretation of *Sein und Zeit* as an 'existentialist' exaltation of man over everything else, including Being and God. Although the Being-man relationship takes place primarily in (human) thought, it is Being which is the superior in this relationship: "Thought brings to fulfillment the relation of Being to the essence of man, it does not make or produce this relation. Thought merely offers it to Being as that which has been delivered to itself by Being."[65] For this communication of itself to human thought, Being makes use of *language* above all else:

Being remains mysterious, the plain closeness of an unobtrusive rule. This closeness is essentially language itself....According to this, language is the house of Being, owned and pervaded by Being. Therefore, the point is to think of the essence of language in its correspondence to Being and, what is more, as this very correspondence, i.e., the dwelling of man's essence.[66]

Heidegger emphasizes the essential though subordinate role of man vis-à-vis Being by describing him as the "guardian of Being" and the "shepherd of Being".[67] It is man's privilege to be the being in which Being manifests itself, but it is through no merit of his own that he enjoys this privilege. Thus, the concept of man as master of beings which is found in both traditional metaphysics and contemporary existentialism is completely mistaken, and as long as man considers himself in this way, he will be unable even to ask the question of Being.

The understanding of Being which Heidegger has gained through his interpretation of thinking and language is essentially determined by his concept of death. Death reveals the finitude of man--that he must die (as in *Sein und Zeit*), that he is able to die (as in the later Heidegger), that he is not the source of his own Being (both early and later Heidegger). Death opens man to his source. It also reveals Being as finite, since it is a primary instrument of Being's (finite) self-revelation to man. But finite Being cannot be the ultimate source of man's Being, precisely because it is finite. Perhaps there is more to Being than its finite aspect. But words such as 'infinite', 'omnipotent', etc., are inadequate to describe this Being because of their metaphysical connotations. 'Being' itself is an equivocal term, since metaphysicians have always spoken facilely of Being as their object, even though this signified only the finite side of Being. In his later works, Heidegger distinguishes this finite Being (Sein) from 'true Being', which he refers to as *Seyn* or ~~*Sein*~~.[68] Can this 'true Being' be the ultimate source of man's own Being?

Heidegger finds it very difficult to say anything positive about 'true Being', for the metaphysical structure of our language dictates that only beings can be the subject of the verb 'to be'.[69] The best that he can do is to use active verbs when speaking of Being--e.g., Being *presences* itself. The primary characteristic of 'true Being', insofar as it can thus be described, is that it reveals itself to man. Man's knowledge of Being, even as finite,

115

is not due to his own initiative, but is 'given' to him by Being. But the knowledge of Being which is thus revealed to man is essential to his own Being, since man is defined as the being which can know Being. We may say, then, that as the source of man's knowledge of Being, 'true Being' is the source of man's Being.

This is not Heidegger's final word on the matter, however. The Being which death reveals as the source of man's Being need not be understood as ultimate--either as God or as some sort of substitute for God. In his 1962 lecture entitled, *Zeit und Sein*, Heidegger suggests a reality beyond Being. The starting-point for this new departure is the phrase, "es gibt Sein." The usual meaning of "es gibt" is: "there is" (as in the French expression, "il y a"). But Heidegger interprets the "es gibt" literally as "it gives," and he asks in what sense Being is a *gift* (Gabe). His answer is that Being is *revealed*, is *brought* into the open;[70] the passive constructions indicate both the verbal-active character of the appearance of Being and also the need for a subject-- one who 'gives'. Is it possible to identify that which gives, the 'es' of the "es gibt Sein"?

The title of this lecture might suggest that time (Zeit) is that which gives Being, especially since Being has traditionally been understood as presence (Anwesenheit)--i.e., with regard to temporality. This is not the case, however, for time, too, is a 'given'.[71] But that which determines the close interrelation of Being and time, that which Heidegger calls the *event* (das Ereignis), is itself the 'es' of the "es gibt Sein."[72] The question now becomes: what is the event?

The word 'event' is not to be understood as a mere occurrence or happening but as "the giving and sending which opens up and preserves" (das lichtend verwahrenden Reichen und Schicken).[73] Event is not a super-concept containing both Being and time; rather, it determines the interconnection of these two concepts. There is really no language to describe the event in itself. The only thing that can be said about it is: "The event brings to pass" (das Ereignis ereignet).[74]

It appears, therefore, that Heidegger has introduced a new factor in his understanding of Being. Whereas previously he had treated Being as the ultimate concept of philosophical thinking, he now seems to be saying that there is something more basic than Being, something which is, in fact, the source of Being, inasmuch as it 'gives' Being to man. He does not attempt to describe this reality beyond Being, but only indicates that there has to be such a reality. Although this aspect of Heidegger's thought appears to be a radical departure from the earlier stages of his philosophical development in which Being was all-important, it can, in fact, be interpreted as the logical outcome of his emphasis on the finitude of Being, especially insofar as Being is known to man. Heidegger no longer speaks of Being giving itself to man, as he did in the *Letter on Humanism*. Much less can one say that man gives or controls Being. No, Being (and time as well) are given to man by the *event*--an inexpressible 'other' which Heidegger can only describe in terms of its 'actions', the giving of time and of Being.

Whatever may be the character of this reality beyond Being, by the very fact that Heidegger postulates such a reality, his philosophy shows itself to be radically open-ended. For just as the analysis of death showed that man cannot be understood as completely self-sufficient but must be open to Being as the source of his own Being, so now Heidegger says that this Being is not self-contained and self-bestowing but is given to man by an indescribable 'other'. Heidegger's concept of death, therefore, reveals not only Being but also and thereby a reality beyond Being as the ultimate source of all that is. It remains to be seen now whether or not Heidegger identifies this ultimate reality as God.

IV. Heidegger and Theism.

For Heidegger, the concept of God belongs to faith (and theology), not to philosophy. Philosophy is neither theistic, atheistic or agnostic--these categories simply do not apply to thinking. Nevertheless, the words 'God' and 'the gods' appear many times in Heidegger's written works. We have already seen that he feels it necessary to criticize the traditional metaphysical concept of God because of its inadequacy for both theology and philosophy. But he also speaks of God in a positive sense, and although he is unable as a philosopher to identify this 'divine God', he seems to consider this matter to be very important for mankind, and he wants to ensure that philosophy will not interfere with theology's asking after God.

Since Heidegger does not deny that there is a God, and indeed at times even seems to encourage such a belief, philosophical theologians have searched his philosophy for the concept which would correspond most closely to their God. The temptation to identify Heidegger's 'Being' with the Christian God has been very great, especially since Heidegger for many years spoke of Being as the ultimate philosophical concept, and to this day still considers the question of Being to be the primary activity of thought. However, he has explicitly rejected the identification of Being and God,[75] and his description of Being as finite is a further indication that these two concepts are not interchangeable.

117

Heidegger also rejects the metaphysical concept of God as the supreme being. But his description of reality, especially with regard to the 'event', indicates that Being is not the ultimate concept, and indeed there 'is' something beyond Being. In order to determine whether or not this region beyond Being is where God is to be found, we must first examine what else he has to say about God.

Because of the failure of the metaphysical concept of God, the predominant experience of God in modern times is of his *absence*. The contemporary world is enthralled with technology, which Heidegger sees as the logical consequence of the metaphysical neglect of Being, and technology is openly antipathetic to the sacred and to God:

The essence of technology only comes slowly to light. This day is the world-night turned into a merely technological day. This day is the shortest day. It threatens a single endless winter. Now not only is man denied a shelter, but the safety of all beings remains in darkness. The wholeness [das Heile] is withdrawn. The world becomes unwhole [heil-los]. Thereby not only does the holy remain hidden as the sign of divinity, but even the sign of the holy, namely wholeness, seems to be obliterated.[76]

The recovery of the dimension of the sacred, in which alone God is to be encountered, is not an easy task. Where there is no respect for the world in itself, the world as 'wholesome', there can be no approach to what transcends the world, the 'holy'. Although Heidegger adopts Nietzsche's expression, "God is dead," to characterize the non-sacred nature of this modern age, he does not mean that the sacred is beyond recovery. It is indeed a time of darkness, a 'world-night', but this situation could change at any time, because it is not man who is responsible for the situation: "Whether God lives or remains dead is not determined by the religiousness of man and still less by the theological aspirations of philosophy and of science. Whether God is God is determined from and within the constellation of Being."[77] This is not to say that God is determined by Being, but the understanding of Being which *is given* to man is a necessary preliminary to the encounter with God in the dimension of the sacred. However, man must do his part in preparing for the reception of this understanding of Being. Heidegger's task is thus to demonstrate why this is a "needy age,"[78] since the inadequacy of the modern technological worldview must first be recognized if it is to be overcome.

In his discussion of theism Heidegger has recourse to three principal concepts: the holy, the quadrant and the event. His understanding of the holy is derived primarily from the poetry of Hölderlin, and his essays on Hölderlin are the richest sources for the study of his concepts of the gods and God.

A. The Holy.

The poet *par excellence* in this needy time is Hölderlin, since
> Hölderlin writes poetry about the essence of poetry--but not in the sense of a timelessly valid concept. The essence of poetry belongs to a determined time. But not in such a way that it merely conforms to this time, as to one which is already in existence. It is that Hölderlin, in the act of establishing the essence of poetry, first determines a new time. It is the time of the gods that have fled *and* of the god that is coming. It is the time of *need*, because it lies under a double lack and a double Not: the No-more of the gods that have fled and the Not-yet of the god that is coming.[79]

Heidegger continues to describe this needy time in terms of night and darkness, but his assessment of the present situation is far from pessimistic: "The night is the mother of the day....The night is the time for sheltering the *departed gods* and concealing gods.... The night, as the mother of the day which brings the holy, is a *holy night*."[80] The sacred aspect of the world is so essential to it that the absence of divinity can only be temporary. Even now, while the technological denial of the sacred holds sway, there are traces of the departed divinities still in evidence, especially to the poet. Heidegger describes these traces as the 'ether' of divinity: "The ether, wherein the gods alone are gods, is their divinity. The element of this ether, that wherein divinity itself is present, is the holy. The element of this ether for the advent of the departed gods, the holy, is the trace of the departed gods."[81] The poet can speak of the god that is to come only in relation to the departed gods and through the intermediary concepts of divinity and the holy: "Only from the essence of the holy can the essence of divinity be thought. Only in light of the essence of divinity can it be thought and said what the world 'God' is to signify."[82]

What then is meant by the 'holy'? For Hölderlin, the holy is Nature, in the sense of the all-creative (die Allerschaffende) and the all-alive (die Allebendige).[83] Nature is the holy because it is "'older than the ages and above the gods' [Hölderlin]. Therefore holiness is in no way the borrowed attribute of an established god. The holy is not holy because it is divine, but the divine is divine because it is 'holy' in its way....The holy is the essence of Nature."[84] Therefore the holy is not God and not the gods or their divinity. The holy is rather that aspect of Nature which is revealed to the poet as he seeks the traces of the departed gods--

119

i.e., it is the sacred aspect of Being:
 'Nature' means here that which is *above* the gods and 'older
 than the ages', according to which every being *is*. 'Nature'
 is the name for 'Being'; for it is prior to all beings, which
 are indebted to it for what they are; and *under* 'Being' as well
 stand all gods, insofar as they *are* and also in the way in
 which they are.[85]
As an aspect of Being, the holy must be encountered before the
essence of divinity or God can be attained, and this encounter is
a task for the poet: "Hölderlin's word speaks the holy and thereby names the once-and-for-all space-time of the original decision
for the essential structure of the future history of the gods and
humanity."[86] The role of the poet is therefore of paramount
importance with regard to the holy, the divine and God.

 Since the poet is a mortal man, yet one who speaks of the gods,
poetry is essentially a relation between the gods and men: "The
essence of poetry is joined on to the laws of the signs of the
gods and of the voice of the people. The poet himself stands between the former--the gods, and the latter--the people. He is
the one who has been cast out--out into the Between, between gods
and man."[87] Heidegger calls the poet the "half-god" (der Halbgott);
he is the one who "thinks from out of this Between that which is
different from both and sanctifies both, and he intends this Between as the subject of his poem. Thinking as a mortal man, he
names poetically the most high."[88] This Between is also called by
Heidegger the 'open' (das Offene); it is the dwelling place of the
poet, where he can welcome the gods as his guests (i.e., in his
poetry).[89] The poet is therefore the privileged mortal who can
experience the holy and name the divine. And yet, all men are
summoned to the life of the poet, which Heidegger feels is best
expressed in Hölderlin's verse: "Poetically, dwells man on this
earth." This expression means: "to stand in the presence of the
gods and to be involved in the proximity of the essence of things.
Existence is 'poetical' in its fundamental aspect--which means at
the same time: insofar as it is established (founded), it is not
a recompense, but a gift."[90] Heidegger does say that the work of
the poet has to be accomplished beforehand if poetical dwelling
is to be possible for men,[91] but his exposition of Hölderlin's
poems indicates that this poet has already shown men how to dwell
on this earth. This poetical manner of dwelling, of living in
the presence of the holy and letting the truth appear, is, needless to say, the exact opposite of the technological form of dwelling which holds sway in modern Western civilization.

 Heidegger's discussion of poetry seems at first sight to be a
strange combination of the mythical (his references to the gods)
and the actual (his criticism of technology). This apparent

120

opposition in his thought can easily be resolved if one considers that he is using the terms 'holy', 'gods' and 'God' with reference to the poetry of Hölderlin and not to theology or religion. In Hölderlin's poem, "The Wanderer," the gods include earth and light, the angels of the house and year.[92] In the elegy, "Homecoming," however, Hölderlin distinguishes between angels and gods:

By the name 'angels' the essence of what were previously called 'gods' is more purely expressed. For the gods are the serenifiers [die Aufheiternden], who in the serenification announce the greeting which the Serene [die Heitere] sends. The Serene is the origin of the greeting, i.e., of the angelic, wherein the innermost essence of the gods consists. By using this word 'gods' sparingly and hesitating to apply the name, the poet has made more apparent the peculiar quality of the gods, as being the heralds through whom the Serene sends greeting.[93]

The gods need not be thought of as real or imaginary personal beings. Heidegger would consider this term rather as the poetic name for an important aspect of man's attitude towards Being, according to which he dwells poetically on the earth. Hölderlin's use of the singular 'God' is more ambiguous, however. He speaks of God as the Unknown; God appears, but he appears precisely as the Unknown. His revelation is mysterious.[94] As the Unknown, God is the limiting factor of the poet's experience of the holy. He remains apart from man, but is at the same time a constant reminder of man's finitude. In this sense, God is the poetic name for Heidegger's Being. As such, it is not a religious concept, and Hölderlin is not a religious poet but a poet of *Being*:

Poets, when they are truly poets, are *prophetic*. But they are not 'prophets' in the Judaeo-Christian sense of this term. The 'prophets' of these religions do not prophesy only the already established word of the holy. They prophesy instantly about the God on whom depends the certainty of salvation for celestial bliss. One should not disfigure Hölderlin's poetry through 'the religious' of 'religion', which remains a matter of the Roman interpretation of the relation between men and gods. One should not overburden the essence of this poetizing by considering the poet as a 'seer' in the sense of a soothsayer. The poetically prophesied holy opens up only the space-time of an appearance of the gods and indicates the place where historical man dwells on this earth. The essence of this poet should not be thought with reference to these 'prophets', but the 'prophetic' aspect of this poetry must be conceived from the essence of poetical prophesy. Its dream is godly but it does not dream of a God.[95]

Whatever one may think of Heidegger's characterization of the Biblical prophets,[96] his main point is clear: Hölderlin's poetry

121

is far more amenable to a philosophical than to a theological interpretation.

It is evident, therefore, that for Heidegger there is an intimate relation between poetry and thinking, and his keen interest in Hölderlin's treatment of the holy and the divine arises out of his dedication to the question of Being. Heidegger looks to the poet for inspiration regarding his search for the truth of Being, yet he insists that the experience of the holy presupposes the thinking about Being, just as any possible encounter with God depends upon a preliminary acquaintance with the holy:

Only from the truth of Being can the essence of the holy be sought....How, then, is the man of the present epoch even to be able to ask seriously and firmly whether God approaches or withdraws when man omits the primary step of thinking deeply in the one dimension where this question can be asked: that is, the dimension of the holy, which, even as dimension, remains closed unless the openness of Being is cleared and in its clearing is close to man.[97]

Heidegger the thinker seeks the truth of Being; Hölderlin the poet names the holy. It would seem to be the same reality that each treats, but Heidegger feels that the two *approaches* are radically different: "poet and thinker...dwell near to one another on mountains farthest apart."[98] The realm of the holy which the poet describes may perhaps be the place where an encounter with God is possible, but Heidegger's views on the relation of thinking and faith prevent him from entering that realm and dealing directly with the problem of God.

B. The Quadrant.

Heidegger's exposition of the holy reveals the mutual dependence of the gods and men upon each other: "Since neither men nor the gods can bring about a direct relation to the holy by themselves, men need the gods and the heavenly beings need the mortals...."[99] The gods can be gods only if there are men, and, conversely, men need the gods in order to be men. This twofold relationship is expanded by Heidegger into the quadrant, in which men and gods are joined by the heavens and the earth as the constituent elements of every 'thing'. In the quadrant, men are consistently referred to as the 'mortals', and the gods ('die Götter' in Hölderlin) are replaced by the less personal expression, 'the divinities' (die Göttlichen).

As was the case with the holy, the introduction of the divine element into the nature of a thing is not to be understood theologically. Heidegger is rather attempting to explain the world in a manner that is compatible with his concept of the ontological difference between Being and beings, and which will indeed help man to realize that difference and come to know the truth of Being. The description of men as the mortals is very apt for this purpose, as we have already seen. This description is complemented by Heidegger's emphasis on the natural elements of man's environment, symbolized by the heavens and the earth, in relation to which man comes to know himself and his position vis-à-vis Being. But this description of the world is incomplete without the divine element, which signifies the hidden truth of Being, the *reason* why there is any being at all (including man) rather than nothing. The appropriate mode of existence of the mortals is called dwelling: "The mortals dwell, insofar as they await the divinities as the divinities....They await the signs of their approach and do not fail to recognize the signs of their absence. They do not make themselves their own gods and do not give homage to false gods. They wait in the unwhole condition for the withdrawn wholeness."[100] The mortals' relation to the divinities, then, is essentially understood as 'awaiting', in the sense that man does not control Being, but Being must rather be revealed to man. And so Heidegger refers to the divinities as the "heralds of deity" (die Boten der Gottheit),[101] according to which Being is revealed in its very concealment.

The description of a jug, which Heidegger gives to illustrate the interplay of the four elements of the quadrant, exemplifies the demythologizing character of his usage of traditionally theological or religious terms. Although he speaks of the out-pouring of the jug's contents as an offering to the immortal gods, it is clear that he wishes only to emphasize the gift-character of this natural object, the jug: "In the gift of the outpour, which is a drink, the divinities abide in their own manner."[102] The mortals must await the messages of the divinities with regard to Being because these messages are gifts to men. Although the ontological difference between Being and beings obtains with regard to every single being, every thing, the realization of this differ-ence is basically a revelation of Being to man--a gift--and is not available to the superficial inquirer.

The appropriate response of man to the gift of his Being is *thanks*. Man shows his gratitude for this gift by doing all that he can to preserve the truth of Being, even if this involves some sacrifice on his part:

This sacrifice is the expense of our human being for the preservation of the truth of Being in respect of what-is [be-ings]. In sacrifice there is expressed that hidden *thanking* which alone does hommage to the grace wherewith Being has endowed the nature of man, in order that he may take over in his rela-tionship to Being the guardianship of Being. Original thanking

123

is the echo of Being's favour wherein it clears a space for itself and causes the unique occurrence: that what-is is.[103] In his book, *What is Called Thinking?* (Was heisst Denken?), Heidegger investigates the close relationship between the words 'thinking' (Denken) and 'thanking' (Danken), and concludes that the activities which these two words name are themselves interrelated. The power of thinking, especially when it is directed towards the question of Being, is essential to our human nature. But this power is a gift--it comes to us from outside ourselves. The best way in which we can show our gratitude for this gift is by using it properly: "Pure thanks is...that we simply think--think what is really and solely given, what there is to be thought."[104] Thus, the thinking of Being and the dwelling in the world are really the same, in that they both emphasize the gift-character of human existence and of Being as well. Can Heidegger as a philosopher say anything definite about the *giver* of this gift, or about the giving itself? It seems that he has attempted to do just this in his discussion of the event.

C. The Event.

The term 'event' (Ereignis) is of capital importance in the later writings of Heidegger. In his essay, "The Meaning of Identity" (1957), he uses this term to describe the relationship of Being and man in language and thinking. Man's attitude towards Being in authentic thinking should be one of service, rather than of control and mastery as in modern technology. The term 'event' is most fitting as an expression of man's serving, care-ful relation to Being. The event is the realm in which "man and Being attain one another in their essence."[105] Essential to man is the fact that he is able to speak, that he is linguistic. Thus the event itself is linguistic: "Insofar as our essence is constituted by language, we dwell in the event."[106] Furthermore, man encounters Being only in thinking upon Being, and so thinking, too, is basic to the event: "Being belongs with thinking in an identity, whose essence is derived from that letting-belong-together that we call the event."[107] The term 'event', then, names the realm in which man encounters Being, a realm in which he dwells linguistically by a care-ful thinking upon Being.

Heidegger thinks further into the linguistic character of the event in his essay, *The Way towards Language* (Der Weg zur Sprache--1959). Here he describes the event as a law of human nature:

The event grants to the mortals a sojourn in their essence--that they are able to be the speakers. If we understand by the law the assembling which allows everything to come to presence in its essence, to belong in its belonging, then the event is the

simplest and mildest of all laws....The event is evidently not
a law in the sense of a norm, which hangs somewhere over us; it
is no decree which orders and rules some outcome. [Para.] The
event is *the* law, insofar as it assembles the mortals in the
coming-to-pass of their essence and holds them therein.[108]
Although man is linguistic in his very essence, every man must
learn to use language properly--i.e., each individual man does not
necessarily realize the complete linguisticality of his nature.
This is why Heidegger speaks of "the way towards language." This
way involves the event:

In this way, which belongs to the essence of language, the
specific nature of language conceals itself. The way is event-
ful.... [Para.] The event brings man to pass for its own use.
Therefore...the event is the way-faring of the saying towards
language. [Para.] The way-faring brings language (the essence
of language) as language (the saying) into language (the tran-
spired word).[109]

Thus, the event is the realm in which man realizes his essence as
the speaking being. The event itself brings-to-pass man in his
linguisticality, an action which Heidegger terms the way towards
language.

This coming-to-pass of language is very difficult to formulate
linguistically, especially in view of the metaphysical character
of European languages. Heidegger speaks of the event as "the
most hidden of the hidden, the simplest of the simple, the near-
est of the near and the furthest of the far, in which we mortals
dwell all our lives."[110] The most that can be said about the
event is that it 'belongs' (es eignet).[111] It belongs to the
nature of man and also to the nature of Being. Indeed, the event
is the "giving-out [Er-gebnis], whose extended giving imparts just
like an 'it gives' [Es gibt], which even 'Being' still needs in
order to attain its essence as presencing."[112] The expression,
'es gibt Sein', indicates that Being is somehow given to man, and
Heidegger implies that the event itself is the giving of Being.
A further clarification of this matter is to be found in his 1962
lecture, *Zeit und Sein*.

In this lecture, Heidegger deals directly with the meaning of
the phrases, 'es gibt Sein' and 'es gibt Zeit'. He interprets
the 'es gibt' literally as 'it gives'. Thus, both Being and time
are gifts.[113] That which gives Being and time, the 'es' of the
'es gibt', is neither Being nor time but rather that which determines both together in their inter-connectedness--i.e., the
event.[114] Since the event is prior to Being and time, and in a
certain sense controls them, it must determine the essence of
man: "So far as time and Being are given only in the event, it
has this characteristic, that it brings man, the one who under-

125

stands Being insofar as he stands in authentic time, into his own essence. Thus determined, man belongs in the event."[115]

It is evident from these descriptions that the event is the ultimate concept in Heidegger's philosophy. Apart from situating the event in relation to man and Being, however, he can say nothing positive about it: "The event neither *is* nor does it *give* the event....What remains to be said? Only this: the event brings to pass."[116] The coming-to-pass of the event is the giving of Being to man. Does this mean that the event is God? Heidegger has been even more reluctant to speak of God in connection with the event than with the holy or the quadrant. Here again, he maintains his separation of philosophy and theology and his belief that God can be described only by theology. Thus, any attempt to locate the concept of God in Heidegger's philosophy must necessarily involve an *interpretation* of his thought—i.e., it must go beyond his own understanding of his philosophy and (to use his own expression) attempt to set forth what has been left unsaid in his writings. If there is to be a theistic interpretation of Heidegger's philosophy, though, the concept which will deserve the closest investigation with regard to its possible identification with God will undoubtedly be the event.

V. Summary.

In order to prepare the way for the evaluation of Heidegger's philosophy in the next chapter, a brief résumé of his treatment of religion is in order. It is clear that Heidegger is keenly interested in this subject. Despite his belief that, as a thinker, he is not competent to deal with religious matters, his philosophy displays many religious characteristics. A number of his key ideas have been adapted from their original religious meaning (e.g., the *revelation* of Being), and his overall description of authentic human existence (in terms of *dwelling*) is closer to the teachings of the major religions than to other philosophers. Furthermore, he has indicated more than once that traditional Christian theology is inadequate *as theology*, and he has urged theologians to produce a theology that reflects more accurately the teachings of the Bible. It is not surprising that his philosophy has evoked such great interest among theologians, although, as we have seen, they have arrived at no consensus with regard to the validity of his reflections on religious topics.

The influence of the Protestant Reformation in general and of Martin Luther in particular is quite evident in Heidegger's discussion of the relation of faith and thinking, and of philosophy and theology. Although he has chosen to be a thinker rather than a theologian, he is quite willing to accept the limits which the

126

Protestant Reformers placed on the competence of human reason, and consequently to regard religious matters (especially God and the divine-human relationship) as off-limits for thinking. Although he says very little about faith as such, it is clear that he regards it as a way of life rather than an intellectual activity, and therefore as impervious to rational criticism. And his distinction between Christianity as a way of life and institutional Christianity (the stronghold of metaphysical theology) reflects the Protestant distinction between the true (invisible) Church of Christ and the historical (visible) Church.

Despite these views on the mutual separation of philosophy from religion, Heidegger finds it impossible to ignore religion altogether. For philosophy in the past and up to the present has been so tangled up with theology that it is necessary to separate the two from each other before either can be attended to properly. The principal subject-matter of philosophy is the question of Being, but traditional metaphysical philosophy has ignored this question, and has dealt instead with beings. One of the major causes of this problem has been the theological character of metaphysics--its concern with the supreme being, God. This concern was evident even in the philosophy of Plato and Aristotle, but it was greatly reinforced by Christianity's identification of its God with the supreme being and first cause of metaphysics. Thus, Christianity is largely responsible for the neglect of the question of Being in philosophy, and Heidegger finds it necessary to criticize this unwarranted intrusion of Christianity into philosophy in order to free both philosophy and theology to deal properly with their respective objects--Being and God.

The identification of God with the supreme being of metaphysics is only one instance of the onto-theo-logical character of traditional Western philosophy. Christianity also adopted the Platonic distinction between the imperfect present natural world and the perfect supernatural world to come, with its consequent devaluation of life on earth. Furthermore, by defining man in relation to God, Christianity has obscured man's more essential (at least for philosophy) relation to Being. Finally, Heidegger considers the preoccupation with certitude of knowledge which is characteristic of modern philosophy to be a direct result of the quest for certitude of salvation which occasioned the Protestant Reformation. In all these respects, Christianity has been a bad influence on philosophy, and at the same time it has been untrue to its own foundation--the Biblical faith--which is essentially incompatible with metaphysical philosophy. As a result, the rejection of metaphysics which Nietzsche began has brought about the rejection of Christianity (the death of God). The metaphysical God is no longer believable, and Christianity has yet to promulgate

a more adequate description of God. The consequent absence of
God is a problem for philosophy as well as theology, since it
refers to the continuing neglect of Being in favour of beings, as
exemplified by modern technology.

Heidegger's explicit treatment of religion is largely negative,
in accordance with his understanding of the philosopher's task.
However, an examination of the major concepts of his thought,
especially man and Being, does reveal that his philosophy is
susceptible of a positive religious evaluation. The principal
aspect of his description of man for this purpose is the importance accorded therein to death. In *Sein und Zeit* man is Being-
towards-death; in Heidegger's later works he is the mortal. In
both instances death refers not just to the ending of life, but
rather characterizes the whole of human life as a distinctive way
to *be*. Heidegger's description of death says nothing either for
or against the possibility of life after death; his concern is
exclusively with this present existence.

The principal implication of this description of man in terms of
death is the radical *finitude* of man. The fact that we are going
to die makes us realize that we are not the source of our own Being, but rather that we depend for our very existence on something
external to us. Since our existence refers not just to the fact
that we are but also to the *way* in which we are (i.e., the beings
that can ask the question of Being), our basic finitude includes
not just the times of our birth and our death but our understanding of Being as well. As human, we have the capabilities of speech
and of thought (which for Heidegger are really the same), and it
is by means of language that we come to know Being. However, this
knowledge of Being is essentially finite, since in all that we do
(including knowing) we are the mortals. Although Being is revealed
by death, it is revealed as finite, since it comes to presence in
man according to his finite way of knowing it. Thus Being is not
God, because there is something beyond Being (i.e., the event)
which *gives* Being to man. Man's proper response to this gift is
described by Heidegger as "serenity with regard to things" and
"openness to the mystery." The domination of beings which characterizes modern technology is totally opposed to this way of dwelling on the earth.

Heidegger's concept of man is thus basically *open*--open to Being
and perhaps also to God. Since he explicitly rejects the identification of Being and God, it is necessary to examine his other
references to God in order to determine whether or not his philosophy is open to a theistic interpretation. His discussion of theism
is complicated by the fact that he speaks of gods, divinities,
divinity, and the holy in addition to God, sometimes with reference
to traditional religion (both Greek and Christian) and sometimes to

128

the poetry of Hölderlin. That his treatment of this topic is
generally consistent, however, is seen in the way he relates his
discussion of these concepts to the question of Being. One of
his dominant themes is the loss of the sense of the sacred in
modern times, which is a loss for both philosophy and religion (he
uses the same term, 'God's absence', in reference to both).
Friedrich Hölderlin was one of the first to recognize this de-
sacralization of the world, and Heidegger feels that his poetry
provides an excellent description of this aspect of modern civilization (which is as valid today as during Hölderlin's own lifetime). According to Hölderlin, this age is one which lies between
the departure of the gods of the past and the arrival of the god
of the future. It is a needy time, but we should not despair,
because the arrival of the god of the future is certain. The poet's
task is to remind men of this fact, so that they can see the
possibility of living fully human lives ('dwelling poetically')
rather than becoming cogs in the machinery of the technological
world-system.

Heidegger considers that the semi-religious imagery used by
Hölderlin is much more appropriate than is the language of traditional metaphysics for expressing the relation of man and Being.
As becomes clear in his discussion of the quadrant, the gods of
Hölderlin are not to be understood as real personal beings, but
refer rather to that aspect of the world in virtue of which men
should have a certain reverence or respect for it. Likewise, the
singular 'God' is the poetic name for Being, and is a particularly
appropriate name because of the way in which man encounters Being—
i.e., Being is *revealed* to man, just as in religion God is revealed (usually by Himself). And just as in religion man can do
nothing by himself to evoke this revelation of God, but must wait
for it to be given to him, so also for Heidegger the revelation
of Being to man is a *gift*, to which man's appropriate response is
gratitude (thinking as thanking).

Despite these obvious analogies between the relation of man and
God in religion and of man and Being in philosophy, Heidegger says
nothing at all about how the God of religion might be described
in relation to Being. The closest he comes to such a discussion
is when he inquires after the 'it' of the 'it gives Being', which
he names the event. The event is his ultimate concept, but
whether or not it can be interpreted as God is a question that
Heidegger has not even raised. He feels that there are too many
preliminary issues to be clarified before this question can be
asked—first, the world must be understood as wholesome, then the
question of Being can be investigated, then the realm of the holy
(the sacred aspect of Being) can be considered, then the essence
of divinity and finally the reality of God. Just where the event

fits in is unclear, except that it does lie beyond Being. Heidegger's primary concern is with the question of Being, and so he can only indicate the existence of the other realms. Thus, we can expect no answer from Heidegger as to the place of God in his thought, because God is not to be found therein, but beyond.

In conclusion we can say that Heidegger does provide us with a certain limited philosophy of religion, despite his aversion to this term. It now remains for us to evaluate his treatment of religion, with particular reference to the viewpoint provided by the American tradition of philosophy of religion.

1. Heidegger, "Brief über den 'Humanismus'", *Wegmarken*, Frankfurt (V. Klostermann: 1967), p. 182 (E.T., p. 294).

2. This work was first published, along with a French translation, in *Archives de philosophie* XXXII (1969), pp. 356-395. We will cite the first German edition published in Frankfurt by V. Klostermann in 1970.

3. Cf. Otto Pöggeler, *La pensée de Heidegger*, Paris (Aubier-Montaigne: 1967), pp. 52-54. Heidegger himself states in *Sein und Zeit*, p. 10: "*Theology* is seeking a more primordial interpretation of man's Being toward God, prescribed by the meaning of faith itself and remaining within it. It is slowly beginning to understand once more Luther's insight that the 'foundation' on which its system of dogma rests [i.e., Greek metaphysics] has not arisen from an inquiry in which faith is primary, and that conceptually this 'foundation' not only is inadequate for the problematic of theology, but conceals and distorts it."

4. Although Heidegger has been most reluctant to reveal what religion means to him personally, the following comment on Bultmann indicates that he may have been somewhat conservative at one time: "When I came to Marburg in 1923, my friend Bultmann had removed so much from the New Testament that there was almost nothing left." Heidegger, *Heraklit*, Frankfurt (V. Klostermann: 1970), p. 222.

5. Heidegger, *Phänomenologie und Theologie*, pp. 14f.

6. *Ibid.*, p. 18.

7. *Ibid.*, pp. 21-27.

8. *Ibid.*, pp. 27-30. Cf. also *Sein und Zeit*, p. 306n.: "The Being-guilty which belongs primordially to Dasein's state of Being, must be distinguished from the *status corruptionis* as understood in theology. Theology can find in Being-guilty, as existentially defined, an ontological condition for the factical possibility of such a *status*. The guilt which is included in the idea of this *status*, is a factical indebtedness of an utterly peculiar kind. It has its own attestation, which remains closed off in principle from any philosophical experience. The existential analysis of Being-guilty, proves nothing either *for* or *against* the possibility of sin. Taken strictly, it cannot even be said that the ontology of Dasein

of itself leaves this possibility open; for this ontology, as a philosophical inquiry, 'knows' in principle nothing about sin."

9. Heidegger, *Phänomenologie und Theologie*, p. 32. Cf. also Heidegger, *Nietzsche*, vol. 1, Pfullingen (G. Neske: 1961), pp. 14f.: "There is no Christian philosophy. There is no genuine philosophy which has to be determined from outside itself. There is therefore no heathen philosophy either, especially since 'the heathen' is still something Christian, the anti-Christian. One ought not to describe the Greek thinkers and poets as heathen."

10. Heidegger, "Vom Wesen des Grundes," *Wegmarken*, p. 55n; "Brief über den 'Humanismus'", *Wegmarken*, p. 181 (E.T., p. 294).

11. Heidegger, "Vom Wesen des Grundes," *Wegmarken*, p. 58n.

12. Heidegger, "Einleitung zu Was ist Metaphysik?" *Wegmarken*, p. 208 (E.T., p. 218).

13. Heidegger, *Einführung in die Metaphysik*, Tübingen (Max Niemeyer: 1953), p. 6 (E.T., p. 6).

14. Heidegger, *Schellings Abhandlung Uber das Wesen der menschlichen Freiheit (1809)*, Tübingen (Max Niemeyer: 1971), p. 61.

15. We will continue to use the term 'philosophy' to designate both traditional metaphysics and Heidegger's thinking.

16. Heidegger, "Platons Lehre von der Wahrheit," *Wegmarken*, p. 141.

17. Heidegger, *Die Frage nach dem Ding*, Tübingen (Max Niemeyer: 1962), pp. 84f. (E.T., pp. 109f.).

18. Heidegger, *Nietzsche*, vol. 2, Pfullingen (G. Neske: 1961), p. 348.

19. *Ibid.*, p. 83. Cf. also Heidegger, *Einführung in die Metaphysik*, p. 80 (E.T., pp. 89f.) and *Nietzsche*, vol. 1, pp. 257, 543.

20. Heidegger, "Nietzsches Wort 'Gott ist tot'", *Holzwege*, Frankfurt (V. Klostermann: 1950), p. 203.

21. Heidegger, *Unterwegs zur Sprache*, Pfullingen (G. Neske: 1959), p. 203.

22. Heidegger, *Einführung in die Metaphysik*, p. 103 (E.T., pp. 113f.). Cf. Heidegger, "Aletheia (Heraklit, Fragment 16)," *Vorträge und Aufsätze*, vol. 3, Pfullingen (G. Neske: 1954), p. 56 for another example of a Christian misinterpretation of Heraclitus: Clement of Alexandria's identification of the imperishable in Heraclitus' thought with the Christian God.

23. Heidegger, *Sein und Zeit*, pp. 49f.

24. Heidegger, *Nietzsche*, vol. 2, pp. 426f.

25. Heidegger, "Wer ist Nietzsches Zarathustra?" *Vorträge und Aufsätze*, vol. 3, p. 77.

26. Heidegger, "Nietzsches Wort 'Gott ist tot'", *Holzwege*, pp. 199f.

27. Heidegger, *Der Satz vom Grund*, Pfullingen (G. Neske: 1957), p. 55.

28. Heidegger, *Identität und Differenz*, Pfullingen (G. Neske: 1957), pp. 64f.

29. Heidegger, "Brief über den 'Humanismus'", *Wegmarken*, p. 179 (E.T., pp. 292f.).

30. Heidegger, "Nietzsches Wort 'Gott ist tot'", *Holzwege*, pp. 239f.

31. Heidegger, "Die Zeit des Weltbildes," *Holzwege*, p. 70.

32. Heidegger, "Wozu Dichter?" *Holzwege*, p. 248.

33. The literal meaning of 'Dasein' is 'there-being'.

34. Cf. James M. Demske, *Being, Man, and Death*, Lexington, Kentucky (The University Press of Kentucky: 1970), p. 3: "...the concept of death is especially well suited to serve as a guide through the labyrinth of Heidegger's thought. It belongs to the area of his central concern, which is the problem of being as appearing to man, or, seen from the other end of the relation, the problem of human existence in

the world of being. Thus, Heidegger's philosophy of death can be understood only against the background of his philosophy of man and of being, and, conversely, his philosophy of man and of being will be appreciated in its full significance and rigorous continuity only insofar as his thoughts on death receive adequate consideration. The problems of death on the one hand, and being and man on the other, mutually illumine and clarify one another."

35. Heidegger, *Sein und Zeit*, p. 233.

36. *Ibid.*

37. *Ibid.*, p. 247.

38. Thus Heidegger is not concerned with what comes after death. Cf. *Sein und Zeit*, pp. 247f.: "If 'death' is defined as the 'end' of Dasein--that is to say, of Being-in-the-world--this does not imply any ontical decision whether 'after death' still another Being is possible, either higher or lower, or whether Dasein 'lives on' or even 'outlasts' itself and is 'immortal'. Nor is anything decided ontically about the 'other-worldly' and its possibility, any more than about the 'this-worldly'; it is not as if norms and rules for comporting oneself towards death were to be proposed for 'edification'. But our analysis of death remains purely 'this-worldly' in so far as it Interprets that phenomenon merely in the way in which it *enters into* any particular Dasein as a possibility of its Being. Only when death is conceived in its full ontological essence can we have any methodological assurance in even *asking* what *may be after death*; only then can we do so with meaning and justification. Whether such a question is a possible *theoretical* question at all will not be decided here. The this-worldly ontological Interpretation of death takes precedence over any ontical other-worldly speculation."

39. Heidegger, *Sein und Zeit*, p. 253.

40. *Ibid.*, p. 263.

41. *Ibid.*, p. 266.

42. *Ibid.*, p. 298.

43. *Ibid.*, p. 308.

44. *Ibid.*, p. 384.

45. Heidegger, *Kant und das Problem der Metaphysik*, Frankfurt (V. Klostermann: 1973), pp. 20-36 (E.T., pp. 27-42).

46. *Ibid.*, p. 222 (E.T., p. 237).

47. Henri Birault gives as the reason for this abandonment the onto-theo-logical character of the notion of 'finitude'. Cf. his article, "Heidegger at la pensée de la finitude," *Revue internationale de Philosophie* 14 (1960), pp. 157-162. We will continue to use this term to signify the subordinate role that man occupies in his relationship with Being.

48. Heidegger, *Einführung in die Metaphysik*, p. 121 (E.T., p. 133).

49. Heidegger, *Erläuterungen zu Hölderlins Dichtung*, Frankfurt (V. Klostermann: 1951), pp. 31f. (E.T., pp. 270f.).

50. *Ibid.*, p. 116.

51. Heidegger, "Wozu Dichter?" *Holzwege*, p. 279.

52. Heidegger, *Unterwegs zur Sprache*, p. 215.

53. Heidegger, "Brief über den 'Humanismus'", *Wegmarken*, p. 145 (E.T., p. 271).

54. Heidegger, *Sein und Zeit*, pp. 148-150, 160-166. Cf. also James M. Demske, *Being, Man, and Death*, pp. 142-144.

55. This term has also been translated as 'quadrate', 'square', and 'foursome'.

56. Heidegger, "Das Ding," *Vorträge und Aufsätze*, vol. 2, pp. 44-46.

57. Heidegger, "Bauen Wohnen Denken," *Vorträge und Aufsätze*, vol. 2, p. 24.

58. *Ibid.*, p. 36.

59. *Ibid.*, pp. 24f.

60. Heidegger, "Gelassenheit," *Martin Heidegger zum 80. Geburt-*

stag, Frankfurt (V. Klostermann: 1969), p. 28.

61. Heidegger, "Das Ding," *loc. cit.*, p. 51.

62. Heidegger, "Bauen Wohnen Denken," *loc. cit.*, p. 25.

63. Heidegger, *Sein und Zeit*, pp. 7, 12.

64. Heidegger, "Was ist Metaphysik?" *Wegmarken*, p. 17 (E.T., p. 346).

65. Heidegger, "Brief über den 'Humanismus'", *Wegmarken*, p. 145 (E.T., p. 271).

66. *Ibid.*, p. 164 (E.T., p. 283).

67. *Ibid.*, pp. 162, 172 (E.T., 281, 288).

68. The crosses illustrate the interplay of the four elements of the quadrant.

69. Heidegger, "Kants These über das Sein," *Wegmarken*, p. 306: "Being can not *be*. If it could be, then it would no longer 'be' Being, but would be a being."

70. Heidegger, "Zeit und Sein," *Zur Sache des Denkens*, Tübingen (Max Niemeyer: 1969), p. 5.

71. *Ibid.*, p. 16: "Die Zeit ist nicht. Es gibt die Zeit."

72. *Ibid.*, p. 20.

73. Heidegger, "Zeit und Sein," *Ibid.*, p. 21.

74. *Ibid.*, p. 24.

75. Heidegger, "Brief über den 'Humanismus'", *Wegmarken*, p. 162 (E.T., p. 282).

76. Heidegger, "Wozu Dichter?" *Holzwege*, p. 272.

77. Heidegger, *Die Technik und die Kehre*, Pfullingen (G. Neske: 1962), p. 46.

78. Heidegger, "Wozu Dichter?" *Holzwege*, p. 248.

79. Heidegger, *Erläuterungen zu Hölderlins Dichtung*, p. 44 (E.T., p. 289). Cf. also Heidegger's own poem, *Aus der Erfahrung des Denkens*, Pfullingen (G. Neske: 1954), p. 7: "We have come too late for the gods and too early for Being."

80. Heidegger, *Erläuterungen zu Hölderlins Dichtung*, p. 104.

81. Heidegger, "Wozu Dichter?" *Holzwege*, p. 250.

82. Heidegger, "Brief über den 'Humanismus'", *Wegmarken*, p. 182 (E.T., p. 294).

83. Heidegger, *Erläuterungen zu Hölderlins Dichtung*, p. 63.

84. *Ibid.*, p. 58.

85. Heidegger, "Vom Wesen und Begriff der *PHYSIS*. Aristoteles' Physik B, 1," *Wegmarken*, p. 310.

86. Heidegger, *Erläuterungen zu Hölderlins Dichtung*, p. 74.

87. *Ibid.*, p. 43 (E.T., p. 288).

88. *Ibid.*, p. 116.

89. *Ibid.*, pp. 139f. Cf. also pp. 98-101 of the same work.

90. *Ibid.*, p. 39 (E.T., pp. 282f.). Cf. also Heidegger, "...dichterisch wohnt der Mensch...," *Vorträge und Aufsätze*, vol. 2, pp. 61-78.

91. Heidegger, *Erläuterungen zu Hölderlins Dichtung*, p. 86.

92. *Ibid.*, p. 19 (E.T., p. 253).

93. *Ibid.*, p. 19 (E.T., pp. 253f.).

94. Heidegger, "...dichterisch wohnt der Mensch...," *Vorträge und Aufsätze*, vol. 2, p. 71.

95. Heidegger, *Erläuterungen zu Hölderlins Dichtung*, p. 108.

96. Cf. Martin Buber, "Gottesfinsternis" (The Eclipse of God), *Werke*, vol. 1: Schriften zur Philosophie, München (Kösel Verlag: 1962), p. 557 for a vigorous critique of Heidegger on this matter.

97. Heidegger, "Brief über den 'Humanismus'", *Wegmarken*, pp. 181f. (E.T., p. 294).

98. Heidegger, "Nachwort zu Was ist Metaphysik?" *Wegmarken*, p. 107 (E.T., p. 360).

99. Heidegger, *Erläuterungen zu Hölderlins Dichtung*, p. 66.

100. Heidegger, "Bauen Wohnen Denken," *Vorträge und Aufsätze*, vol. 2, p. 25.

101. *Ibid.*, p. 24. Cf. also "Das Ding," *loc. cit.*, p. 51.

102. Heidegger, "Das Ding," *loc. cit.*, p. 45.

103. Heidegger, "Nachwort zu Was ist Metaphysik?" *Wegmarken*, p. 105 (E.T., p. 358).

104. Heidegger, *Was heisst Denken?* Tübingen (Max Niemeyer: 1954), p. 94 (E.T., p. 143).

105. Heidegger, *Identität und Differenz*, p. 24.

106. *Ibid.*, p. 26.

107. *Ibid.*, p. 27.

108. Heidegger, *Unterwegs zur Sprache*, p. 259.

109. *Ibid.*, pp. 260f.

110. *Ibid.*, p. 259.

111. *Ibid.*

112. *Ibid.*, p. 258.

113. Heidegger, "Zeit und Sein," *Zur Sache des Denkens*, pp. 6, 18.

114. *Ibid.*, p. 20.

115. *Ibid.*, p. 24.

116. *Ibid.*

Heidegger and the Americans

Our topic in this work has been the religious significance of Heidegger's philosophy. The first chapter dealt with previous (mostly theological) interpretations of Heidegger, and it was seen that none of them has won general acceptance. The principal reason for this lack of consensus is the division among Heidegger's interpreters with regard to the validity of the philosophical study of religion, whether independent (philosophy of religion) or in the service of theology (philosophical theology). Furthermore, there seemed to be no agreement among philosophers as to the possibility or the necessity of philosophy of religion. However, there does exist at least one major philosophical tradition in which the philosophy of religion plays a very important part, namely the American 'pragmatic' tradition, and so the second chapter was devoted to an exposition of this tradition, first by way of its major representatives, and then by a summary of its principal features. The result of this study was a realization that the philosophy of religion is a valid enterprise, and consequently a confidence that an investigation of the religious significance of Heidegger's philosophy would not be an automatic failure. Chapter three was devoted to an exposition of Heidegger's treatment of religious topics, and revealed that he does indeed have a philosophy of religion, despite his own rejection of that term. It now remains for us to evaluate the religious significance of his philosophy in the light of the American approach to the philosophy of religion. This evaluation can be divided into four sections: 1) Heidegger's views on the relation of philosophy and religion; 2) his own treatment of religion; 3) a sketch of a more complete Heideggerian philosophy of religion; and 4) his significance for philosophical theology.

I. Philosophy and Religion.

It is obvious by now that Heidegger and the Americans do not share the same view of the relation of philosophy and religion. Although they both criticize traditional metaphysical theology, only the Americans attempt a reconstruction of the concepts of God and the divine-human relationship. For Heidegger, this is a task for the theologians; the concept of God has no place in philosophy. The basis of his attitude is his belief that faith and reason (or thinking) are two different human activities, and any attempt to synthesize them is bound to fail.

This attitude of Heidegger is understandable as a reaction against the admixture of Greek metaphysical philosophy and the Christian faith whose inadequacies have become all too obvious in recent times. It would seem, however, that Heidegger has overreacted in this regard. To separate faith and reason to the degree which he seems to require would be to deprive religion of any objective standard of evaluation, since every man's faith, no matter how bizarre or harmful, would be impervious to rational criticism. Furthermore, Heidegger distinguishes faith and reason according to the unconditional character of the former and the problematic character of the latter.[1] But given the results of recent scholarship with regard to the historically and culturally conditioned character of religious faith, Heidegger's distinction appears misfounded. Indeed, the radical separation of faith and reason is a carryover from the very Greek onto-theo-logy which Heidegger is attempting to overcome. In this tradition, as one of the Americans treated above has shown, "faith is but a sub-stitute for knowledge, made available to us in the absence of the possibility of real knowledge,"[2] and is therefore something different from 'real' human experience. Heidegger himself has said very little about faith in his published works, although he is reported to have treated this matter in his early teaching years at the University of Freiburg.[3] At this stage of his career Heidegger was very interested in the views of Martin Luther on the relation of philosophy and theology, and it would appear that he has accepted Luther's understanding of faith with-out subjecting it to a philosophical critique. But whether or not he derived his understanding of faith from theology, it is clear that his philosophy displays a positivistic rejection of the philosophy of religion—a rejection that he nowhere justifies on strictly philosophical grounds.

American philosophy of religion, on the contrary, does not eliminate religion from the outset as an appropriate object of its investigation. Even those Americans who display a certain hostility to religion feel that they cannot ignore it, since it plays a significant role in man's understanding of his place in the universe. The empirical approach to reality, which is so characteristic of American philosophy, reveals the certain existence of human religious experience, and although the Americans do not always agree as to the nature and especially the object of that experience, they do feel that to ignore these problems is to allow a serious gap in their interpretation of reality.

In opposition to Heidegger's uncritical understanding of reli-gious faith and its relation to reason (or thinking), the Americans have subjected faith to philosophical analysis. As a result, they feel that faith is better understood as the perfection of ordinary experience than as its imperfect substitute or opponent. The validity and usefulness of religious faith can be judged by philosophical criteria, such as those associated with pragmatism, since faith is a *human* activity (notwithstanding the superior role that God may play in the divine-human relationship).

The use of philosophy in theology is a further point of disagreement between Heidegger and the Americans. Although Heidegger allowed a limited use of philosophy in theology in what concerns the scientific character of the latter discipline—namely, its logical consistency and certain of its concepts—he insisted that the object of theology, the Christian way of life, is entirely distinct from the object of philosophy, Being. Nor can the concept of God in theology be compared with philosophy's concept of Being, since the latter is finite while the former has always been understood as infinite. Thus, Heidegger would not only reject the attempts of Tillich and Macquarrie to describe God in terms of Being, but would maintain that no philosophical concept is capable of describing the God of religious faith.

The theologians among the Americans treated above do not accept the limitations which Heidegger has placed on their use of philosophy, whether his own or any other. They all agree with Tillich that neither philosophy nor theology is complete in itself—philosophy's analysis of human existence raises questions to which theology has the answers, but unless the theologian is aware of these questions, his message will go unheard. In addition, the theologian requires a philosophical explanation of the nature of language and of thinking; these are essential theological tools but ones which are not investigated by theology as such. Therefore, the Americans hold that every theologian is, whether he recognizes it or not, a philosophical theologian. Heidegger's view to the contrary must be rejected.

It is evident, therefore, that the a priori refusal by Heidegger to consider religion as an object of philosophical investigation and his severe limitations on the use of philosophy in theology must be regarded as inadequacies of his thought. This is not to say, however, that his philosophy has no value for religion. For, in spite of his own views, he does treat of topics that are important in religion, and his philosophy compares much more favourably with American philosophy of religion on these topics than on the relation of philosophy and religion.

II. Heidegger and Religion.

As a result of his attitude towards the philosophy of religion, Heidegger's explicit treatment of religious topics is somewhat

141

uneven--he has much more to say on some topics than on others.
American philosophy of religion is generally more complete, and
therefore provides a useful basis for the evaluation of Heidegger's work. This is not to say that American philosophy of religion is superior to Heidegger's thought in every respect. Rather,
it will be shown below that each of the two approaches has its
strong points and its weaknesses, and that what is needed is a
critical synthesis of the two.

In determining the meaning and content of the expression,
'philosophy of religion', as used here, we shall continue the
practice established earlier in this work of allowing the philosophers and theologians treated here to suggest their own
topics for consideration as the subject-matter of philosophy of
religion and philosophical theology. In our evaluation of the
theological interpretations of Heidegger, we saw that there were
four principal topics of concern to the relationship of philosophy and theology, namely: man, God, language and revelation.
The first two of these topics proved to be of major interest to
the American philosophers of religion as well, in addition to the
relation of faith and reason and the pragmatic aspect of religious
experience. Finally, we saw that Heidegger himself deals with
certain religious topics (although he does not acknowledge them
to be religious), namely: man's relation to reality, especially
to that which is greater than him, and the various aspects of this
relationship: death, thinking, language and dwelling. It is
apparent, therefore, that notwithstanding the differences of
emphasis among the various individuals treated above, they all
share the same general understanding of what constitutes the
meeting-place of philosophy and religion--namely, the description
of God and the relationship of man to God (which also includes
the relationship of man to the rest of reality). And so, it is
on the basis of this understanding of the philosophy of religion
that we are going to compare Heidegger and the Americans. This
is not to deny that there are other, perhaps equally valid,
approaches to the philosophy of religion. It means simply that
we are choosing to deal with what Heidegger and the Americans
have actually said about the philosophy of religion rather than
with what they might have said. Thus, we can give a complete
comparison of their approaches to the philosophy of religion by
dealing with their views on the following three topics: a) traditional theology; b) man; and c) God.

A. Traditional Theology.

On this topic more than any other Heidegger and the Americans
are in fundamental agreement. They are all reacting against the

Greek metaphysical tradition of philosophy, which they feel has been quite inadequate both as philosophy and as the philosophical basis of Christian theology. Although Heidegger would consider the American critique of metaphysics to be insufficiently radical, since it concentrates on the attributes of beings (especially the relation of man to other beings through knowledge) rather than on the question of Being, nevertheless he has come to many of the same conclusions as the Americans with regard to specific inadequacies of metaphysics (e.g., the concept of knowledge as the overcoming of an original separation between knowing subject and known object and the correlative concept of truth as the conformity of the mind to reality). Since metaphysics is inadequate as philosophy, it is ipso facto unsuitable for theological use.

Although Heidegger's critique of traditional metaphysical theology is undertaken for philosophical reasons (i.e., the purification of philosophy from theological concepts), his treatment of this topic is no less thorough than the Americans', who consider themselves quite free to evaluate religion as religion. They all criticize the adoption by Christianity of the Platonic view of reality, according to which the present natural world is inferior to the supernatural world of the beyond. The traditional theological description of God is also regarded by both as inadequate. Heidegger is especially critical of the description of God as the highest being, the uncaused cause and the supreme value, while the Americans concentrate on the unseemliness of the traditional divine 'attributes'--infinity, immutability, impassibility, etc. Heidegger's reaction to the metaphysical description of God would be readily acceptable to the Americans: "To this God man can neither pray nor offer sacrifice. Before the causa sui man can neither fall to his knees nor sing and dance."[4] But whereas Heidegger criticizes the traditional theological concept of God because of its incompatibility with the God of the Bible, which he seems to accept as normative (at least for Christians), the Americans generally feel that the critique of the metaphysical God need not lead back to the Biblical God but rather forward to a concept of God which surpasses all previous descriptions of divinity.

The most severe critics of traditional theology among the Americans are Alfred North Whitehead, Charles Hartshorne and Leslie Dewart. Whitehead objected to traditional theological formulations, such as the description of God as unchangeable, on *philosophical* grounds: "God is not to be treated as an exception to all metaphysical principles, invoked to save their collapse. He is their chief exemplification."[5] (Heidegger would agree with the first part of this formulation, but not the second.) The categories of Greek metaphysical philosophy, which have in the past been used to explain the Christian faith, are as inadequate for that task as they are for providing a sound philosophical explanation of the world today, and Whitehead would agree with Heidegger that theologians must rid their discipline of this Greek metaphysical heritage.

This critical analysis of traditional metaphysical philosophy is developed at considerable length by Charles Hartshorne, with particular emphasis on the classical description of God as absolute in all respects. Since God is the key concept in theology, the inadequacy of the classical description of God renders all of traditional theology suspect, and until theologians come to grips with Hartshorne's arguments in favour of panentheism, their theological enterprises will rest on foundations of sand.

Finally, Leslie Dewart has been most outspoken in his criticism of traditional theology, and he feels that a systematic 'dehellenization' of both philosophy and theology is urgently needed. The classical explanations of truth, reality and being are quite inadequate in the light of contemporary human self-consciousness, and they must be reinterpreted in meta-metaphysical terms. Thus, it can be seen that these Americans are in basic agreement with Heidegger as to the philosophical shortcomings of traditional theology, and together they argue a very strong case for the need to undertake a radical revision of theology in the light of modern philosophical developments.

As we saw in the first chapter, the critique of the metaphysical basis of traditional Christian theology by Heidegger and the Americans has been appreciated by most Christian theologians (at least to a certain extent). The same cannot be said for the disparagement of institutional Christianity which Heidegger practises along with some of the Americans (not the philosophical theologians among them), and on this point both Heidegger and the Americans need to be corrected. Heidegger's distinction between Christianity as a way of life and institutional Christianity, while valid to a certain degree, still ignores the communitarian aspect of religious faith and the necessity for an institutional structure of some sort to preserve and develop the faith. Furthermore, the historical basis of his distinction between the primitive New Testament Christian faith and the Christian Church of later times is at best hypothetical, and at any rate should not be confused with the adoption of a Greek philosophical framework by the developing Church for the elaboration of its faith into a theology. And this very adoption should not be criticized because of the inadequacy of this theology for our own times; it was rather the untimely *retention* of this theology, the failure to continue its development, which has resulted in the present situation.[6] The rejection by Heidegger and the American philosophers of *all* institutional religion because of the inadequacy of its past forms betrays a certain unjustified arbitrariness on their part, which is out of keeping with an open-minded approach to the philosophy of religion.

Thus, the comparison of Heidegger and the Americans with regard to their attitude towards traditional religion reveals a basic agreement among them. Their critiques of metaphysics are complementary rather than identical, and thus would benefit from greater familiarity with each other (which has been extremely limited in the past, particularly on Heidegger's part). Together they show that any adequate philosophy of religion in the future must be developed on a non- (or meta-) metaphysical basis. However, such a future philosophy of religion will have to take into account something which both Heidegger and the Americans have failed to deal with sufficiently—namely, the communitarian (institutional) aspect of religion.

Needless to say, there is more to this communitarian aspect of religion than church buildings and clergy, especially as these have functioned traditionally. The institutional forms of religion must be just as open to change and development as religious doctrines. Throughout this change, however, they remain necessary, since human religious experience is not simply individual, but social as well. There are three major aspects of the social character of religion: 1) some sort of institutional framework is necessary to ensure that a particular religious tradition survives from generation to generation; 2) each individual human being requires religious instruction if he or she is to be capable of interpreting religious experience; this instruction is provided, at least indirectly, by religious institutions; 3) finally, the religious experience itself often occurs in a social setting—notable occasions include birth, marriage, and death—and cannot therefore be relegated to the realm of individual solitude.

The role of the Church has been a central issue in traditional Christian theology, but is generally neglected by philosophy of religion. It would seem from the above considerations, however, that there would be no fully-developed religion without some sort of 'church', and therefore a complete philosophy of religion cannot exclude this social dimension of religion. The development of a Heideggerian 'ecclesiology' is a task for the philosophical theologian rather than the philosopher of religion, but the latter should be ever aware that he, too, is dealing with a social, not just an individual, phenomenon.

145

B. Man.

Whereas traditional theology defines man in relation to an already established concept of God, philosophy must do just the reverse. The concept of man is logically prior to the concept of God in philosophy, and indeed the latter depends to a considerable extent on the former. Although Heidegger does not develop a specific concept of God, his description of man can be evaluated in terms of its suitability for a theistic interpretation. American philosophy of religion, on the other hand, is quite prepared to speak of God in relation to man, and to the extent that it does deal with God, its concept of man is already theistic.

Although Heidegger does not treat of human religious experience as such, his description of man is very suggestive of a religious interpretation. The role of death in his concept of man emphasizes the openness of man beyond himself to Being and to that which gives Being. He has elaborated the gift-character of thinking, language, time and Being itself--those factors which are constitutive of human existence. His contrast between human existence as an unthinking technological mastery of the world and as a poetic dwelling upon the earth and his analysis of the holy dimension of Being both contribute to a picture of contemporary man as one who needs to ask the question of God.

For the Americans, too, man is such that he cannot be explained adequately without reference to that which transcends him. Their analysis of human nature reveals the existence there of religious experience, which is just as valid as any other type of experience and cannot be explained away by psychology or sociology. Although the object of religious experience--God--is not subject to immediate empirical verification, nevertheless the religious experience itself can be evaluated by philosophy according to the same standards of pragmatic verification--"By their fruits shall you know them"--as with any other type of experience.

This general agreement among American philosophers of religion regarding the religious component of human existence does not prevent them from developing different specific aspects of this topic in their respective systems. William James, for one, devoted considerable attention to such aspects of religious experience as saintliness and mysticism. He felt that these human qualities provided evidence for both the existence of God--"God is real since he produces real effects"[7]--and for our knowledge of the divine nature--in order to inspire fear, hope and expectation, the foundations of the saintly life, God must possess such moral attributes as holiness, justice and love. John Dewey, too, stressed the essentially religious nature of certain important human activities, although he was more reluctant than James to describe God as the object of religious experience. For Dewey, religion refers more to the way in which we act than to our relationship with a God; he speaks more freely of faith in intelligence and faith in democracy than of faith in God. Nevertheless, his description of human existence is quite compatible with a belief in a non-metaphysical God, and Dewey himself was willing to use the term 'God' in this sense.

Alfred North Whitehead and Charles Hartshorne both concentrated on the metaphysical status of God, and said little about human religious experience. However, Whitehead's differentiation of God's consequent from his primordial nature, especially as developed by Hartshorne, John Cobb and Schubert Ogden, has important implications for the description of man's religious nature. It allows for a more genuine interaction between God and man than was the case in traditional metaphysical religious thought; man will naturally act differently towards a deity who can really respond to his changing needs than to one whose desires and actions are fixed for all eternity.

Finally, Paul Tillich, John Macquarrie and Leslie Dewart all consider man's experience of his contingency to be a key element of human religious experience. The realization that we might not have existed at all leads us to ask the question of the source and the meaning of our existence, and this, it is felt, is an essentially religious question. Thus, it can be seen that all the American philosophers of religion (and philosophical theologians) treated above agree that religious experience is a valid and important component of human nature.

In comparing Heidegger's description of man with that of the Americans, one can see that there is a fundamental compatibility between the two, and they complement each other extremely well. Despite Heidegger's reluctance to deal with human religious experience, his analysis of human existence shows that the most important questions that man faces are precisely those which the Americans designate as 'religious'--those which deal with the ultimate meaning of human life. Apart from this basic similarity between Heidegger and the Americans, we can see that the Americans supplement Heidegger's thought in two important respects: 1) they treat religious experience as *religious*, thereby enabling themselves to explore this topic in all its dimensions; and 2) they deal explicitly with the *object* of religious experience (i.e., God). On the other hand, Heidegger's superiority over the Americans is manifested in his rigorous analysis of human nature as such, which is not equalled by any of the Americans. And so, it would appear that neither of the two approaches is sufficient in itself, but taken together they provide a valuable interpretation of human religious experience, and in addition, they offer a

147

sound basis for an elaboration of one of the most important questions for philosophy of religion, how best to describe God.

C. God.

Since Heidegger says nothing at all about God apart from his criticisms of the metaphysical concept of God, it is evident that the American philosophy of religion is much more complete than his own. As with the other major aspects of religion, the Americans feel that the concept of God is a legitimate object of philosophical investigation, and that the 'God of philosophy' cannot be other than the 'God of religion'. For both philosophy and religion, God is the source of meaning and value for the universe (which is *not* to say that he is the highest value). Apart from this, however, the Americans have not produced a common understanding of what God is and what he does. John Dewey, for one, would be reluctant to conceive of God as in any sense personal, whereas most of the others would not reject this traditional attribute of God, however much they may reinterpret it. On the other hand, A. N. Whitehead and Charles Hartshorne describe God from a strictly philosophical point of view, which ignores the specific details of God's interaction with man which are of interest to theologians such as Tillich and Macquarrie. Despite these differences, however, a close examination of the Americans' treatment of God does provide some valuable suggestions for supplementing Heidegger's philosophy of religion on this topic.

The first consequence of the rejection of the traditional metaphysical description of God, as agreed to by both Heidegger and the Americans, is the awareness that God's supremacy must have some limitations. If there is to be any genuine interaction between God and man, then God must in some sense be relative to man, rather than absolute in all respects. For William James, this meant that God is finite. Most of the other Americans have hesitated to describe God in this way, but they all realise the necessity of dealing with this question. Whitehead's solution to the problem was to distinguish two natures in God--his primordial nature, which refers to his absolute superiority over all else, and his consequent nature, which refers to his capacity for interacting with human beings. It is through his consequent nature that God is in process. Charles Hartshorne accepted this way of describing God, and attempted to be more specific about the way in which God relates to the world. He compares this relationship to that of the human mind and body--the world is in a certain sense God's body. Although God is superior to all other beings at any given point in time, he can surpass himself by, for example, learning new things. According to Hartshorne,

God's knowledge of the future is limited.

Whereas John Cobb and Schubert Ogden carry on the Whitehead-Hartshorne understanding of a God in process, Paul Tillich and John Macquarrie feel that the traditional term 'being', if properly understood, is the best one for describing God. In order to distinguish their use of this term from its use in traditional metaphysical philosophy and theology, Tillich speaks of God as the "ground of being" and Macquarrie calls him "holy being." They both feel that 'being' is a more appropriate name for God than 'becoming', which would be the choice of Hartshorne, Cobb and Ogden. In this they are reflecting Heidegger's early emphasis on Being as the most fundamental philosophical concept. However, it can be argued that the description of God in terms of becoming (or of 'presence', as Leslie Dewart would have it) is more compatible with Heidegger's thought, given his wholesale rejection of traditional metaphysical thinking.

It would appear, therefore, that the lack of consensus among the Americans as to the nature of God prevents them from complementing Heidegger's thought on this question as successfully as they do on the rejection of traditional theology and on the religious aspect of human existence. Although the description of God as the source of meaning and value for the universe is evidently compatible with Heidegger's philosophy, it is a matter for debate whether his description of human existence is more suggestive of a God conceived as being, as becoming, or as presence. If a decision on this question can be made on the basis of Heidegger's philosophy, however, it may well help the Americans to overcome the disagreement among themselves on this matter.

We are now ready to draw certain conclusions from our comparison of Heidegger with the American philosophers of religion: 1) the creative approach to the philosophy of religion, as exemplified by the American tradition, is possible, and indeed is superior to the other approaches; 2) according to this understanding of the philosophy of religion, Heidegger's philosophy does contain a valid, albeit limited, philosophy of religion; 3) American philosophy of religion supplements Heidegger's thought at several crucial points (his understanding of the relation of faith and thinking, and his refusal to deal with God). By studying Heidegger's philosophy from a perspective other than his own, we can see that it is of greater significance for religion than he himself (and, indeed, the majority of his theological interpreters) realise. It now remains for us to indicate, if only briefly, the full significance of his thought for the philosophy of religion and for philosophical theology.

III. A Heideggerian Philosophy of Religion.

It should be evident by now that Heidegger's views on the relation of faith and thinking must be rejected in order to derive
the greatest benefit from his philosophy. We shall accept instead the American view that religion is a legitimate object of
philosophical inquiry (and not just of faith), and on this basis
we shall attempt to show how Heidegger's thought is valuable for
the understanding of religion. This section will accordingly deal
first with Heidegger's analysis of human existence, especially
insofar as it reveals the existence of a reality which can be
identified as God, and second, with that reality itself, insofar
as it can be known and described by man.

A. Man and God.

The key factor of Heidegger's analysis of man with regard to
religion is his constant emphasis on the openness of man beyond
himself. Man is not sufficient unto himself and wholly independent of any transcendent reality, but is first of all Being-in-
the-world, and thereby a Being-with-others. Although the rigorous description of human existence which is given in *Sein und
Zeit* concentrates on the individual rather than the communitarian
aspects of man, Heidegger's understanding of language as deter-
minative of human nature and his constant references to mankind
(Mensch) and the mortals (die Sterblichen) prove that he considers
the individual man to be essentially related to other men as well
as to the world in general.

This openness of man to what is outside him is expressed very
clearly in Heidegger's discussion of 'dwelling'. Rather than
attempting to dominate nature, man should respect it. Heidegger
sees a direct link between modern technology and metaphysical
subjectivism--both represent attempts to assert the supremacy of
the human individual over that which lies outside him, and are
therefore fundamentally opposed to Heidegger's ideal of openness
to what lies beyond. The surpassing of metaphysics in all its
forms--thinking, language, and technology--is necessary if man
is to be capable of a genuine encounter with other men, nature,
Being, or God.

The fundamental openness of man to Being is especially evident
in Heidegger's interpretation of death. As a Being-towards-death,
man is essentially finite. The fact that man is going to die
reveals that he is not the master of his destiny. The realization
of his finitude opens man beyond himself in an effort to ascertain
the meaning of his existence. To realize one's finitude is to ask
the question of Being: why is there any Being at all; why is

there not rather nothing? Since death is thus constitutive of man's encounter with Being, Heidegger considers man's most proper name to be 'the mortal'. The mortal is the one who, because he is mortal, can encounter Being. As finite, the mortal encounters Being as finite; death is man's ultimate limitation and is therefore the basis of his limited (finite) understanding of Being.

Man's encounter with Being as finite entails that Being, although constitutive of man's very essence, is not the ultimate source of human existence. Being is not God nor a substitute for God. Being is itself given to man by some reality beyond it, some indescribable 'other'. Thus Heidegger's description of Being and its relation to man confirms the fundamental openness of man and points beyond both man and Being to a source of all that is.

Heidegger's limitation of the meaning of death to its significance for this life neither affirms nor denies the possibility of some sort of continued human reality after death. A philosophical exploration of this problem would not be incompatible with his thought, however, especially if it were to be shown that man's openness to some reality beyond Being could be fulfilled and perfected in an actual encounter with that reality at the moment of death.

Man's fundamental openness does not of itself necessitate a religious interpretation, especially since we are concerned primarily with the understanding of religion in the Western Christian tradition. In this tradition, the notion of *God* is generally considered to be essential to religion, but it would be possible to conceive of Heidegger's reality beyond Being as other than God: as fate, the devil, space-time, etc. Since Heidegger does not attempt to name this reality, much less describe it, his philosophy is theistically neutral. It does seem, however, that this reality which Heidegger indicates can be fittingly described as God, and therefore that his philosophy contains implicitly the essential elements of the philosophy of religion.

B. God and Man.

What meaning can be ascribed to the term 'God' for it to be compatible with Heidegger's thought? The traditional metaphysical concept of God is evidently inadequate, and Heidegger has done religion a great service by demonstrating this inadequacy. But since Heidegger has not attempted a reformulation of the traditional description of God, we must look elsewhere for a more adequate description--one which can serve as a standpoint from

151

which to evaluate the theistic potential of his thought. It would appear that this service can be provided by American philosophy of religion, which, despite its lack of unanimity on all aspects of the nature of God, has at least investigated this problem very thoroughly and has come to some agreement on certain important points. With regard to both the concept of God and man's relation to God, the significance of Heidegger's thought for religion can best be understood from the standpoint of American philosophy of religion.

Heidegger's most explicit references to God are negative--God is neither Being nor a being. Thus, it is necessary to go beyond Being for an appropriate description of God, and Heidegger has indicated in his discussion of the 'event' that he does envisage some sort of reality beyond Being. Although he does not speak of this reality as God, he does describe it as the source of Being and of time, a description which is quite compatible with most concepts of God. This refusal of Heidegger to limit all of reality to being is therefore the key to a theistic interpretation of his philosophy, especially from the standpoint of American philosophy of religion. For the Americans have been no less concerned than Heidegger to free both philosophy and religion from their metaphysical heritage. As far back as Peirce, they were describing God in terms of *meaning* rather than being, and this emphasis has continued into the most recent works of Macquarrie and Dewart. Likewise, the description of God in terms of *process* begun by Whitehead and continued by Hartshorne, Cobb and Ogden represents another attempt to overcome the limitations of the metaphysical concept of God. Thus, it is evident that a Heideggerian philosophy of religion can easily accommodate the description of God contained in American philosophy of religion.

If, then, Heidegger's reality beyond Being is to be interpreted as God, what, in fact, can be said about it? Since we are dealing with a philosophy of religion rather than a revealed theology, it is evident that we must begin with man's experience of God rather than with God's description of himself. Man's first and foremost indication of God is his realization of the contingency of being--in Heidegger's expression, why is there any being at all and not rather nothing? This contingency is especially evident with regard to man's own being, since he knows that he is finite--that he is going to die. Since our being is contingent-- that is, since there seems to be no reason why we might never have come to be--Heidegger feels that we should regard our being as a *gift*. The question of the meaning of human existence necessarily involves a search for the giver of this gift--i.e., for the source of our being. Heidegger himself feels that the ultimate source of our being is beyond the scope of philosophical investigation, and he is content simply to point out the openness of man to this source of his being and the duty of man to acknowledge the gift of his being by living a fully human--i.e., thinking--life (thinking as thanking). The Americans, however, feel that more can be said about the source of human existence, especially with regard to the *meaning* of existence.

The American description of God in terms of meaning finds its best expression in the writings of Leslie Dewart. He maintains that the meaning of human existence, and of being in general, is not to be found within being itself, since the latter is no less contingent than human existence and cannot, therefore, be the source of its own meaning. Man can make being meaningful in part, inasmuch as he can know being. But he is not able to give meaning to his own being, since his primary relation to his own being--i.e., consciousness--is an awareness of himself precisely as being (since consciousness is the presence of being to itself) and therefore as contingent. But the absolute contingency of all being, including man's own, implies that there is a reality beyond being, a reality in which the meaning of existence is to be found. Since this reality is not directly evident to man, it must be appropriated in faith. The alternative to such a faith would be the denial of meaning to existence. This reality which gives meaning to human existence is the very source of all being, God.

Man's relation to God can best be described in terms of religious experience or faith. Although God is a reality beyond being, he is encountered only in being, and especially in human existence. In his experience of the contingency of being, man can choose to regard being as meaningful in terms of God; he can choose to believe. This integration of faith and 'ordinary' human experience means that man can encounter God in all his actions and in all beings, since God is there precisely as the ultimate meaning of being. This does not mean that God has predetermined the precise meaning of every being and every action in advance, and that we must somehow ascertain that meaning and act accordingly. Faith in God means rather living one's life as a fully mature conscious being, aware of man's privilege and responsibility for creating the future, yet confident that human existence is ultimately meaningful because of the presence of God.

This description of God in terms of meaning fits in well with Heidegger's discussion of poetry. Although as we have seen, Heidegger uses religious terminology in this discussion solely in reference to Hölderlin's poetry and not to theology or religion, it nevertheless remains possible to give a religious interpretation to his thinking on this subject as elsewhere. Heidegger describes poetry as a relation between men and Being;

153

the poet is the privileged mortal who can experience and name the sacred aspect of reality. To dwell poetically on the earth means to let things be; i.e., it is the exact opposite of the technological domination of things which holds sway in modern western civilization. Thus, the poet is engaged in determining the true meaning of existence. Since Heidegger contends that every person should dwell poetically on the earth, it would seem that we all have the duty and responsibility to investigate the meaning of our existence. If we are prepared to look beyond ourselves and beyond Being for the meaning of our existence, then Heidegger's poetic dwelling becomes one with faith in God.

Although the description of God in terms of meaning is the major contribution of American philosophy of religion to a Heideggerianism theism, it is by no means the only such contribution. The Americans have also attempted to explain the cosmic function of God—that is, the role of God in the establishment and the operation of the world-order (including the lives of humans). Like Heidegger, they regard the traditional metaphysical descriptions of God as inadequate—God as first cause, supreme value, infinite, omnipotent, omniscient, etc. There is a general reluctance to assign to God the credit for having created the universe out of nothing, since this notion is scientifically problematic. However, the description of God as the source of law in the universe is widespread among the Americans, especially the scientists among them, Peirce and Whitehead. And with regard to the relation of God and man in particular, the Americans have produced some of their most original insights. Especially among the process philosophers and theologians we find an understanding of God as capable of change and development, and therefore as genuinely involved with and affected by human beings. The development of this panentheistic conception of God represents an important innovation in the philosophical understanding of Western Christianity, and is of major significance for a Heideggerian philosophy of religion since it accords so well with the elements of Heidegger's thought which are relevant to religion, such as the openness of man to that which lies beyond Being. The panentheistic conception of God is not the only one which is compatible with Heidegger's philosophy, but if it proves to be superior to other conceptions of God, it can readily take its place in any future Heideggerian philosophy of religion.

It is evident, therefore, that there is 'room' in Heidegger's thought for a non-metaphysical concept of God, and that the American description of God can serve to fill this significant gap in Heidegger's philosophy of religion. But what then? Even if we develop a systematic philosophy of religion based on Heidegger's description of man and his relation to Being, will this

provide us with all that religion has to offer? Will the God
of this philosophy of religion be, any more than the God of
metaphysics, the one to whom man can pray and offer sacrifice,
fall to his knees, and sing and dance? Or are these responses to
God themselves inappropriate for the divine-human relationship,
rightly understood? These questions have usually been treated by
theologians rather than by philosophers, but given the freedom
with which American philosophers of religion deal with religious
topics, it is questionable whether or not there are *any* religious
topics which are the exclusive concern of theologians. A fully-
developed Heideggerian philosophy of religion would need to
include a treatment of all aspects of the divine-human relationship. For the present we shall consider just two of these
aspects: mysticism and ethics.

The word 'mystic' means many different things to different
people. We shall use it here to designate a person who attempts
to experience union with the divine or the absolute. Since this
union is strictly speaking inexpressible, mystics communicate
their experiences in language which is highly symbolical. This
has resulted in a widespread dismissal of mysticism by positivistic
philosophers as meaningless self-deception, incapable of objective
verification.

Heidegger's philosophy has not infrequently been referred to as
a species of mysticism. And indeed there are some superficial
similarities between his writings and those of the mystics. They
both are convinced of the inadequacy of ordinary language (including traditional metaphysical language) to express their
ideas. And they both attempt to overcome this difficulty by using
language in novel ways. We have seen examples of this in Heidegger's discussion of Hölderlin's poetic imagery and in his description of a thing in terms of the 'quadrant'. But this creative
approach to language is hardly enough to qualify Heidegger as a
mystic. More important in that respect is the *content* of his
philosophy. Here, the apparent parallel between the mystic's
attitude towards the divine and Heidegger's attitude towards
Being is complicated by Heidegger's subordination of Being to the
'event' in his later works. It is therefore quite problematical
to speak of a mystical union with Being in Heidegger's philosophy.
It may indeed be possible to envisage such a union of man and the
event, but as we have seen, Heidegger says so little about the
event that the possibility of such a union cannot be determined
by reference to him.

Apart from Heidegger's own silence on this matter, it would
seem that the mystical union of man and God is not ruled out by
the other elements of his philosophy of religion, especially if
the panentheistic concept of God were assimilated into his

155

thought. Indeed, such a union might not then be nearly as unusual as it has been in traditional religion, since the presence of God to man would be more easily understood and accepted. The 'God beyond Being' could turn out to be much closer to man than 'God the Supreme Being'.

The second major aspect of the divine-human relationship for which a place should be made in a Heideggerian philosophy of religion concerns man's relations with other human beings, i.e., the field of ethics. Even though this is often treated as an independent branch of philosophy, it cannot be omitted from the philosophy of religion, since God, according to most descriptions of him, is concerned with how humans act towards one another. Here again, Heidegger's philosophy shows itself to be quite amenable to a religious interpretation. Although he says little about inter-personal relations as such, his description of authentic human existence shows that each person has a fundamental responsibility for the well-being of others, and indeed for the whole world. This is brought out very well in his discussion of dwelling, where he carefully explains the ill-effects of modern technological civilization, based as it is on subjectivism rather than on the respect for others which he prescribes.

This critique of the technological mentality is perhaps the key to a Heideggerian religious ethics. It is an integral part of his description of man as open to what lies beyond him, since it is only by overcoming his subjectivism (of which technology is but a manifestation) that man can attain Being and what lies beyond Being. Thus, until man comes to question the validity of our technological civilization, he is incapable of encountering God. And once he has had this religious experience, he will be all the more concerned to overcome his subjectivism and instead dwell 'caringly' on the earth. This latter expression can be seen to contain in germ all the elements of religious ethics: relations with oneself, with others and with all of nature. Heidegger's own writings do no more than provide the basis for such an ethics, but it is clear that such a religious ethics is not incompatible with the rest of his philosophy.

This concludes our outline of a Heideggerian philosophy of religion, to be constructed in accordance with the understanding of philosophy of religion provided by the Americans. However, since we promised to consider here the full religious significance of Heidegger's philosophy, we need still to treat the relevance of Heidegger's thought for philosophical theology. This task is all the more necessary now that the philosophy of religion seems to be dealing with topics which were once considered by many as the exclusive subject-matter of theology. It would seem that in order to determine the limits of philosophy of religion, whether

Heideggerian or any other, we must first specify the relationship between philosophy of religion and theology. Only then will we be in a position to evaluate Heidegger's significance for theology.

IV. Heidegger and Philosophical Theology.

Theology may be defined as the rational interpretation and development of religious beliefs (i.e., of the faith). It is evident both historically and logically that faith *needs* theology. Religious people have always sought reasons for their beliefs, since the acceptance of a belief without sufficient reason is not faith but credulity (belief in the belief rather than in the object of belief). Thus, theology is an essential aspect of any religious tradition. But just as faith needs theology, so also does theology need philosophy. For the explanation of the faith, if it is to be understood at all, must conform to the rules of human understanding, and it is precisely the task of philosophy to formulate these rules. In addition, there are other functions which philosophy performs for theology, such as analyzing the meaning of human existence and even the meaning of God. And, as we have seen, philosophers do not hesitate to criticize previous theological formulations which they consider to be inadequate on philosophical grounds. We might wonder, then, whether there is any need for theology if we have recourse to a fully developed philosophy of religion.

This question can be raised but not answered on historical grounds. For the history of religions provides much evidence that the major religious traditions can be accounted for without reference to any supernatural divine intervention. Religion is very much a human affair, but whether it is *solely* a human affair cannot be answered by history (nor, for that matter, by philosophy). Thus, the question as to whether philosophy of religion (understood in its widest sense) was responsible for the *origin* of religious faith, and is therefore anterior to theology, cannot be answered one way or the other.

Whatever their origins, most religious traditions have come to regard themselves as divinely inspired and consequently as impervious to merely human (philosophical) criticism, at least with reference to their central beliefs. Theology is considered as the interpretation and elaboration of beliefs which are accepted as *given*, and theologians usually feel obliged to interpret positively the beliefs of their religious tradition. The philosopher of religion is not bound to accept as true the beliefs of any religious tradition, but nevertheless he cannot work in isolation from these traditions, for it is there that religion-- the object of his study--is to be found. It would be very

157

difficult if not impossible for the philosopher to produce an entirely new religion; he must rather deal with what already exists, although he is free to modify this religion to a considerable extent.

In the light of these limitations for both theology and philosophy of religion, it would appear that both disciplines are necessary, and that neither is sufficient in itself. The philosopher depends upon previous theological formulations of religion for his subject-matter, and cannot even mention terms such as 'God' without defining his meaning of the terms in relation to those employed by theology. Thus, the philosophy of religion is theological philosophy, although it is theological in but a limited sense. At the same time, theology must be philosophical theology, if it is to have any success in making itself understood. The theologian is in a sense the guardian of a religious tradition, and it would seem that his distinctive task is to ensure that the continual reconceptualization of religious beliefs remains true to the tradition of his faith. He has much to learn from the philosopher with regard to the understanding of reality, including God and the divine-human relationship, but he also has something to teach the philosopher--namely, how and why religion has manifested itself the way it has in his own religious tradition. The philosopher of religion who is ignorant of or unsympathetic to the history of theology is just as badly off as the theologian who knows nothing of philosophy.

With regard to Heidegger's philosophy in particular, we have seen that many Christian theologians have found his thought useful for their explanation of Christian beliefs. Heidegger is generally reluctant to investigate the relevance of his ideas for theology, but he makes an exception to this rule in his critique of metaphysics. Theology, no less than philosophy, has suffered from the predominance of metaphysical thinking, and Heidegger has recommended to theologians that they rid themselves of this metaphysical heritage. This advice has been generally well-received by Christian theologians, although its application has not been uniform. Among the theologians treated above, Jean-Paul Resweber and Leslie Dewart have attempted the most radical critique of metaphysical theology. They have tried to show that theology must begin with an explanation of human experience in general, with special reference to the nature of thinking and language. Only when such an understanding of experience and knowledge has been reached can the more specific task of explaining religious experience and theological knowledge be attempted. Insofar as Heidegger's critique of metaphysical thinking and his alternate explanation of human knowledge are valid, they are applicable in equal measure to philosophical and theological

158

thinking.

Although few if any theologians have explored the implications of Heidegger's critique of metaphysics as deeply as Resweber and Dewart, many of them have recognized the need for the non-metaphysical reinterpretation of at least some theological concepts. An early example of this was Bultmann's existential anthropology, in which he adopted Heidegger's description of Dasein in order to express more faithfully the Biblical understanding of man than had traditional metaphysical theology. Bultmann has not been alone in his recognition of Heidegger's importance for theological anthropology; John Macquarrie and Schubert Ogden, among many others, have continued to explore this dimension of his thought. Although Heidegger does not deal with man's relation to God, which is a central element of the theological concept of man, he does describe man's relation to Being in a manner which is very suggestive of a theological interpretation. Heinrich Ott and John Macquarrie have both shown the close parallels between man's attitude towards Being in Heidegger's thought and man's attitude towards God in Christian theology. Likewise, the relation of Being towards man, which Heidegger describes in terms of 'revelation', is similar to the Christian understanding of God's relation to man. Although it would appear that Heidegger has appropriated many of these ideas from Christian theology, his non-metaphysical reinterpretation of these ideas can be accepted by the theologian as a novel contribution to the development of Christian theology.

The major component of a Heideggerian philosophical theology, as with any theology, would be the concept of God. As we have seen, Heidegger has nothing positive to say about God. However, his criticisms of the metaphysical concept of God as the supreme Being, the first cause, the highest value, etc., have stimulated theologians to develop non-metaphysical concepts of God. Although the theologians, like the philosophers of religion, will have to supplement Heidegger's thought with other resources in order to achieve an adequate description of God, they can get their work off to a good start by accepting Thomas O'Meara's assessment of Heidegger's philosophy that God is neither Being nor a being but is beyond Being. Thus, it is the American theologians--Cobb, Ogden and Dewart--rather than those more directly influenced by Heidegger--Tillich, Ott and Macquarrie--whose concept of God is more suitable for use in a Heideggerian philosophical theology.

Whether or not Heidegger's philosophy is valuable for the reinterpretation of other elements of Christian theology, such as Jesus Christ, the Church, morality, services, etc., must be left to the theologians themselves to decide. It would seem, however, that a knowledge of Heidegger's philosophy with regard to the topics discussed above is important, if not indispensable, for the modern theologian. His treatment of religious topics is valuable for theology as well as for philosophy of religion, and to the extent that his descriptions of traditional theology, man and God are accurate, they *must* be assimilated by the theologian. Thus, the full significance of Heidegger's philosophy for religion is to be determined by the cooperative efforts of philosophy and theology as they work together to further the development of the religious consciousness of man.

1. Heidegger, *Was heisst Denken?*, p. 110 (E.T., p. 177).

2. Leslie Dewart, *The Foundations of Belief*, p. 449.

3. Cf. Otto Pöggeler, *La pensée de Heidegger*, pp. 47-59 for a description of Heidegger's courses, "Introduction to the Phenomenology of Religion" (winter semester 1920-1) and "Augustine and Neo-Platonism" (summer semester 1921).

4. Heidegger, *Identität und Differenz*, p. 64.

5. Whitehead, *Process and Reality*, p. 405.

6. For a criticism of Heidegger's (and Luther's) interpretation of St. Paul's characterization of philosophy as 'foolishness', cf. Otto Pöggeler, *La pensée de Heidegger*, p. 264n.

7. James, *The Varieties of Religious Experience*, p. 491.

Bibliographies

A separate bibliography is given for each of the three major chapters of this work. Only those writings which have proved useful in the preparation of this work are included in the bibliographies. Heidegger's own writings are listed in the bibliography for chapter three, "Heidegger's Philosophy of Religion." In general, they are presented in chronological order according to the date of first publication. When an English translation has been used, it is noted alongside the original version. The specific editions of Heidegger's works which have been consulted are given. This bibliography of Heidegger's writings and translations does not pretend to be complete, especially in view of the recently announced project to publish (in some 80 volumes) all of Heidegger's lectures and writings, and because of the incomplete and haphazard appearance of Heidegger's previously published works in English translation.

1. Heidegger and the Theologians

Barth, Karl. "Gott und das Nichtige," *Heidegger und die Theologie*, ed. by Gerhard Noller, München: Chr. Kaiser, 1967, 197-225.

------. "Philosophie und Theologie," *Philosophie und Christliche Existenz*, Festschrift for Heinrich Barth, ed. by Gerhard Huber, Basel: Hebling & Lichtenhahn, 1960, 93-106.

------. *Rudolf Bultmann: Ein Versuch, ihn zu Verstehen*, Zollikon: Evangelischer Verlag, 1952.

Barth, Karl and Bultmann, Rudolf. *Briefwechsel 1922-1966*, ed. by Bernd Jaspert, Zürich: Theologischer Verlag Zürich, 1971.

Bleistein, Roman and Klinger, Elmar, eds. *Bibliographie Karl Rahner 1924-1969*, Freiburg: Herder, 1969.

Brechtken, Josef. *Geschichtliche Tranzendenz bei Heidegger*: Die Hoffungsstruktur des Daseins und die gott-los Gottesfrage, Meisenheim am Glan: Verlag Anton Hain, 1972.

BIBLIOGRAPHIES

Brunner, Emil. "Theologie und Ontologie--oder die Theologie am Scheidewege," *Heidegger und die Theologie*, ed. by Gerhard Noller, München: Chr. Kaiser, 1967, 125-135.

Buber, Martin. *Werke*, vol. I--Schriften zur Philosophie, München: Kösel Verlag, 1962.

Bultmann, Rudolf. *Existence and Faith*, ed. and tr. by Schubert M. Ogden, New York: Meridian, 1960.

------. *Foi et Compréhension*, ed. and tr. by André Malet, Paris: Editions du Seuil, 1969.

------. *Kerygma and Myth*, ed. by Hans Werner Bartsch, tr. by Reginald Fuller, New York: Harper Torchbooks, 1961.

------. "Die Geschichtlichkeit des Daseins und der Glaube. Antwort an Gerhardt Kuhlmann," *Heidegger und die Theologie*, ed. by Gerhard Noller, München: Chr. Kaiser, 1967, 72-94.

Bultmann, Rudolf and Jaspers, Karl. *Myth and Christianity*, New York: Noonday Press, 1958.

Cobb, John B., Jr. "Nihilism, Existentialism and Whitehead," *Religion in Life* 30 (1961), 521-533.

Cochrane, A. C. *The Existentialists and God*, Chicago: University of Chicago Press, 1956.

Collins, James. *The Emergence of Philosophy of Religion*, New Haven and London: Yale University Press, 1967.

------. *The Existentialists*, Chicago: Regnery, 1959.

------. "The German Neoscholastic Approach to Heidegger," *The Modern Schoolman* 21 (1943-4), 143-152.

Corvez, Maurice. *L'Être et la conscience morale*, Louvain: Editions Nauwelaerts, 1968.

------. *La philosophie de Heidegger*, Paris: Presses Universitaires, 1966^2.

Danner, Helmut. *Das Göttliche und der Gott bei Heidegger*, Meisenheim am Glan: Verlag Anton Hain, 1971.

164

Dewart, Leslie. *The Future of Belief*, New York: Herder & Herder, 1966.

Dinkler, Erich. "Martin Heidegger," *Christianity and the Existentialists*, ed. by Carl Michalson, New York: Charles Scribner's Sons, 1956, 97-127.

Diem, Hermann. *Gott und die Metaphysik*, Zollikon: Evangelischer Verlag, 1956.

Ebeling, Gerhard. "Verantworten des Glaubes in Begegnung mit dem Denken M. Heideggers," *Zeitschrift für Theologie und Kirche* 58 (1961) Beiheft 2, 119-124.

Fabro, Cornelio. *God in Exile*, tr. by Arthur Gibson, New York: Paulist-Newman, 1968.

Franz, Helmut. "Das Denken Heideggers und die Theologie," *Heidegger und die Theologie*, ed. by Gerhard Noller, München: Chr. Kaiser, 1967, 249-289.

Fuchs, Ernst. *Marburger Hermeneutik*, Tübingen: J. C. B. Mohr, 1968.

------. "Theologie und Metaphysik. Zu der theologischen Bedeutung der Philosophie Heideggers und Grisebachs," *Heidegger und die Theologie*, ed. by Gerhard Noller, München: Chr. Kaiser, 1967, 136-146.

------. *Zum Hermeneutischen Problem in der Theologie*, Tübingen: J. C. B. Mohr, 1959.

Funk, Robert. *Language, Hermeneutic and Word of God*, New York: Harper and Row, 1966.

Gadamer, Hans-Georg. "Martin Heidegger und die Marburger Theologie," *Heidegger*, ed. by Otto Pöggeler, Köln and Berlin: Kiepenheuer & Witsch, 1969, 169-178.

Gethmann-Siefert, Annemarie. *Das Verhältnis von Philosophie und Theologie im Denken Martin Heideggers*, Freiburg/München: Karl Alber, 1974.

Gilson, Etienne. "L'Etre et Dieu," *Revue Thomiste* 62 (1962), 181-202 and 398-416.

BIBLIOGRAPHIES

Gray, J. Glenn. "Heidegger's 'Being'", *Journal of Philosophy* 49 (1952), 415-422.

Grene, Marjorie. *Dreadful Freedom*, Chicago: University of Chicago Press, 1948.

Guibal, Francis. "Martin Heidegger et l'attente du 'Dieu Divin'", *Etudes* (1971), 595-623 and 753-774.

Hinners, R. C. "Being and God in Heidegger's Philosophy," *Proceedings of the American Catholic Philosophical Association* 31 (1957), 157-162.

Hodgson, Peter C. "Heidegger, Revelation, and the Word of God," *Journal of Religion* 49 (1969), 228-252.

Jolivet, Régis. *Le problème de la mort chez Heidegger et Sartre*, Abbaye Saint Wandrille: Editions de Fontenelle, 1950.

Jonas, Hans. "Heidegger and Theology," *Review of Metaphysics* XVIII (1964), 207-233.

Kegley, Charles W., ed. *The Theology of Rudolf Bultmann*, New York: Harper and Row, 1966.

Kegley, Charles W. and Bretall, Robert W., eds. *The Theology of Paul Tillich*, New York: Macmillan, 1952.

Kroner, Richard J. "Heidegger's Private Religion," *Union Seminary Quarterly Review* 11 (1956), 23-37.

Kuhlmann, Gerhardt. "Zum theologischen Problem der Existenz. Fragen an Rudolf Bultmann," *Heidegger und die Theologie*, ed. by Gerhard Noller, München: Chr. Kaiser, 1967, 33-58.

Langan, Thomas. *The Meaning of Heidegger*, New York: Columbia University Press, 1959.

Lehmann, Karl. "Christliche Geschichtserfahrung und ontologische Frage beim jungen Heidegger," *Heidegger*, ed. by Otto Pöggeler, Köln and Berlin: Kiepenheuer & Witsch, 1969, 140-168.

Lotz, J. B. "Das Sein selbst und das subsistierende Sein nach Thomas von Aquin," *Martin Heidegger zum 70. Geburtstag*, Pfullingen: G. Neske, 1959, 180-194.

------. *Sein und Existenz*, Freiburg: Herder, 1965.

Löwith, Karl. "Phänomenologische Ontologie und protestantische Theologie," *Heidegger und die Theologie*, ed. by Gerhard Noller, München: Chr. Kaiser, 1967, 95-124.

Macquarrie, John. "Bultmann's Understanding of God," *The Expository Times* 79 (1967-8), 356-360.

------. *An Existentialist Theology*, London: S.C.M. Press, 1955.

------. *God-Talk*, London: S.C.M. Press, 1967.

------. *Principles of Christian Theology*, New York: Charles Scribner's Sons, 1966.

------. *The Scope of Demythologizing*, New York: Harper Torchbooks, 1966.

Martelet, Gustave. "Pour une définition de la théologie: à travers trois textes de Martin Heidegger," *Foi et Vie* 70 (1971), 196-213.

Mehl, Roger. *La condition du philosophe chrétien*, Neuchatel and Paris: Delachaux & Niestlé, 1947.

Meyer, Hans. *Martin Heidegger und Thomas von Aquin*, München: F. Schöningh, 1964.

Noller, Gerhard. "Ontologische und theologische Versuche zur Überwindung des anthropologischen Denkens," *Heidegger und die Theologie*, München: Chr. Kaiser, 1967, 290-315.

------. *Sein und Existenz*, München: Chr. Kaiser, 1962.

Ogden, Schubert M. "Bultmann's Demythologizing and Hartshorne's Dipolar Theism," *Process and Divinity*, ed. by William L. Reese and Eugene Freeman, LaSalle, Illinois: Open Court, 1964, 493-513.

------. *The Reality of God*, New York: Harper and Row, 1966.

O'Meara, Thomas F. "Heidegger on God," *Continuum* V (1967-8), 686-698.

------. "Tillich and Heidegger: A Structural Relationship," *Harvard Theological Review* 61 (1968), 249-261.

Ott, Heinrich. "Die Bedeutung von Martin Heideggers Denken für die Methode der Theologie," *Durchbliche. Martin Heidegger zum 80. Geburtstag*, ed. by Vittorio Klostermann, Frankfurt: Klostermann, 1970, 27-38.

------. *Denken und Sein*. Der Weg Martin Heideggers und der Weg der Theologie, Zollikon: Evangelischer Verlag, 1959.

------. "Language and Understanding," tr. by Thomas Dean, *New Theology no. 4*, ed. by Martin Marty and Dean Penman, New York: Macmillan, 1967, 124-146.

------. "What is Systematic Theology?" *The Later Heidegger and Theology*, ed. by James M. Robinson and John B. Cobb, Jr., New York: Harper and Row, 1963, 77-111.

Rahner, Karl. "Introduction au concept de philosophie existentiale chez Heidegger," *Recherches de Science Religieuse* XXX (1940), 152-171 (tr. by R. Celle).

------. *On the Theology of Death*, tr. by C. H. Henkey, Montréal: Palm, 1965^2.

Resweber, Jean-Paul. *Essai sur le discours théologique à la lumière de la critique heideggérienne de la métaphysique*, Lille: Service de Réproduction des Thèses, Université de Lille III, 1974.

Richardson, William. "Heidegger and God--and Professor Jonas," *Thought* 40 (1965), 13-40.

Roberts, David E. *Existentialism and Religious Belief*, New York: Oxford University Press, 1957.

Robinson, James M. and Cobb, John B., Jr., eds. *The Later Heidegger and Theology*, New York: Harper and Row, 1963.

------. *The New Hermeneutic*, New York: Harper and Row, 1964.

Sartre, Jean-Paul. *Existentialism and Humanism*, tr. by Philip Mairet, London: Methuen, 1948.

Siewerth, Gustav. "Martin Heidegger und die Frage nach Gott," *Grundfragen der Philosophie in Horizont der Seinsdifferenz*, Düsseldorf: L. Schwann, 1963, 245-259.

Tillich, Paul. "Autobiographical Reflections," *The Theology of Paul Tillich*, ed. by Charles W. Kegley and Robert W. Bretall, New York: Macmillan, 1961, 3-21.

------. *The Courage to Be*, New Haven: Yale University Press, 1952.

------. *On the Boundary*: An Autobiographical Sketch, New York: Charles Scribner's Sons, 1966.

------. *Perspectives on 19th and 20th Century Protestant Theology*, London: S.C.M. Press, 1967.

------. *Systematic Theology*, Chicago: University of Chicago Press, vol. I--1951, vol. II--1957, vol. III--1963.

------. *Theology of Culture*, ed. by Robert C. Kimball, New York: Oxford University Press, 1959.

Vorgrimler, Herbert. *Karl Rahner*, tr. by Edward Quinn, Montréal: Palm, 1965.

de Waelhens, A. *La philosophie de Martin Heidegger*, Louvain: Publications Universitaires de Louvain, 1955.

Weischedel, Wilhelm. *Der Gott der Philosophen*, 2 vols., Darmstadt: Wissenschaftliche Buchgesellschaft, 1972.

Welte, Bernhard. "Die Gottesfrage im Denken Martin Heideggers," *Auf der Spur des Ewigen*, Freiburg: Herder, 1965, 262-276.

Wittgenstein, Ludwig. *Lectures and Conversations*, ed. by Cyril Barrett, Oxford: B. Blackwell, 1966.

Wisser, Richard, ed. *Martin Heidegger im Gespräch*, Freiburg and München: Karl Alber, 1970.

Yannaras, Christos. *De l'absence et de l'inconnaissance de Dieu*, tr. by Jacques Touraille, Paris: Editions du Cerf, 1971.

2. American Philosophy of Religion.

Adams, James Luther. *Paul Tillich's Philosophy of Culture, Science and Religion*, New York: Schocken Books, 1965.

BIBLIOGRAPHIES

Baum, Gregory, ed. *The Future of Belief Debate*, New York: Herder & Herder, 1967.

Blau, Joseph L. *Men and Movements in American Philosophy*, Englewood Cliffs, N.J.: Prentice-Hall, 1952.

Brown, Delwin, James, Ralph E., Jr., and Reeves, Gene, eds. *Process Philosophy and Christian Thought*, Indianapolis, Indiana: Bobbs-Merrill, 1971.

Cobb, John B., Jr. *A Christian Natural Theology*, Philadelphia: Westminster Press, 1965.

------. *God and the World*, Philadelphia: Westminster, 1969.

------. *Living Options in Protestant Theology*, Philadelphia: Westminster, 1962.

------. "Nihilism, Existentialism and Whitehead," *Religion in Life* 30 (1961), 521-533.

------. "Perfection Exists: A Critique of Hartshorne," *Religion in Life* 32 (1963), 294-304.

------. *The Structure of Christian Existence*, Philadelphia: Westminster, 1967.

------. "What is Alive and What is Dead in Empirical Theology," *The Future of Empirical Theology*, ed. by Bernard E. Meland, Chicago: University of Chicago Press, 1969, 89-101.

------. "A Whiteheadian Christology," *Process Philosophy and Christian Thought*, ed. by Delwin Brown, Ralph E. James, Jr., and Gene Reeves, Indianapolis: Bobbs-Merrill, 1971, 382-398.

Cousins, Ewert H., ed. *Process Theology*, New York: Newman Press, 1971.

DeMarco, Joseph P. "God, Religion and Community in the Philosophy of C. S. Peirce," *The Modern Schoolman* XLIX (1972), 331-347.

Dewart, Leslie. *The Foundations of Belief*, New York: Herder & Herder, 1969.

Dewart, Leslie. *The Future of Belief*, New York: Herder & Herder, 1966.

------. *Religion, Language and Truth*, New York: Herder & Herder, 1970.

Dewey, John. *A Common Faith*, New Haven: Yale University Press, 1960.

------. "Creative Democracy--The Task Before Us," *The Philosopher of the Common Man*, New York: Greenwood Press, 1968, 220-228.

------. *Experience and Nature*, New York: W. W. Norton, 1929^2.

------. "From Absolutism to Experimentalism," *The Golden Age of American Philosophy*, ed. by Charles Frankel, New York: George Braziller, 1960, 385-395.

------. "The Philosophy of Whitehead," *The Philosophy of Alfred North Whitehead*, ed. by Paul Arthur Schilpp, New York: Tudor Publishing Co., 1951^2, 641-661.

------. *The Quest for Certainty*: A Study of the Relation of Knowledge and Action, New York: Minton, Balch & Co., 1929.

------. *Reconstruction in Philosophy*, Boston: Beacon Press, 1967^2.

------. "What I Believe," *Pragmatism and American Culture*, ed. by Gail Kennedy, Boston: D. C. Heath & Co., 1950, 23-31.

Evans, Robert A., ed. *The Future of Philosophical Theology*, Philadelphia: Westminster Press, 1971.

Feibleman, James K. *An Introduction to the Philosophy of Peirce*, Cambridge, Mass.: M.I.T. Press, 1970.

Ferré, Nels F. S., Hartshorne, Charles, Dillenberger, John, Livingston, James C. and Harouturian, Joseph. *Paul Tillich: Retrospect and Future*, Nashville and New York: Abingdon Press, 1966.

Fisch, Max H., ed. *Classic American Philosophers*, New York: Appleton-Century-Crofts, 1951.

BIBLIOGRAPHIES

Frankel, Charles, ed. *The Golden Age of American Philosophy*, New
York: George Braziller, 1960.

Halferty, Brian J. *John Dewey and the Religious Elements of
Experience*, unpublished M.A. thesis, University of St.
Michael's College, Toronto, 1969.

Hartshorne, Charles. *Beyond Humanism*: Essays in the Philosophy
of Nature, Lincoln, Nebraska: University of Nebraska
Press, 1968.

------. *Creative Synthesis and Philosophical Method*, London:
S.C.M. Press, 1970.

------. "The Development of My Philosophy," *Contemporary American
Philosophy*, ed. by John E. Smith, London: Allen &
Unwin, 1970, 211-228.

------. "The Development of Process Philosophy," *Process Theology*,
ed. by Ewert H. Cousins, New York: Newman Press, 1971,
47-64.

------. *The Divine Relativity*: A Social Conception of God, New
Haven and London: Yale University Press, 1967.

------. "Introduction" to *Saint Anselm: Basic Writings*, ed. by
S. N. Deane, LaSalle, Illinois: Open Court, 1962^2,
1-19.

------. *The Logic of Perfection* and other Essays in Neoclassical
Metaphysics, LaSalle, Ill.: Open Court, 1962.

------. *Man's Vision of God* and the Logic of Theism, Hamden,
Conn.: Archon Books, 1964.

------. *A Natural Theology for Our Time*, LaSalle, Ill.: Open
Court, 1967.

------. "A Philosopher's Assessment of Christianity," *Religion
and Culture: Essays in Honor of Paul Tillich*, ed. by
Walter Leibrecht, New York: Harper & Bros., 1959,
167-180.

------. *Reality as Social Process*: Studies in Metaphysics and
Religion, New York: Hafner Publishing Co., 1971.

172

Hartshorne, Charles. "Tillich's Doctrine of God," *The Theology of Paul Tillich*, ed. by Charles W. Kegley and Robert W. Bretall, New York: Macmillan, 1961, 164-195.

------. "Tillich and the Nontheological Meanings of Theological Terms," *Paul Tillich; Retrospect and Future*, by Nels F. S. Ferré et al., Nashville and New York: Abingdon Press, 1966, 19-30.

------. "Whitehead's Idea of God," *The Philosophy of Alfred North Whitehead*, ed. by Paul Arthur Schilpp, New York: Tudor Publishing Co., 1951^2, 513-559.

------ and Reese, William L., eds. *Philosophers Speak of God*, Chicago: University of Chicago Press, 1963.

Hook, Sidney. *John Dewey: An Intellectual Portrait*, Westport, Conn.: Greenwood Press, 1971.

James, William. *The Varieties of Religious Experience*, London: Fontana Press, 1971.

------. *The Will to Believe*, New York: Dover, 1956.

------. *The Writings of William James*, ed. by John J. McDermott, New York: Random House, 1967.

Kegley, Charles W. and Bretall, Robert W., eds. *The Theology of Paul Tillich*, New York: Macmillan, 1952.

Kennedy, Gail, ed. *Pragmatism and American Culture*, Boston: D. C. Heath & Co., 1950.

Leclerc, Ivor, ed. *The Relevance of Whitehead*, London: Macmillan, 1961.

Leibrecht, Walter, ed. *Religion and Culture: Essays in Honor of Paul Tillich*, New York: Harper & Bros., 1959.

Lundeen, Lyman T. *Risk and Rhetoric in Religion: Whitehead's Theory of Language and the Discourse of Faith*, Philadelphia: Fortress Press, 1972.

Mack, Robert D. *The Appeal to Immediate Experience*: Philosophic Method in Bradley, Whitehead and Dewey, Freeport, N.Y.: Books for Libraries Press, 1968.

BIBLIOGRAPHIES

Macquarrie, John. *An Existentialist Theology*, London: S.C.M.
        Press, 1955.

------. *God and Secularity*, London: Lutterworth Press, 1968.

------. *God-Talk*, London: S.C.M. Press, 1967.

------. "God and the World: One Reality or Two?" *Theology* 75
        (1972), 394-403.

------. *Principles of Christian Theology*, New York: Charles
        Scribner's Sons, 1966.

------. *Studies in Christian Existentialism*, Montreal: McGill
        University Press, 1965.

------. *Twentieth Century Religious Thought*, London: S.C.M.
        Press, 1971^2.

Meland, Bernard E., ed. *The Future of Empirical Theology*,
        Chicago: University of Chicago Press, 1969.

Moore, Edward C. *American Pragmatism*, New York: Columbia Univer-
        sity Press, 1961.

Ogden, Schubert M. "Bultmann's Demythologizing and Hartshorne's
        Dipolar Theism," *Process and Divinity*, ed. by William
        L. Reese and Eugene Freeman, LaSalle, Ill.: Open
        Court, 1964, 493-513.

------. *Christ Without Myth*, London: Collins, 1962.

------. "A Christian Natural Theology," *Process Philosophy and
        Christian Thought*, ed. by Delwin Brown et al., Indiana-
        polis: Bobbs-Merrill, 1971, 111-115.

------. *The Reality of God*, New York: Harper & Row, 1966.

------. "The Task of Philosophical Theology," *The Future of
        Philosophical Theology*, ed. by Robert A. Evans, Phila-
        delphia: Westminster, 1971, 55-84.

------. "The Understanding of Theology in Ott and Bultmann,"
        The Later Heidegger and Theology, ed. by James M.
        Robinson and John B. Cobb, Jr., New York: Harper &
        Row, 1963, 157-173.

Peirce, Charles Sanders. *The Collected Papers of Charles Sanders Peirce*, ed. by Charles Hartshorne and Paul Weiss, Cambridge, Mass.: Harvard University Press, 1931-35, six volumes.

Perry, Ralph Barton. *The Thought and Character of William James* (briefer version), New York: George Braziller, 1954.

Peters, Eugene H. *The Creative Advance*, St. Louis: Bethany Press, 1966.

Pittenger, Norman. *Alfred North Whitehead*, Richmond, Virginia: John Knox Press, 1969.

Ramsey, Paul, ed. *Religion* (Humanistic Scholarship in America: The Princeton Studies), Englewood Cliffs, N.J.: Prentice-Hall, 1965.

Reese, William L. and Freeman, Eugene, eds. *Process and Divinity*, LaSalle, Ill.: Open Court, 1964.

Robinson, James M. and Cobb, John B., eds. *The Later Heidegger and Theology*, New York: Harper & Row, 1963.

Schilpp, Paul Arthur, ed. *The Philosophy of John Dewey*, New York: Tudor Publishing Co., 1951^2.

-------. *The Philosophy of Alfred North Whitehead*, New York: Tudor Publishing Co., 1951^2.

Smith, John E. "Philosophy of Religion," *Religion*, ed. by Paul Ramsey, Englewood Cliffs, N.J.: Prentice-Hall, 1965, 355-450.

-------. "Religion and Theology in Peirce," *Studies in the Philosophy of Charles Sanders Peirce* (first series), ed. by Philip P. Wiener and Frederic H. Young, Cambridge, Mass.: Harvard University Press, 1952, 251-267.

-------. *The Spirit of American Philosophy*, New York: Oxford University Press, 1966.

-------. *Themes in American Philosophy*, New York: Harper Torchbooks, 1970.

175

Smith, John E., ed. *Contemporary American Philosophy* (second series), London: Allen & Unwin, 1970.

Thomas, J. Heywood. *Paul Tillich*, Richmond, Virginia: John Knox, 1965.

Thompson, Kenneth F., Jr. *Whitehead's Philosophy of Religion*, The Hague: Mouton, 1971.

Tillich, Paul. "Autobiographical Reflections," *The Theology of Paul Tillich*, ed. by Charles W. Kegley and Robert W. Bretall, New York: Macmillan, 1952, 3-21.

------. *The Courage to Be*, New Haven, Conn.: Yale University Press, 1952.

------. *The Dynamics of Faith*, New York: Harper & Row, 1957.

------. *The Future of Religions*, ed. by Jerald C. Brauer, New York: Harper & Row, 1966.

------. *On the Boundary*: An Autobiographical Sketch, New York: Charles Scribner's Sons, 1966.

------. *Perspectives on 19th and 20th Century Protestant Theology*, London: S.C.M. Press, 1967.

------. *The Protestant Era*, tr. by James Luther Adams, Chicago: University of Chicago Press, 1948.

------. *The Shaking of the Foundations*, Harmondsworth, Middlesex: Penguin, 1966.

------. *Systematic Theology*, Chicago: University of Chicago Press, vol. I--1951, vol. II--1957, vol. III--1963.

------. *Theology of Culture*, ed. by Robert C. Kimball, New York: Oxford University Press, 1959.

Welch, Claude. "Theology," *Religion*, ed. by Paul Ramsey, Englewood Cliffs, N.J.: Prentice-Hall, 1965, 219-284.

Weiner, Philip P. and Young, Frederic H., eds. *Studies in the Philosophy of Charles Sanders Peirce* (first series), Cambridge, Mass.: Harvard University Press, 1952.

Whitehead, Alfred North. *Adventures of Ideas*, New York: Macmillan, 1933.

------. *Modes of Thought*, Cambridge: Cambridge University Press, 1956.

------. *Process and Reality*, New York: The Free Press, 1969.

------. *Religion in the Making*, New York: Meridian Books, 1971.

------. *Science and the Modern World*, New York: The Free Press, 1967.

3. Heidegger's Philosophy of Religion.

A. Heidegger's Works.

1927 *Sein und Zeit*, Tübingen: Max Niemeyer Verlag, 1967. (E.T., *Being and Time*, by John Macquarrie and Edward Robinson, New York: Harper & Row, 1962, from the 7th German edition, 1953.)

1929 *Was ist Metaphysik?*, *Wegmarken*, Frankfurt am Main: Vittorio Klostermann, 1967, 1-19. (E.T., "What is Metaphysics?" by R. F. C. Hull and Alan Crick, *Existence and Being*, ed. by Werner Brock, Chicago: Regnery, 1949, 325-349.)

Kant und das Problem der Metaphysik, Frankfurt: V. Klostermann, 1973. (E.T., *Kant and the Problem of Metaphysics*, by James Churchill, Bloomington, Indiana: Indiana University Press, 1962.)

Vom Wesen des Grundes, *Wegmarken*, 21-71.

1942 *Platons Lehre von der Wahrheit*, *Wegmarken*, 109-144.

1943 *Vom Wesen der Wahrheit*, *Wegmarken*, 73-97. (E.T., "On the Essence of Truth," by R. F. C. Hull and Alan Crick, *Existence and Being*, 292-324.)

Nachwort zu Was ist Metaphysik?, *Wegmarken*, 99-108. (E.T., "Postscript to What is Metaphysics?" by R. F. C. Hull and Alan Crick, *Existence and Being*, 349-361.)

1944 *Erläuterungen zu Hölderlins Dichtung*, Frankfurt: V. Klostermann, 1963. (Partial E.T., "Remembrance of the

Poet" and "Hölderlin and the Essence of Poetry," by Douglas Scott, *Existence and Being*, 243-270 and 270-291.)

1947 *Brief über den 'Humanismus'*, *Wegmarken*, 145-194. (E.T., "Letter on Humanism," by Edgar Lohner, *Philosophy in the 20th Century*, ed. by W. Barrett and H. Aitken, New York: Random House, 1962, vol. 2, 270-302.)

1949 *Einleitung zu Was ist Metaphysik?*, *Wegmarken*, 195-211. (E.T., "Introduction to What is Metaphysics?" by Walter Kaufmann, *Existentialism from Dostoevsky to Sartre*, ed. by Walter Kaufmann, New York: Meridian, 1957, 207-221.)

1950 *Holzwege*, Frankfurt: V. Klostermann, 1963.

1953 *Einführung in die Metaphysik*, Tübingen: Max Niemeyer, 1966. (E.T., *An Introduction to Metaphysics*, by Ralph Manheim, New Haven, Conn.: Yale University Press, 1959.)

1954 *Aus der Erfahrung des Denkens*, Pfullingen: Günther Neske, 1965.

Vorträge und Aufsätze, Pfullingen: G. Neske, 1967 (3 vols.)

Was heisst Denken?, Tübingen: Max Niemeyer, 1971. (E.T., *What is Called Thinking?* by J. Glenn Gray, New York: Harper & Row, 1968.)

1956 *Was ist das--die Philosophie?*, Pfullingen: G. Neske, 1956.

Zur Seinsfrage, *Wegmarken*, 213-253.

1957 *Der Satz vom Grund*, Pfullingen: G. Neske, 1971.

Identität und Differenz, Pfullingen: G. Neske, 1957.

1958 *Vom Wesen und Begriff der PHYSIS, Aristoteles' Physik B, 1*, *Wegmarken*, 309-371.

1959 *Gelassenheit, Martin Heidegger zum 80. Geburtstag*, Frankfurt: V. Klostermann, 1969, 16-30. (E.T., "Memorial Address," by John M. Anderson and E. Hans Freund, *Discourse on Thinking*, New York: Harper & Row, 1966, 45-57.)

Unterwegs zur Sprache, Pfullingen: G. Neske, 1965.

1960 *Hölderlins Erde und Himmel, Hölderlin-Jahrbuch* 11 (1958-60), 17-39.

Hegel und die Griechen, Wegmarken, 255-272.

1961 *Nietzsche* (2 volumes), Pfullingen: G. Neske, 1961.

1962 *Die Frage nach dem Ding*. Zu Kants Lehre von den transzendentalen Grundsätzen, Tübingen: Max Niemeyer, 1962. (E.T., *What is a Thing?* by W. B. Barton, Jr., and Vera Deutsch, Chicago: Gateway, 1970.)

Kants These über das Sein, Wegmarken, 273-307.

Die Technik und die Kehre, Pfullingen: G. Neske, 1962.

1963 *Ein Vorwort. Brief an P. William J. Richardson*. (E.T., "Preface" by W. Richardson). *Heidegger, Through Phenomenology to Thought*, by William J. Richardson, The Hague: Nijhoff, 1963.

1964 *Aus der letzten Marburger Vorlesung, Wegmarken*, 373-395.

1967 *Wegmarken*, Frankfurt: V. Klostermann, 1967.

1969 *Zur Sache des Denkens*, Tübingen: Max Niemeyer, 1969.

Martin Heidegger zum 80. Geburtstag, Frankfurt: V. Klostermann, 1969.

1970 *Heraklit*, Frankfurt: V. Klostermann, 1970.

Phänomenologie und Theologie, Frankfurt: V. Klostermann, 1970.

1971 *Schellings Abhandlung über das Wesen der menschlichen Freiheit (1809)*, ed. by Hildegard Feick, Tübingen: Max Niemeyer, 1971.

B. Other Works.

Biemal, Walter. *Heidegger*, Reinbek bei Hamburg: Rowohlt, 1973.

Birault, Henri. "De l'Etre, du divin et des dieux chez Heidegger," *L'existence de Dieu*, Tournai: Castermann, 1961, 49-76.

BIBLIOGRAPHIES

Birault, Henri. "La foi et la pensée d'après Heidegger," *Philosophies Chrétiennes*, Paris: Fayard, 1955, 108-132.

------. "Heidegger et la pensée de la finitude," *Revue internationale de Philosophie* 52 (1960), 135-162.

Brechtken, Josef. *Geschichtliche Tranzendenz bei Heidegger*: Die Hoffungsstruktur des Daseins und die gott-los Gottesfrage, Meisenheim am Glan: Verlag Anton Hain, 1972.

Danner, Helmut. *Das Göttliche und der Gott bei Heidegger*, Meisenheim am Glan: Verlag Anton Hain, 1971.

Demske, James M. "Heidegger: Wisdom as Death," *Continuum* V (1967-68), 504-518.

------. *Being, Man, and Death*: A Key to Heidegger, Lexington, Kentucky: University of Kentucky Press, 1970.

Gethmann-Siefert, Annemarie. *Das Verhältnis von Philosophie und Theologie im Denken Martin Heideggers*, Freiburg/München: Karl Alber, 1974.

Guibal, Francis. "Martin Heidegger et l'attente du 'Dieu Divin'", *Etudes* (1971), 595-623 and 753-774.

Haumann, Adolphe. *La philosophie éludant le théisme de M. Heidegger et quelques faits precurseurs*, unpublished doctoral thesis, Université de Strasbourg, 1959.

Hodgson, Peter C. "Heidegger, Revelation, and the Word of God," *Journal of Religion* 49 (1969), 228-252.

Müller, Max. *Existenzphilosophie im geistigen Leben der Gegenwart*, Heidelberg: F. H. Kerle, 1964^3.

Nichols, Francis W. *The Question of God in the Philosophy of Martin Heidegger and its Theological Prolongations*, unpublished doctoral thesis, Université de Strasbourg, 1969.

Ott, Heinrich. *Denken und Sein. Der Weg Martin Heideggers und der Weg der Theologie*, Zollikon: Evangelischer Verlag, 1959.

180

Perotti, James L. *Heidegger on the Divine*, Athens, Ohio: Ohio
    University Press, 1974.

Pöggeler, Otto. "Heidegger Today," *Martin Heidegger in Europe and
    America*, ed. by Edward G. Ballard and Charles E. Scott,
    The Hague: Martinus Nijhoff, 1973, 1-36.

------. *La pensée de Heidegger*, Paris: Aubier-Montaigne, 1967
    (translation by Marianna Simon of *Der Denkweg Martin
    Heideggers*, Pfullingen: G. Neske, 1963).

Resweber, Jean-Paul. *Essai sur le discours théologique à la
    lumière de la critique heideggérienne de la métaphysique*,
    Lille: Service de Réproduction des Thèses, Université
    de Lille III, 1974.

Richardson, William. *Heidegger: Through Phenomenology to
    Thought*, The Hague: Nijhoff, 1963.

Sass, Hans-Martin. *Heidegger-Bibliographie*, Meisenheim am Glan:
    Anton Hain, 1968.

Schrag, Calvin O. "Whitehead and Heidegger: Process Philosophy
    and Existential Philosophy," *Dialectica* 13 (1959), 42-
    54.

Vycinas, Vincent. *Earth and Gods*, The Hague: Nijhoff, 1961.

Index of Names

183

INDEX OF NAMES

Index of Subjects

INDEX OF SUBJECTS

SUPPLEMENTS

---

1. FOOTNOTES TO A THEOLOGY
The Karl Barth Colloquium of 1972

Edited and with an Introduction by
MARTIN RUMSCHEIDT

1974   149 pp.
ISBN 0-919812-02-3 $3.50 (paper)

2. MARTIN HEIDEGGER'S PHILOSOPHY OF RELIGION
JOHN R. WILLIAMS

ISBN 0-919812-03-1 $4.00 (paper)

3. MYSTICS AND SCHOLARS
The Calgary Conference on Mysticism 1976

Edited by
HAROLD COWARD
and
TERENCE PENELHUM

ISBN 0-919812-04-X $4.00 (paper)

Available from:

WILFRID LAURIER UNIVERSITY PRESS
Wilfrid Laurier University
Waterloo, Ontario, Canada N2L 3C5

EDITIONS

1. LA LANGUE DE YA'UDI

Description et classement de l'ancien parler de Zencirli dans le cadre des langues sémitiques du nord-ouest

PAUL EUGENE DION, O.P.

1974   509 pp.
ISBN 0-919812-01-5 $4.50 (paper)

STUDIES IN RELIGION / SCIENCES RELIGIEUSES
Revue canadienne / A Canadian Journal

Abonnements / Subscriptions

Abonnement personnel: $10.00 (quatre fascicules)
Abonnement pour les institutions: $15.00 (quatre fascicules)
Fascicule isolé : $4.00

Individual subscriptions: $10.00 (four issues)
Institutional subscriptions: $15.00 (four issues)
Individual issues: $4.00

ISSN 0008-4298

Tout chèque doit être fait à l'ordre de Wilfrid Laurier University Press.

Make cheques payable to Wilfrid Laurier University Press

WILFRID LAURIER UNIVERSITY PRESS
Wilfrid Laurier University
Waterloo, Ontario, Canada N2L 3C5